Prayer for All Times

Prayer for all Times

Translated by Maud Monahan
from
LA PRIERE DE TOUTES LES HEURES
by
PIERRE CHARLES, S.J.
Professor of Theology in Louvain

With a Foreword by
REV. C. C. MARTINDALE, S.J.

(Complete edition containing First, Second and Third Series)

THE NEWMAN PRESS
Westminster, Maryland

FIRST PRINTED	1929
FIFTH IMPRESSION	1937
SIXTH IMPRESSION	1942
SEVENTH IMPRESSION	1949
ELEVENTH IMPRESSION	1961

NIBIL OBSTAT
G. H. JOYCE, S. J.
Censor Deputatus.

IMPRIMATUR
EDM: CANON SURMONT
Vic. Gen.

WESTMONASTERII,
Die, 18 Maii, 1925.

Made and printed in England by
STAPLES PRINTERS LIMITED
at their Rochester, Kent, establishment

CONTENTS

FIRST SERIES

SECOND SERIES

Contents

THIRD SERIES

FOREWORD

WE are familiar with St. Paul's words which tell us to "pray without ceasing" (i *Thess.*, v. 17) and we may have felt that it was impossible to do so. But he was fond of those two little words "without ceasing". In the same Epistle (ii, 13) he says he thanks God "without ceasing"; he tells Timothy (ii *Tim.*, i, 3) that he remembers him without ceasing; and elsewhere (e.g., *Rom.*, i, 9) that without ceasing he makes mention of certain names in his prayer. And in the Acts, St Luke tells us (xii, 5) that prayer was made "without ceasing" for St Peter. Even in the last case, we are hardly to suppose that an endless chain of prayer was arranged for, so that someone, night and day, was explicitly praying for the Apostle: nor can St Paul have been literally praying for his friends, or thanking God, without a break. He must mean "very often", and no doubt "regularly". We all of us probably have a kind of litany of names or topics that we recall, perhaps nightly, before God. But we may feel in our hearts that we could do still better than that and come somewhat nearer to a ceaseless prayer. And it is towards this that Fr Charles hopes to help us.

He certainly does not undervalue "ejaculatory prayer", yet he would not recommend to many Fr S. Doyle's vast multiplicity of "acts" of, for example, worship. Nor does he undervalue a set time or method of "meditation"—in fact, reverence itself dictates that we should not drift or crash into God's presence or lounge out of it or leave Him abruptly without, so to put it, saying a humble and loving goodbye—some such "framework" for our prayers is good. Yet "prayers" are somehow different from "prayer".

Fr Charles wishes our *life* to be a "prayer-life". "As for me, I was praying", says the Psalmist in our version (*Ps.* cviii, 4), but the Hebrew is more bold, and says: "I was—I am—*prayer.*" How can I be that? Undoubtedly we must have taken trouble. Fr Charles does not disguise the austerity devolved in our Faith, especially if we wish to be anything like an "embodied prayer". I shall at first have to drill myself, if I am to thank God for anything that I like, but after a while it will come spontaneously to me and as my *first* "reaction", to thank and praise God for anything that strikes me as lovely, like a sunset, or flowers, or music. W. G. Ward said— impishly, but quite sincerely—that he never made so many acts of pure love of God as at the opera. . . . "Thou hast enraptured me, Lord, with what Thou hast made! I exult in the works of Thy hands!" (*Ps.* xci, 5.) One's mind can "be prayer" even though one does not exclaim into the words of praise or of thanksgiving, though the very words "Thank God! Praise God!" may come often and easily on our lips. Again, it will need long self-discipline if we are at once to pray for anyone we meet, have to speak to, or just see in the street or at a party. But it may become almost impossible *not* to. This certainly needs no words nor even very clear thought. I " know" that I am putting this person wholly into the hands of God. I do not know what his spiritual condition is—unawakened, in a state of temptation, even sinful; but I do know that he has need of God and is meant to receive always more grace, always more of the Holy Spirit. And we can pray almost instinctively for anyone we hear of as having died, especially if we think that not many will pray for him. But there are times when I am plodding away at my job, not enjoying anything, meeting no one, and just keeping on at something quite uninteresting or even distasteful. This is the time especially suited to what may be the best prayer of all, which is simply the loving abdication of self-will and the unvoiced desire that God may have His own way in us and through us. No words are needed for that nor any separate "ideas". It is the "back of the mind" that prays; it is the will which is the prayer. I am giving up all "property" in myself; I abdicate self altogether, but lovingly, childlikely. Then my humblest action becomes God's action!

This may be why Fr Charles tells us not to be frightened of using "ordinary words", if we pray "vocally"; or of praying about "ordinary things". Certainly modern taste itself is hostile to rhetorical prayers, just as it is to "pulpit oratory"; we are rather apt to feel hypocritical if we so much as tell God that we love Him above all things . . . that we are longing for heaven. Well, whatever words we use, let us wish to mean them with all the meaning that God sees in them, to pray the "Our Father" with the mind that was our Lord's when He taught it, to trust to the meaning of the Holy Spirit who is ceaselessly praying within us. We may not know what to pray for, or how, but "the Spirit joins hands with our weakness", and intercedes for us with a cry that is beyond all words, and God who reads the very depths of hearts, knows what is the meaning of His own Spirit (see *Rom.* viii, 26, 27).

Much, in this book, consists of "colloquy". The author will not expect us to reproduce his own words in what must be our own prayer, but he provides a wonderful stimulus—makes us see not so much new things, as "into" what we had been but superficially aware of; and will excite in us a reaction which will be proper to ourselves, and yet, due to his very personal habit of mind and aspiration. That, I think, is how he would wish us to use his book, which has already been of such help to innumerable souls.

C. C. MARTINDALE, S.J.

London 1948.

FIRST
SERIES

PROLOGUE

Gloria Tibi Domine
Liturgy. The Mass

IF the place of our prayer is but alongside of our life, even if it is close at hand, it is as though we put the yeast beside the dough, or fumbled with the key on the edge of the keyhole. The life of a Christian should be a life of prayer. Why? Because however trivial it may be in appearance and however wanting in external brilliancy, it can become divine.

By the mere fact that the conventional observances which so often surround prayer have been chosen and arranged beforehand, a cold shadow is at times cast over our devotion, and it is enveloped in a vague feeling of insincerity. For not having dared, in their dealings with God, to be such as He Himself has made them, many people have debarred themselves from all experience of the life of prayer; a life which is fed and upheld by light-giving sincerity. The scrupulous anxiety to be punctiliously correct has overthrown, within many souls, the happiness of being true. They have never joyously dared to put their trust in the real, and in God who is its Master; their one fear has been lest they should fail in carrying out the prescriptions of some meticulous and unattractive formulary.

Now, however, the custom of daily Communion, bringing us as it does to the God of every day, is gradually dispelling these awe-inspiring prejudices from our minds. The God of each of our days interests Himself in the events of each day; in that very prosaic crowd of little occupations and of little worries; He moves among them, as formerly He moved among the dust-stained children of Nazareth, the unknown crowds of Galilee, and the thousands of very ordinary poor country folk among whom He sowed the good tidings of His beatitudes.

Why should not our prayer be spent in sanctifying this life which God has given us, and which we should love divinely, by associating ourselves more and more consciously and more and more peacefully with the silent work of Grace.

People say at times: When I kneel down before God, I banish everything else . . . and when I speak to Him, I at once suppress three-quarters of my every-day vocabulary; I search out the rarest words and I avoid mentioning common things; I pretend to be quite other than I am, I should never dare to tell God that the North wind makes my head ache, nor that my feet, the feet of a weary pilgrim, burn painfully in my badly made shoes.

Why should we have this pagan shyness and reserve with God? Must we pretend and make-believe in the presence of substantial Truth? At the marriage feast of Cana did He not Himself repair a want of foresight which was not in the least of a dramatic order? With what simplicity did He not advise Jairus to give food to the little child whom He had just raised to life! Did He not complain that when Simon the Pharisee invited Him to his house, He was not welcomed with the customary salutation, nor given water for His feet, nor perfume for His hair?

If then in this "Prayer for all Times" simple words are used and lowly things are mentioned, let not this scandalize anyone, as though it were a want of respect, nor should these humble things be driven out of the divine presence, as if they were intruders. These daily, lowly realities are at home in the house of the Father, where, in fact, the only misplaced and ridiculous things are our pride, our stiff courtier-like manners, our classic nicety in the use of words and our off-hand disdain. The God of heaven and of earth, the Word, Creator of all that is, Sustainer of all in virtue of His power, the Father, the Son, and the Holy Spirit have never rejected anything that they have made: *nihil eorum odisti quæ fcistei.* (*Wisdom* xi. 25.) To accept the actualities of life with simplicity is the first of duties and the final one. Little children learning their A B C begin their lesson by the Sign of the Cross, and it is In the Name of the Father and of the Son and of the Holy Ghost that they chant in monotonous chorus for an hour, twice two are four. And it is in the Name of the Blessed Trinity that, in Catholic countries, the farmer's wife cuts the great loaf on which she has first marked a cross with the blade of her knife. It is likewise in the same Blessed Name and after having signed himself with the sacred sign that a Catholic drinks a glass of water or eats a bit of bread. If it offends our ears to hear that we who are but as little ants of a day, have God for our partner in our smallest actions, it is a certain proof that we have not understood yet what we are, nor realized the meaning of our life.

It has not seemed advisable to put this "Prayer for all Times" into a methodically reasoned form, nor to divide it into preludes, points, affections and colloquies; nor do the various chapters follow each other in any clearly marked order. The hours in the lives of men follow no rigid law, and virtues do not become necessary to us successively, one after another, following the learned hierarchical order of the *Secunda Secundæ.* The reader will however, realize that the play of thought in these papers is not haphazard, nor are the ideas running riot in uncontrolled anarchy. The end aimed at (which it was perhaps hardly possible to attain) was to make smooth the ways of the Spirit, of that Spirit which ever breathes how and where He

will, and Whom none can bind down to follow rigid methods. To show God as near to us—*Dominus enim prope est*—(*Philippians* iv. 5) is to continue the work of the Apostles, and to unfold the eternal message.

The texts of Scripture have been used in these pages *only as a help to devotion*. "The Scriptures must be understood through the Spirit that inspired them, that is to say through the Holy Spirit," wrote Cardinal Bellarmine in a very neatly turned phrase: *Omnis scriptura eo Spiritu debet intelligi quo scripta est, id est Spiritu Sancto*. It is unquestionably allowable to glean invitations to thought and encouragements to pray from the Sacred pages and from the leaves of the Missal. The Fathers of the first centuries did so. And in her introits and antiphons the Catholic Church sets before us allusions to the Sacred Text and adaptations of its meaning. Children have the right to use their mother's language. They have the right to believe that God has hidden lights and lessons for them beneath the inspired words, and where no infallible decision intervenes, they are free to gather from Holy Writ that peace-bringing consolation which the author of the *Imitation* with many others before him, urges them to seek there, and which the Holy Spirit, the Father of the Poor, has prepared for them in secret.

PIERRE CHARLES, S.J.

Louvain, Pentecost 1922.

I

Ubi caput reclinet
Where to lay His Head
(*Matt. viii.* 20.)

OUR Lord God seeks a place to rest in the shelter of a strong and watchful love. He would sleep in peace, as in the ship with His disciples, far off from the clamorous crowd and the uproar of the tumultuous world. He seeks, that is to say, for a soul that will receive Him, and be content to watch in silence by Him; a soul that will find all its happiness in possessing Him, even when no words are uttered, and He remains motionless and as it were overcome with sleep; a friendly and self-sacrificing soul, that will be to Him as the homeliest home: *ubi caput reclinet*, in which He can find rest in His weariness.

He seeks, but hardly does he find such a one, for the greater number of men are too much taken up with themselves to find their happiness in that rest which God enjoys within them. We want someone who will talk to us. All long waiting wearies us, and silence seems full of emptiness. We cannot understand a God who is mute. Faith fails us, and we cannot believe that He is present, acting and Divine, Who seems to sleep and do nothing.

Ubi caput reclinet: He seeks a soul matured and strong in virtue, without roughness and harshness, one that will yield without difficulty to His Will, and which will not draw back as into a stronghold to escape from the pursuit of grace. *Super cervical dormiens* (*Mark* iv. 38): a gentle and submissive soul—yielding as the rower's cushion in the ship of the Apostles, a soul that knows how to forget itself, to hold itself cheap, to be flexible in His hands and wholly self-surrendered.

But we are full of self; hard, rough, wounding and domineering, without courtesy or gentleness. Never do we let Him lean on us or rest within us. That He may do so, all plunging and jolting should be avoided, whereas good as well as evil troubles and disturbs us. The good desires in the soul are all entangled with human eagerness, and even when we wish to obey, the thoughtless impetuosity of our start carries us generally far beyond the goal. We delight in making schemes, in drawing up the most wonderful programme of sanctity. We set up before ourselves entrancing ideals of virtue, which must be attained, but we rarely stop to purify these desires by passing them through the filter of God's will, nor do we wait to consult Him and correct our views by comparing them with His: *non omnis affectio puœ videtur bona statim est sequenda.* (*Imit. Bk.* iii. ii.)

And so it comes to pass that after a time nothing is left of all these magnificent programmes, of these resolutions, so admirable in theory, but a sense of disappointment, a bruised and wounded feeling, a harmful irritation with ourselves, and a paralyzing discouragement, which is wholly unchristian. *Ubi caput reclinet.* Could He possibly be safely and tenderly harboured in such a soul? Could He rest His divine head on such a heart, full of earthly and conflicting interests? To assure His rest, our inner peace should be unbroken, but to preserve that interior peace not even a good desire may be followed unless His spirit has counselled it. Schemes for the acquisition of virtue, plans for reform of life are doubtless good, but if they are to be anything more than day-dreams and pastimes, they must be rooted in complete interior freedom of soul, and in an entire and courteous acceptance of all the arrangements of God's Providence in our regard. Mould me, O my God, in the form which You have chosen for me. I wish for nothing unless You also will it, I shall always be content to be such as You have desired to have me.

Ubi caput reclinet. I cannot leave Him outside in the storm and dust of the road and in the falling dews of night. I cannot let Him rest that Divine and suffering Head on the stones by the wayside, that Head whose "locks were full of the drops of the night" before they were saturated with the sweat of Blood. *Caput meum plenum est rore.* (*Canticle* v. 2.) My soul must be to Him a hiding place, a house of repose, in which as in a sanctuary we walk with measured tread; and where we speak with lowered voice, as watching by those who sleep.

This overpowering and yet loving reverence for the God at rest within our heart will be both the reason of our restraint and the best means of acquiring it. *Mansionem apud eum faciemus.* (*John* xiv. 23.) This restraint becomes then an act of faith, and it is the Spirit of Christ which must put it in our souls. It is a restraint made up of silence and of waiting, for we do not watch by Him as by one that is dead, but as by one who is risen gloriously from the dead. We watch by Him with hearts all illuminated by desire, for we know that He has conquered darkness, and that His dawn has a midday radiance. When His hour is come, the hour of His own choice, He will awake from His apparent inaction, and all eyes shall behold Him . . . *et qui eum pupugerunt* (*Apoc.* i. 7) . . . even those who have afflicted Him. This tranquillity which is blended of silence, of waiting, and of love which adores and thanks, is in itself a perfect homage and as a breath of incense. It is difficult for us to attain to it, for our souls are full of strange and clamorous troubles, of secret and exacting ties, of rough and commonplace emotions. All our scattered love should be united and fused into one clear flame. But the inner anarchy has dispersed all our powers, and reposeful, quiet sleep is impossible for Him in the midst of our confusion and disturbance.

And yet, my God, I am not unmoved by Your appeal, nor passive and cold in presence of Your need. I long to make my own, the eternal blessing promised to those who, seeing You wandering without shelter, have opened their doors wide and welcomed You within. *Hospes eram et collegistis Me. (Matt.* xxv. 35.) In receiving You, we find ourselves again; the calm and stillness we secure for You become our own given back to us as a reward. When You can rest within our hearts in peace, our poor heads are likewise quieted, and our troubled thoughts have fled . . . *in pace sunt ea quæ possidet. (Luke* xi. 21.)

You know, O Lord, that all our good inclinations come from You, and that apart from You we can never please You; *tibi sine te placere non possumus. (Collect* xviii. *Pent.)* Receive my soul which wishes to receive You, and let us remain thus one within the other, prisoners of the same divine love, that love which You have first borne to me, and with which Your grace fills my heart for You. Grant that I may desire nothing but only You, that I may prefer You to all Your gifts, and should You wish to be silent in my company, and to remain inactive, even for long, as in a tomb, give me a spirit of Faith, strong enough to accept Your way with me, to love that way as a special favour, and to rejoice in it into the day eternal.

II

Cœnabo cum Illo

I shall sup with Him

(*Apoc. iii.* 20.)

OUR Lord has Himself said it, else we could never have aspired to such intimacy. He has said "I shall come" as one, that is, who both wishes it and has been invited. He has said that He will seat Himself at our humble board, and share our evening meal, that homely meal of the day, which is so often prolonged under the calm and quiet influence of the night, coming as it does at the hour which shrouds and seems to invite a loving interchange of secrets, and the out-pourings of purest friendship. We should learn to know Him thus, the Christ who is at rest with us and gives us rest; the guest of our twilight hour when the great feast of glaring daylight is extinguished and all creation speaks with lowered voice, as though murmuring marvellous secrets in our ears.

Cœnabo cum Illo: I shall sup with Him, as long ago the disciples did in the little town of Emmaus, as His own in the Upper Chamber, when all the doors being closed—*januis clausis*—(*John* xx. 19), His love brought Him into their midst; as His friends at Bethany, and as all their mystic descendants ever since. At this divine feast, I, who have nothing, I who am poor and a beggar will offer Him my daily actions, for that is an acceptable gift, one on which He does not disdain to feed His redeeming love. *Ego cibo invisibili qui ab hominibus videri non potest, utor.* (*Tobias* xii. 19.) His invisible food is the perfect accomplishment of the Will of His Father. *Meus cibus est ut faciam voluntatem ejus qui misit me.* (*John* iv. 34.) All then that I have of conformity to the Will of God, all that goes under the name of resignation, gentleness, courage, abnegation, docility, detachment, all *that* can be offered to Him. All my humble and frail virtues, inspired as they are by His grace . . . all in a word that grows in my poor furrows.

My provisions, Lord, are very scanty. I have thought so little of laying in supplies of supernatural food, and I blush at the sight of what I have to offer You. My want of foresight, my improvidence, has produced my present dearth.

Bring it here, bring Me what there is, even if it should be but a few barley loaves and two fishes. My invisible blessing will multiply your offerings, and I have never yet rejected anything that has been given to Me.

Lord, I dare not offer You the remnants of a love on which others have already fed, I have given part of my life as a prey to the devil

and to my own selfishness, how can I venture to put on Your table
that for which men have no further use?

Bring it here, bring always. I only ask that your offering to-day
shall be made in sincerity, and that you will keep back nothing
secretly. In the Upper Chamber they offered Me, at my own request,
the remains of some broiled fish—*partem piscis assi*. (*Luke* xxiv. 42.)
Understand the mystery hidden in each word of My Gospels, and
be neither less simple nor more pretentious than your fathers in the
faith.

Lord, I bring You all I have, and my ardent desire is to refuse You
nothing. But, You, what do You bring, O noble and beneficent
Guest, when You come to this divine supper, which is renewed each
evening in the soul that serves You?

What does He bring? He brings His familiar converse, the light
and warmth of His speech; He brings words which captivate and
bind us to Him for ever. Speak, Lord, speak to me of Yourself, for
that is what rests my soul. I am weary of always talking about myself
and my affairs, as though I alone were of interest and as if my personality and not Yours were the alpha and the omega of all things. Tell
me what You feel, what You have to go through, what You desire,
what grieves You. Tell me, not briefly, but in detail, what You have
done, and what You still plan to do. Tell it to me sweetly and confi-
dentially, to me Your poor redeemed one. Teach me to play my
part as a Mary at Bethany, and may I at length know how to listen
when You speak only of Yourself.

And He will tell me over again the story of His hidden life in my
soul. He will tell of all the efforts He has had to make, all the divine
strategy He has employed to capture me: He will relate my own life
to me as seen by Him, and tell me how often He has been obliged
to begin His work again, His work within me, which my folly has
made so heavy for Him. He will explain how it is that He has never
ceased to pursue after me, nor ever given up the struggle to gain me
in spite of all disappointments and failures. My life, my poor human
life shown thus, my life related to me by God, in which there is
nothing that is not sacred since all speaks of His love; my life, which
appears to me now as a divine success, because it brings Him each
evening as a guest to my table, this life . . . I accept it all. I shall
no longer complain of anything. The remembrance of my sins will
even become sweet to me, since My Saviour has sanctified it. *Semper
et ubique gratias agere*. (*Preface—Mass*.)

He will tell me also of His plans, of the difficulties He meets with
and of the way in which He means to overcome them. He will
initiate me into the mysterious secret of His work on earth, and I
will give Him all that I have, and humbly try to comfort Him, when

the remembrance of bitter sorrow endured will blind His eyes, the eyes of the Good Shepherd, with tears. He will tell me of His great longings; I have other sheep that are not yet of My Fold, *illas oportet me adducere* . . . (*John* x. 16) these I must capture and bring home. Speak to me of those strayed sheep, O Lord, and make me great-souled, even as an Apostle.

Rogate Dominum messis. (*Matt.* ix. 38.) The harvests are white in the fields, entreat the Master of the fields to send in the reapers. Speak to me, O Lord, of Your mystic ears of corn, and may my hand be restless till it grasps the sickle.

Vigilate et orate. (*Matt.* xxv. 41.) You must watch and pray, while I suffer and expiate, so that no trial may be able to overthrow the hopes I have founded on you. Where are those who can watch one hour with Me?

Speak to me of your loneliness, Lord, of the neglect You have met with, teach me Yourself, *tu mihi loquere solus.* (*Imit. Bk.* i. 3.) Make known to me all Your desires, I listen to You speaking in the stillness of my thoughts, when the day declines and evening falls, and the shadows of my life grow long: *donec aspiret dies et inclinentur umbræ.* (*Cant.* ii. 17.)

And even as He speaks with me, He is being glorified in heaven, the angels extol Him and voices thunder through the clouds in praise of Christ, *et in laudem Christi voces tonant per nubila.* (*Ant. Procession: Palm Sunday.*) But He talks with me; He abides in my house—the house of His publican. It is as if all that glory were as nothing to Him, and I alone were all His care.

We speak together, I listen . . . and thus a lifetime passes. Then comes a moment . . . Who can tell what happens? It is as though a veil were rent, and blind eyes opened. A radiance not of earth surrounds Him . . . It is the moment of my passing hence. Blessed death approaches; that death which never interrupts the converse of the soul with its God; but which lets fall all earthly coverings, all mists and veils of faith, and shows us, face to face, our long-loved Guest and Sovereign Master . . . *Jesu, quem velatum nunc aspicio.* (*Adoro Te.*) Rising from our humble supper board we pass to the supper of the Lamb in the Kingdom of the Father, and for ever.

III

Et Galilæus es

For thou art also a Galilean
(*Mark xiv.* 70.)

HIS love is tenacious and He marks all that is His with an indelible mark, a seal of eternity. Even should we leave Him and lose ourselves in evil company, and stray, through weakness or through malice, into the midst of His most implacable enemies, even then we can be recognized by a something in our views, in our speech, in our actions, that can only have been learnt in His school. The accent betrays the soul that Christ has loved. *Et Galilæus es*—we too are Galileans. We are strangers everywhere unless with Him. Once we have belonged to Him we not only lose the power of withdrawing this gift of ourselves, without incurring loss or danger, but to do so altogether, becomes impossible.

To learn to know Him thus attaches us to Him by a new bond, and makes us fathom something of His unmerited love; it makes us understand a little better the wonderful power of this love; it opens, by faith, the fountains of sorrow and of trust in the very heart of a desert—*in inaquoso*. (*Psalm* cv. 14.)

Let us learn to recognize Him under the modest disguise of grace, which when roughly turned away, does not leave us wholly: *O amator peccatorum* (*Salve mundi . . . Arnulphus Abb. of Villers*); let us discern Him in the divine fire, which, smothered beneath the ashes of dissipation and accepted selfishness, yet hides in the deepest hollow of the soul, one last spark, and with it the hope of a radiant resurrection.

Let us learn to know Him following in the track of the soul which has escaped from the fold of the Good Shepherd, following it patiently in all its wandering fancies, its foolish extravagances and its dangerous adventures . . . then shall we understand that His love never lets go, that never again can we think and judge exactly as an unbeliever, nor hinder Him from being in reality Our Master.

A Galilean! Lord, when I postpone the total surrender of myself to You to some later day; when I wait for the advent of some magic hour in order to give myself to You and to abdicate my last rights and make over to Your keeping my most sacred hopes; when I evade and dissemble before honestly acknowledging You as Lord and Conqueror; when I count upon possible to-morrows whose dawn, however, is constantly deferred to suit the inclinations of my selfish indolence . . . in all these moments, I am yet a Galilean, and something of You still lives in me. . . . For to *put off* the date

25

of Your final and absolute triumph over my pride, is to confess that sooner or later this triumph will be Yours, and to own that I cannot do without You. It is an acknowledgment that every position we assume, which is not that of utter loyalty, is after all but provisional, and that all our boasted security is false. To refuse to pay my debts *at once*, is a lame recognition of the fact that You are my Creditor ... *Et Galilæus es* ... Our awkwardness betrays us, as it betrayed Your Apostle in the courtyard of the High Priest; our awkwardness betrays us and reveals to whom those souls belong who are following afar off indeed, and putting off, till later, the day of faithful service.

Et Galilæus es! We walk with Him for a time, then suddenly, with a vacant look, we turn away our heads and leave Him. We fear that He is about to ask for some service that will call for generosity; that He is perhaps about to ask divinely for an alms, and we don't want ... at least for the moment we don't want to give it. But we dare not look Him in the face, for we know so well that at one glance from those eyes all our opposition would fade away, and we should fall prostrate at His feet. So we pretend to be busy and absorbed in things outside His service; in this very pretence it is easy to read the secret dread of His power, and the fear of His inevitable exactions.

Et Galilæus es! In order not to hear His call, and in the hope of stifling His unwelcome complaints or loving reproaches in the purposely planned tumult of a conscience that is in hiding, we talk very loud to ourselves, and laugh boisterously with others, we keep up a wearisome and perpetual commotion in our souls; our souls ... that seek to forget His winning invitations, that amuse themselves and cry aloud like frightened children in the dark, to make others think they are not afraid, and whose childish trick makes known their secret terrors. *Galilæus es!* All these cowardly tricks, these devices and schemes, this great anxiety to haggle, to evade, to put off, to quibble ... all these half measures betray a disciple who is ashamed of his discipleship, and who yet cannot destroy its divine mark upon him, nor escape from the strong grasp of redeeming love.

My God, how is it that You are not weary of me, when even in my own eyes my degrading meanness has destroyed all dignity? I meet with tenderness from You in the midst of my unfaithfulness, and I am able in fact to gather ripe grapes from the thistles of my sins! *Quia amabas me! fecisti me amabilem. (St. Augustine.)* Because You have loved me, you have made me lovable. All my cunning skill applied to throw Your grace off the scent; all my wicked efforts to make myself unlovable in Your sight; all this but makes Your freely-given love glow with a deeper splendour. That love which has first put in me that which it must ever love there; that love which is all-embracing, and from which nothing can escape, any more than a fish can escape from the surrounding waters of the sea.

Quid dicam de te? (*Imit. Bk.* iii. x.) Tell me Your thoughts, and let me learn to judge myself as You will judge me; teach me not to bruise, by unneedful roughness, the bent and quivering reed; nor to crush by impatience and contempt, by a harshness that You never counsel, the still smouldering taper. Teach me to treat myself with respect and love, for Your sake, and out of reverence to that which it has seemed good to You to put within me. Let me keep my un-measured contempt for everything in my soul or in my life that tries to free itself from Your loving guardianship, and to assert imaginary claims and pretensions. But, show me, O My God, You who love our souls, how I can, and why I should find everywhere, even in the remembrance of my guilty weakness, tokens of Your persevering love. A ciborium cannot be turned to common uses without profa-nation, but even after profanation it is still a sacred vessel, and its true place is in the Tabernacle. All my desecrations of my own soul have not hindered You from being still and ever my one Master, and Your sovereign rights have not been impaired either by my persistent refusals, or by my loud-voiced rebellions. I belong to You . . . my very accent has always betrayed me; I am of Your family, of Your homeland of Galilee since the day of my baptism and even before it, since that eternity in which You chose me . . . *ante tempora sæcularia.* (2 *Tim.* i. 9.)

IV

Pone me juxta Te

Place me very near You

(*Job xvii.* 3.)

THAT I may wrench myself free from all that is mediocre, therefore above all from self, may He deign to place me very close to Him, in His shadow and in His light. Very near to Him, as a little child, simple and awkward, who must be helped and held up, and whose natural clumsiness turns the most useful things and the most serviceable realities into so many death-bringing perils and dreaded enemies; as a child who wounds itself by catching hold of knives by their blades and who burns itself by playing with the captivating fire. My God . . . I am that child, that simple, curious, weak child, whatever may be the high figure to which the days of my mortal pilgrimage have attained. Yes, that child is myself, and if I refuse to recognize this fact You will never be able to complete the education of my soul, and I shall not enter with the little ones into the kingdom of heaven. It is I who wound myself so stupidly, taking hold of knives by their blades. I do so each time that I rebel against the trials that Your Providence chooses for me, each time that I complain and murmur, each time that by selfish preoccupations I allow the divine peace, which descends from above, to be troubled in my soul.

There is, however, a way of taking hold of knives and of trials, a way which makes it easy to use them, but which must be learnt that it may be known and put in practice. Your trials have also, as it were, a handle, they have a side, an aspect, by which they can be adjusted to our souls. It is called submission. But submission demands detachment, and that is a word we refuse to hear.

Teach me, O Lord, to avail myself of every occasion, to make use of every event without wounding or bruising myself, teach me to distinguish between good and evil, to resist the mad fascination of all that shines and dances, and is in reality but a cruel and death-bringing flame. There is, however, a way of making use of fire; without it our life itself would be extinguished. Lord, I am a frail and ignorant child; show me how to make use of all that heats and even of all that sparkles and flares so pleasantly while still keeping the distance prescribed by caution and not overstepping the limits of prudence. Teach me to suffer without wounding myself, and to enjoy without being imperilled.

Pone me juxta Te. Place me very close to You, like the mischievous child, giddy and half-wild, whom it is necessary to watch and restrain, off whom we cannot take our eyes for long, and who needs to feel some protecting presence round him, else he would break out in the most nonsensical whims, in the most inconsistent follies and in the most senseless deeds and exploits. For, again, I am that child whose mind is yet unbalanced, and who is incapable of resisting the sudden impulses of his nature; and the only merit I can claim by Your grace is, perhaps, that I do not dream of hiding this fact. Yes, it is I who, coming from prayer, returning from Communion, suddenly break out into the most ridiculous impatience, impulsive anger, peevish roughness, and aggressive remarks, without being even able to state clearly the cause of these extravagances. It is I who change my mood because the sky is over-clouded, or who throw up all resolutions guided by the secret counsel of my laziness. Watch over me, Lord, may I be always very near to You, for if I do not know that You see me, and that I am in Your presence, if my faith, increased by Your grace does not vouch for this, I shall be undone through my folly, and my heedlessness will be the death of Your work within me . . . *Kyrie eleison.*

Pone me juxta Te. Place me very close to You again as the familiar tool, on which You can count, and which will not fail in its work. I see all round me on my writing table those lowly and reliable instruments which, as it were, lengthen my fingers to enable me to write, support my limbs, show me at what pace time is passing, and preserve the memory of all that I forget. Lord, I should like to be able to prolong Your action in the same way, to be Your docile instrument, as near to You as the sword is to the soldier, and the prayer book to the hands which hold it. I wish that You could rely upon me, and make use of all that I have by Your grace, without having first to ask my permission and without fearing to wound my susceptibility. For You have need of fellow-workers, and You have willed not to complete the work of Your redemption all alone. Place me very close to You, and while You make use of me, teach me to be useful to You.

Pone me juxta Te. Put me very near to You, as the intimate friend to whom is whispered our most secret confidences and our dearest hopes. I know that I am not worthy to hear Your eternal thoughts, and that my heart is not pure enough for You to pour into it Your divine wishes, Your tender and loving desires . . . *Desiderio desideravi* . . . (*Luke* xxii. 15). But, O Lord, would it not be the only way of purifying it? If You wait to come to me till I, by my own means, heal my poverty and dislodge my misery, I shall be dead, laid low between the boards of my coffin, before I have experienced Your friendship which makes holy.

He binds us to Himself by a mysterious tie; we are to possess Him by our very destitution, and feel ourselves driven towards Him by all the power of our trouble, and the weight of our weakness. Foolish as we are, we should be tempted no longer to believe Him to be indispensable to us on the day we did not feel that without Him all was lacking to us. Therefore He does not wish to cure us all at once, nor to remove all our blemishes; but like the sunlight which returns each day, He never ceases helping us, and it is through our poverty that we get to know Him better, and unite ourselves more closely to Him.

My God, is not all that I need to be found in this one wish: *juxta Te*, near, very near to You? Is not every infidelity a withdrawing from You, and at the starting point of all real misfortunes do we not find a desertion? When we remain in our place, everything, even death, becomes meritorious and glorious; and the place for me, weak, heedless and capricious as I am, yet loving and longing for You, cannot be far from You. *Juxta Te* . . . this word prolongs itself in the echoes of eternity, since my paradise will be nothing else; it is wholly enclosed in that little formula. May Your watchfulness and Your divine loving-kindness be ever with me, *quia non-desinis propitius intueri quos talibus auxiliis concesseris adjuvari.* (*Collect SS. Tiburtius and Susanna.*) All I ask is asked for Your sake, Lord, in remembrance of all You have done for my soul; keep me in Your grace and do not let me escape from You.

V

Rabbi, ubi habitas?

Master, where dwellest Thou?
(*John* i. 38.)

IT is not enough to meet Our Lord by chance, as it were, and to speak with Him by the way. That which satisfies a momentary curiosity is not enough for a faithful friend. The faithful friend, the ardent disciple who has heard him speak to the crowd, must be able to meet Him again at leisure, and stay near to Him—*et apud eum manserunt die illo* (*John* i. 39), the disciple must know where He dwells, and where amongst us is the place of His retirement—*habitavit in nobis* (*John* i. 14), the place to which we are sure to see Him return if we are willing to wait a little; the place where He cannot escape us.

Ubi habitas? We shall not know His permanent dwelling place unless He Himself shows it to us, unless He Himself leads us to it. *Venite et videte.* (*John* i. 39.) We can only reach Him through Himself. We can only make our way to Him, by Him. He is at the same time the road and the goal, the door and the sheep-fold, the beginning and the end, the alpha and omega of all things—*principium et finis.* (*Apoc.* xxii, 13.) Thus only those hearts which His light enlightens, only those souls which His will directs can find Him and dwell with Him. Overstepping all methods, or rather in the heart of every method and of every practice of perfection, it is His spirit which gives life and sight and movement and light: *Venite et videte.*

His dwelling place? *In nobis* . . . (*John* xvii. 21) amongst us; for the whole world is filled with His unseen presence, and if He appears to be absent our faith assures us that He can only be hidden. He is at the fountain-head of all loyal and pure thoughts, and of all genuine and heartfelt sorrow; and it is my poor soul, innocent or penitent, which is still His dwelling place, the one He wishes never to leave. Master, where dwellest Thou? Make known to me the roads which lead to myself. Disclose to me that deepmost sanctuary which Your voluntary love has contrived for itself in the inmost core of my being, and grant that as I reascend one by one all the paths of my waking life, I may always find Your pitiful grace at their starting-point, forestalling all my beginnings and giving me whatever true worth is mine. Since You have willed to save us all, the mystery of my free will can only be explained by Your presence and Your action. *Ego in eis.* (*John* xvii. 23.) My intellect, too, is illuminated by the brightness of Your revelation, and deep beneath my thoughts I meet again with You.

Ubi habitas? Lord, where dwellest Thou? Lead me to Your home.

And he will lead us to that resting-place of His choice in the souls of His saints and of those who love Him, of all those men, known or unknown, who have let themselves be penetrated by His spirit and have opened to Him the gates of eager docility. That I may see Him in His chosen ones, He must lend me His own eyes, for He alone knows Himself—*sui perfectus cognitor,*—(*St. Thomas: De Fide*) and when, by my fault, this view of faith is darkened in my life, my whole action becomes rough and commonplace, and I profane His dwelling, by disturbing the peace of my neighbour with whom He dwells. Teach me Lord, to reverence You in virtuous souls, make me learn the sweet and restful joy of watching You in silence in hearts devoted to You, in all those who love You, and whom You sanctify. *Venite et videte.* It seems to me that You could make me understand what is that mysterious place within the soul, for that place is You Yourself, *omnia in omnibus.* (*I Corinthians* xv. 28.) It seems to me that if my faith increased, if my inner sight were illuminated, I should see them all—Your chosen ones here below—as real "Christophers," Christ-bearers, God-bearers, and that there would be no place in my judgment, appreciation or behaviour for anything mediocre or base.

Ubi habitas? Lord, where dwellest Thou? He also dwells in the little chances which arise of doing well, or of suffering well. He dwells in these humble homes as in His consecrated Hosts, and beneath the appearances of chance annoyances, of importunate visitors, of disagreeable illnesses, of unprofitable work, of sacrifices claimed, of meritorious obedience . . . under these appearances He is morally present as He is corporally present under the Eucharistic species. And my life passes close to these His dwellings: and the meandering course of my days meets them at each moment; but I am too blind to notice them and I pass by the chances of doing or of suffering well, as we pass by empty shanties or ruined hovels on our road. *Venite et videte.*

Open my eyes for me, Lord, and may I learn to know You in the humility of these Your lowlinesses, and to meet You in the sanctifying prose of daily duties. For *there* is in truth Your dwelling place; it is in this unpretentious duty, no matter what form it may take, that I am sure to meet You, not only passing by, and as it were by stealth, but stationary, and always present. There, I need never fear illusion. Those who obey You, those who uncomplainingly consent to love their duty, those embrace no phantom when they clasp Your merciful loving-kindness in their suppliant arms; and their voices are not lost in empty air, when in their anguish they call to You for help. You are with them, and quite close to them, or more truly, doing their duty and remaining faithful to it, they dwell with You throughout their whole life . . . *et apud eum manserunt die illo.*

The question we should really ask Him is: *Rabbi, ubi non habitas?* Master, where dost Thou not dwell? You are in me. You are in my neighbour. You are in the events of my life, in my work, in my drudgery, in my sufferings, in all my sacrifices . . . Where then do You not abide, and where can that place be, here below, which shall be without You? He will answer what He has said long since to man, the place where He does not abide is there where self-will dwells and selfishness, the all-usurping and restless self, aggressive, insolent, sullen and crafty. He will tell us that every place is void of Him which we refuse to yield up to Him, and that His almighty love is stopped short before doors which some meanness, acquiesced in, shuts in His face, and before barriers raised against Him by the desire of an illusory independence, and of a sham emancipation. *Ab omni proprietate evacuatus* . . . (*cf. Imit.* iii. 37, ii. 8), may I be free from all spirit of proprietorship, from all deliberate clinging to myself, so that no secret cell may remain within me impenetrable to His action, so that He may abide as Sovereign in His mansion; in His mansions, rather, for here below as above in the house of His Father, *mansiones multæ sunt.* (*John* xiv. 2.)

Lord, I am an inattentive disciple, and a forgetful student. The lesson of Your unseen presence, which I have understood to-day, will have to be repeated daily to me, for each day I let it escape my mind, and each day, I am recaptured by that common illusion which relies only on what is perceptible to the senses. Increase my love and my reverence, and may I at last learn to see You where You are, until the day, when to my ever recurring question: *Ubi habitas?* You will usher me in for ever to Your eternal Paradise.

C

VI

Verba delictorum meorum

All that my sins say
(*Psalm xxi.* 1.)

SINCE You do not refuse to forgive them, Lord, our sins also have a message of love to convey, and if we know how to question them aright, they will answer us with a Gospel . . . a good tiding of Redemption. They speak of repentance and of sorrow, but to my natural and earthly-minded soul their language is obscure and confused, and I have never really known what they wished to make me understand. Enlighten me, O my God, refine me through the power of Your Spirit: *qui corda fidelium Sancti Spiritus illustratione docuisti.* (*Collect Pentecost.*)

There is a way of pondering over sins, of meditating on evil done, of regretting past faults, which weakens, paralyses and makes faint-hearted. Perhaps I have not protected myself sufficiently on this side. At times compunction has been made to appear to me as a lonely sadness confronting a vast expanse of ruins; as a mournful verification of an irreparable bankruptcy . . . of a total and final defeat. My poor good desires resulting in nothing; each stage of my spiritual life marked by a crushing defeat; each of my efforts broken in its flight; each of my resolutions collapsing upon itself. And I am invited to walk for long and all alone in the midst of this debris. I am urged to go through this necropolis, to count carefully all that has failed, all that has been unable to keep its word, or to make good its promise. *Sedebit solitarius et tacebit* . . . (*Jeremias* iii. 28.) This pilgrimage is always heart-breaking when made thus; we do not return stronger from it, but only more desolate and at times more bitter; and when we are told that this pilgrimage must be begun again each day, that it is our best occupation while here below, and that to think of anything else is but to fall into illusion and to expose ourselves to irreparable failure, we accept these exhortations or these commands as a sentence of condemnation, and the remembrance of our sins disgusts and crushes us. Compunction—this word and thing which should be so moving and so familiar—appears to us to be nothing more than a funereal order; and those are not few, perhaps, who had turned away from it, not wishing to take this useless load upon their already too wearied shoulders, and thinking it wrong, or at least not wise, to be for ever reviving a dead past, excavating in swamps, instead of leaving behind us for ever that which no thought, no regret can repair or undo.

Compunction which should feed the Christian soul, which should be supernaturally attractive, cannot surely be this cake of sand, this acrid gluey bitumen bringing illness in its train, which no one can assimilate nor desire to take. And yet when compunction has been reduced to solitary sadness in the presence of our own incapacity, a sadness which, in defiance of all logic, we associate with a firm determination to act quite otherwise in the future! when compunction is nothing more than the earnest and persevering contemplation of the periodic collapse of a building, backed up by the resolution to rebuild it all—every day!—it is necessarily hard, morose and paralysing, a councillor of discouragement and of deep-felt vexation, the enemy of all that has wings.

Compunction is a means of knowing God, and our past faults are roads which lead us to Christ, since it is down their course that His pardon has come or will come to us. Children count the stars in the hazy firmament of our summer evenings; and each of these stars is a path of light; sinners—we should count our sins in the firmament of our life, for each is a mysterious pathway which divine mercy has trodden in order to overtake us.

Compunction does not consist in being moved to pity over myself, over my weakness and my wanderings—of what use could those solitary tears be! It consists in weeping *together* over a common misfortune and in understanding better a misjudged love. And these tears are lights. There are things which can never be seen but with tear-brimmed eyes, and love that has saved us is one. Far from chilling stoically, or depressing uselessly, compunction softens and strengthens, as every really Christian feeling does. Love grows greater through reparation; love needs regret and avowals and repentance, and those know this well, who in the things of earth, to rekindle the flame of a love that is failing, seek instinctively for some motive or at least some pretext for a "reconciliation," for tender reproaches. Love forgiven is strong as death, and our sins should be a fresh bond, rebinding us to God: *funiculus triplex* (*Ecclesiastes* iv. 12) . . . a threefold cord.

The joint work, bungled by my carelessness, my idleness, my ridiculous folly, is His Redemption in me. When I wish then to repent, I must first of all call to Him. Far from imagining that I must keep timidly in my lonely corner, weeping in solitude like a child that has been punished, until my regrets shall have made me worthy of Him, I must understand that without Him I can repair nothing, reconquer nothing, and that the very first movement which brings me back towards Him is the effect of His grace, which has come to seek me. *Pastor agnorum relagium!* (*Clement of Alexandria.*)

Then repentance becomes sweet to me; instead of being a solitary and heart-breaking walk in the midst of tombs, it is a pilgrimage of love on which I shall set out with Him. I examine myself as carefully as ever. But I no longer fear to find that I am guilty, on the contrary, I seek with holy eagerness for all my failures, I accuse myself almost without measure, even there where Jesus gently excuses me; I pile up the injuries done, I increase and exaggerate my debts . . . for each of my faults is a magnificent and indisputable proof of His love, being as it is a relic of His pardon. How easily then we understand the Christian need of truth even if it is humiliating truth, a need that false wisdom has declared to be morbid, the need of repeated confessions, of examinations of conscience renewed each day: and how far removed from the Catholic mind, from the mind of the Redeemer are all those—even though they do not know it—who reject, distrust and lessen these holy practices of repentance, of remembrance of our faults, of contrition and of tears of sorrow. Compunction is divine and revealing—for it shows us God the Comforter. *Lætitia sempiterna* . . . (*Isaias* xxxv. 10) everlasting joy . . . is it my sin or my virtue that is its cause? And to repeat my *peccavi* (*Luke* xiv. 18) to rehearse my old *mea culpa* is sweet to me as an assurance of His love, and as a pledge of His infinite mercy. It is He who then says to me "Weep not, be comforted" . . . *Noli flere; confortare—consolamini; popule meus.* (*Luke* vii. 13; *Isaias* li. 6, l. 1.) He can console to the uttermost, for it is He alone, in reality, who has suffered from all that has made me guilty.

VII

Fatigatus ex itinere
Weary from the journey
(John iv. 5.)

TO become like Our Lord there is no need to change the conditions of our earthly existence, there is no need to cease to be a man; we have only to cease being human in the wrong way, that is to say, to keep apart and cut off from Him. He has sanctified the lowliest realities of our life, for He has made His own the "weakness of our substance" *fragilitatis substantiam. (Preface, Ascension.)* And because He has Himself known what it is to be wearied out, weariness has become a divine thing.

This poor human frailty, this weariness which we know so well, and which always seems to us to be a dull and senseless barrier between our soul and God; this miserable weariness which fetters our prayer, benumbs our energies and slows down the first transports of zeal, this age-long languor of our race, which all men look on as an enemy, may yet be the bearer of a message of light to our souls. Lacking the true spirit of a Christian, we have perhaps misunderstood it, been troubled as at an apparition—*putaverunt quia phantasma est. (Mark vi. 49.)* It is a sign to be contradicted.

The weariness that follows on days of exhausting labour, when, as evening falls, the poor body falters and gives way, when sleep clouds our thoughts and physical discomfort, reaching almost to an agony, takes entire possession of us . . . Can it be that we are of any more worth than a senseless machine, since this periodic collapse of our powers reduces us to this pitiable helplessness! Can it be possible that in the slow hours of this our physical weakness we are still worthy to appear before God? To be admitted to the Divine presence should we not have an awake and vigorous mind, a prompt and eager will, eyes that sparkle and arms stretched forth to labour? . . . *Fatigatus ex itinere* . . . To be like God there is no need to strain to reach these dizzy heights, no need to stretch the springs of our soul to breaking point. To meet God we need not first escape from human weakness, nor pretend that it is non-existent. We need play no lying part, need borrow no conventional attitudes. It is enough to be merely a man to become like to the Son of Man. So long as we never descend to the level of sin, we are on a footing with Him who has known in His own person each one of our miseries: *tentatum . . . per omnia pro similitudine absque peccato (Heb.* iv. 15) . . . One tempted in all things like as we are, without sin.

37

He has known this pitiable weariness of ours. He has known it as
we know it, felt its weight, its constraint, its humiliation. Those who
refuse to believe in such condescension on His part, and who deny
that He has felt our frailties, and been weary with our weariness,
measure the things of God by human standards, and know nothing
of the spirit of God. "If Christ be not risen, our hope of resurrection
is vain." So, too, if Christ has not suffered, it will only be in spite of
suffering, outside its realm, and by opposing it that we may join
ourselves to Him, and hope to meet Him. But Christ is the Truth,
and when in the days of His pilgrimage He rested on the edge of a
well, it was because He felt very weary. He had exhausted His
strength in traversing the long roads of earth. Thus weariness is a
divine thing, and when I can do no more I am like to Him.

Help us, O Lord, to understand this mystic sacrament of Christian
weariness; teach us that to be tired may yet be sanctifying, because
something of You is found therein. Every worn-out man recalls the
Man of Sorrows, and at the root of all our physical weakness is
hidden that secret bond which binds them to the One who has first
borne them all—*dolores nostros ipse portavit (Isaias* liii. 4) . . . He has
borne our sorrows.

We often ask ourselves what is there we can offer to God that
will not be unworthy of His acceptance. We look all round about
and see how few are our possessions and how great that misery
which is so well known to Him—*tibi undique notam—(Imit. Bk.* iii. 20)
and we can find no incense to place on the glowing embers of His
invisible censers—*habens thuribulum aureum. (Heb.* ix. 4.)

Now, however, we begin to understand, and our poverty may
even become sweet to us. Nothing is worthy of His acceptance
unless He first makes it so, not only by accepting it from without, as
offered by command, but by sanctifying it from within by the
penetrating action of grace. That alone can be offered to Him which
is already His, that alone can delight Him which He has first made
lovable. We may then offer our weariness and our weakness, our
tedious languor and that dark heaviness which takes possession of
us periodically and only at rare intervals leaves us wholly free. We
may place all this in the invisible censer as a perpetual and silent
homage. We can put there all that "*odor mortis*" (2 *Corinth.* ii. 16)
which since He has slain the slayer—*extinctor necis—(Hymn Brev;
Paschal time*) has about it the fragrance of eternity.

Our pitiable fatigue! The weariness that humbles us, that turns
the thoughts in our mind and the words in our sentences upside
down! That weariness so full of aching stupidity, of gloomy stupor,
of nervelessness and powerlessness, that seems the inheritance of a
slave, that was familiar to the chosen people when they carried their

baskets full of clay and bricks in the land of Egypt . . . even this can trace His likeness sweetly in us, if we accept it with and for Him, resigned, and without bitterness or anger. All human weariness belongs to Him, as long as it is not sinful. It may then all be offered to Him, for nothing that is His is unworthy of Him. Our poverty wins the kingdom of heaven for us, and when we are powerless it is in order that He who is Almighty may alone uphold us.

We have then found our morning and our evening sacrifice: *sacrificium vespertinum, matutinum.* (*Psalm* cxl. 2.) We know now that we can put into our "baskets" at the moments when we seem most destitute. And when at length the weariness of life becomes too great for our sick and worn-out bodies, when at last all struggle and all war shall have ceased within us; when weariness has conquered in our death, then, O Lord, receive this last act of homage, this last breath of the perfume of Your love within us—*fatigatus ex itinere.* Yes, weary from our journeyings on the many roads of life, weary from having walked so far! When we can no more, and when our hour—Your hour—has come, the hour that no man knows, remember, O Lord, that You too learnt, with labour, to suffer as we suffer, and that as a deposit entrusted to Your keeping all our weakness is laid up: *didicit ex eis quæ passus est.* (*Heb.* v. 8.)

We can then love this blessed weariness, this heaviness which You have sanctified. And we can understand those friends of Yours who rejoice to feel their body wear out, their strength fail, their life fade away in the hard labour that Your sweet Providence imposes in mercy on us. O joy of weary evenings, of days of fasting, of nights of watching, when the body moaning forth, after its fashion, some mute misery, the soul yet gives the answering cry of Alleluia.

VIII

Lecythus olei
A cruse of oi
(3 *Kings xvii.* 14.)

THE disciples of Our Lord are always distrustful and their restless anxiety hinders His peaceful actions and puts an obstacle to His work of grace. He described us all in a word when, on the road to Emmaus, He reproached us with being "foolish and slow of heart to believe," with not daring to rely upon His word.

That anticipated discouragement, which we call mistrust, is too natural to us to be anything but folly. Hearts are rare indeed which have never been invaded by this cunning enemy. Even when it has withdrawn for a time, even when some realization of Divine goodness forces back the inundation of pusillanimity and the rising flood of mistrust, there remains behind a death-bearing deposit, in which, as in a bed of adhesive clay, our good desires are choked, and every glow of genuine trust in God is stifled as it comes to birth.

What is this false wisdom, through which the old error is kept alive within us, and what blessing of God can drive it into exile? *Vetus error abiit.* (*Isaias* xxvi. 3.) This error old as the race, which is seated, like a beggar in rags, on the threshold of so many souls, whence comes it? This old mistake of cowardice and distrust is so often met with that it seems in the end to be almost a necessity of our nature. Whence comes it, and by what right has it established itself so close to us?

We are at times discouraged, always pusillanimous because we stake our security on a fragile and tottering support. We aim at establishing the peace of our soul and the pledge of our worth on the purely natural opinion which we are ourselves able to form of our capabilities and of our deserts. We question ourselves anxiously, we try to estimate the reserve of energy which we have at our command, we busy ourselves with the stethoscope that we may know ourselves more intimately, we analyse ourselves that no appearances may deceive us; we lose endless time in calculating what we might have done formerly, if . . . what we may yet perhaps be able to do later, when . . . and it is on all these empty speculations that we hope to build up our confidence. Precarious, frail supports, and crazy props, which have themselves to be underpinned daily, and yet totter at the slightest shock.

It is not on the consciousness that we have of our own abilities, that our trust should rest, but on the merciful goodness of Him who never abandons those whom His Father has given to Him, that He might keep them in life: *quos dedisti mihi non perdidi ex eis quemquam.* (*John* xviii. 9.) Our certainty and our security rest on faith, and that which keeps us at peace with ourselves is something which has a very real existence though it is invisible.

When the prophet Elias, in the name of God, blessed the oil of the poor widow of Sarepta, this blessing also remained invisible. At the bottom of the little earthen pot there were still but a few drops of oil—*pauulum olei in lecytho*—(3 *Kings* xvii. 12), and at the sign of the prophet the vessel was not filled, it remained apparently just as it had been . . . but as these drops were poured out they renewed themselves in proportion to the need of the moment, no more, so that the pot while always on the point of becoming empty, yet always contained enough oil to secure the household against want.

God works in our souls in just this same way. Each day He gives us the measure of grace that is sufficient for us; but He never allows us to feel that we are plentifully supplied for all our needs, and that we possess a store that is inexhaustible. This ordinary sense of security which comes with the assured possession of our hoarded wealth; this quiet confidence of the farmer who has gathered in his harvest; this security that comes with ownership has nothing in common with the spirit of faith, and yet it is just the kind of security that we all long to attain.

To *feel* that we are strong and rich and powerful; to *feel* at least that the divine coffers into which we are allowed to thrust our hands, are inexhaustible and are open to our every call; to *feel* that we are not depending on anything, but may sleep in peace sheltered from all risk and from all need, that is the state which always appears to us to be the most enviable. The condition, that is, of those who possess. It is with difficulty that we can bring ourselves to do without marks of esteem, not so much because we long to be flattered, as that we pine to be reassured: less that is to say from vanity than from weakness, less from the desire to know what others think of us, than from the hunger to know what we may think of ourselves. God wishes to free us from this bad habit. He wishes to teach us to place our confidence in Him and to disengage ourselves from the opinions we have formed about ourselves. *Quod es hoc es, nec major dici vales quam Deo teste sis.* (*Imit.* Book ii. 6.) As soon as we give up this search for security within ourselves, when we relinquish the right to appraise our souls at their true worth to Him who has been appointed judge of the living and the dead, then a great peace will settle down upon us, and an immense sense of relief. For the burden of anxiety as to what we are really worth and what we can count upon ourselves to do, a burden borne by so many, is a heavy one and has never yet been of the smallest use to any one.

Our confidence rests upon unceasing dependence. Each day God will give us the drop of oil that is necessary for us, at each moment the measure of grace that is sufficient, and thus, feeling ourselves perpetually upheld, yet never able to walk alone; realizing that we are fed each day and yet never cease to be hungry, we attach ourselves to God by one of the deepest fibres of our being; our poverty itself binds us straitly to Him. It is this very destitution, perpetually made good, yet never removed, which renews, as it were, the Redemption within us by making us realize how much we need our God. *Lecythus olei non est imminutus.* (3 *Kings* xvii. 16.) The cruse of oil was not diminished. I know God well enough to be sure that He will not forget me to-morrow any more than He forgot me to-day, and I know that His mercy is everlasting. And so when I rejoice, when in the midst of deeply felt and even overwhelming trouble I can yet sing and work as though as free from care as the birds of the air, my trust is full of adoration, and my joy is a worship that nothing could replace. *Scio cui credidi.* (2 *Tim.* i. 12.) I know in whom I have believed.

Unhappily our short-sighted wisdom understands little of these lessons. Preoccupied as we are with the desire to please God, we do not realize that Without God, or far from Him, we cannot become worthy to please Him; *tibi sine te placere non posumus.* (*Collect* xviii. *Pent.*) Longing to meet Him we have not understood that it is by His side that we must walk to meet Him; He alone can bring us to that trysting-place which His love has chosen for us. Wishing to appear of worth in His eyes, we forget, or rather we have never known that we can have no other value than that which He recognizes in us, having first placed it there Himself. We find it hard to put all our glory, and to find all our joy in being just simply the redeemed. Bought back at a price! At the starting point of all that we are, we must establish His grace, and this one word kills all distrust.

IX

Colligite fragmenta
Gather up even the crumbs
(*John vi.* 12.)

THERE is nothing little for a real love; and he who says "it is only a little thing," in speaking of the suffering which he has caused, or of the happiness which he has destroyed, has never known what love is, nor understood the meaning of charity.

Little things, therefore, have always been sacred in the eyes of faith; and not to trouble about them, to assume towards them the contemptuous arrogance of the wise ones of the world, is to condemn ourselves to remain fundamentally commonplace, and to be strangers to all that is refined.

These little things are a hidden treasure which supernatural insight enables us to find in the field of the Father of the family; these little things are our whole life which passes through our fingers in minute grains of time; these little things are the sum of courage, which our will divides among short-lived actions; these little things are dew-drops of divine grace—*stillæ super gramina*—(*Deuteronomy* xxxii. 2.).), portions of the Holy Sacrifice, the lamp of the sanctuary, the bell of the altar, the silent curling wreaths of incense which scent the air. *Colligite fragmenta:* let nothing be lost of that which Christ has sanctified; the only great thing is the harvest gathered of the little sheaves, and the sheaf made up of the slender stalks, and the ear of corn in which cluster the little grains of wheat given to us by God.

But if the care of little things is obligatory, it is no less so to understand the spirit which should animate this solicitude, and to know why it is good to glean in the furrows where the sickle has passed.

Is it a fatigue-duty that is imposed on us? Is it a heavy and painful obligation? Are we as those working by the piece who will be called upon to settle their accounts, and who think of nothing unless it be how to keep their countenance, and prepare answers for that decisive moment? Is it only by a kind of minutely detailed fidelity, a meddling scrupulosity, that we are to constrain ourselves to finish all our tasks, and to avoid all negligence? We shall work throughout the livelong day, watching ourselves unceasingly, carrying out our programme point by point, verifying, collating, comparing, to be sure that we have passed over nothing, letting all our attention be absorbed in our tasks; and by dint of wishing to do well we shall become unable to think of anything but our business. We shall develop into something as regular and as passive as a mechanical movement, and shall know no other joy than that of saying to ourselves each evening: All is as it should be; I have counted everything, verified everything, I may sleep on the pillow of my precision.

Does the care of little things mean no more than a command to be precise? No, we must go further than that: the care of little things is the homage of fidelity, and the gratification of one of love's great needs. We are never far from Him! We do not work under His eyes, for He is not a mere onlooker, He is a fellow-worker and a friend. Before He exacts anything from us, He forestalls all our wants. Precision in the accomplishment of His will is but submissive fidelity to correspond with His inspirations. How attractive little things should be to me, O God my Redeemer, Who love me such as I am!

Nothing in me is negligible in Your eyes, and that is why all is important, why all should be sanctified, why all is a response and a homage. We shall work together then to make me such as You would have me to be.

Colligite fragmenta . . . He notices the way in which I walk and when my pace is more precipitate than it should be, or more languid than is becoming, He is pained, as one is pained by a defect in a person loved. My bearing and my gestures preoccupy Him: and when they are exaggerated, or too frequent, unruly or merely flippant, He is saddened, for He wants me to keep them simple and restrained. He observes the expression of my countenance, and the tone of my voice: when I raise it, when it grows loud in a wave of anger, when it grates with irritability or temper, when it drawls with nonchalance and listlessness, He suffers as one suffers from a want of good manners, an uncouthness more or less accepted, in those one loves and of whom one wishes to be proud. He cares about everything, since nothing is unconnected with His will; the paper I take to write upon, the words which my mind dictates to my pen, even the stains on my clothes, and the details of my dress, the swiftness of my glance, and the curl of my lip . . . everything is noted by Him, to be approved or deplored by His love.

And this is what I must understand if I would grasp what is really meant by the care of little things. These tiny details are not small change with which to pay for future glory and eternal rewards; they are first and foremost demands made by Him, but demands full of friendliness. They are an answer and a homage which I can and should offer to Him.

Colligite fragmenta. Nothing seems trivial to a great love, and if I believe in the love of my God, if I am convinced that this love is all embracing, that He takes me as I am and intends to change me wholly; if I succeed in persuading myself that nothing is trivial, but that all is but proof of tender fidelity, then I shall be able to avoid, on the one hand, that cramping cowardice which is engrossed in itself, and on the other that false liberty of spirit which disdains to gather up the fragments of the divine gift which is our life, the crumbs of heavenly food which is the grace of Christ.

Give me, O my God, that which is wanting to me. I waver perpetually between a meticulous and frightened narrowness, and a cool and dreamy negligence. You alone can establish me in truth, which is justice, and which, putting each thing in its rank and each being in its place, and illuminating all with true light, re-establishes order in our souls and harmony in our efforts. I know too well the sorrowful remorse felt for having failed You in what is called a "little thing." I know by experience that there are sacred and unspoken pacts between us, which no one has ever guessed at, and which gently call for attentions towards You, for the courtesies of fidelity, and for a proud and filial glory in the accomplishment of all duties, which in fact are Your desires. When people encourage me or seek to console me for my failures, even for those which are but passing weaknesses, by saying "it is nothing or not much," You know, Lord, that those trivial words, those commonplace expressions pain me like the touch of a hot iron. I know Your love too well to measure out thus what I owe You, to reserve my own part in the holocaust and not to wish for Your reign to be absolute. Guide me and help me to understand that You exact nothing from afar off, as a heavy burden, but that, very nigh unto the souls that are Your own—and all are that by their calling—You entreat. Let us work together; my misery will become sweet and fruitful, and having nothing that is mine, I shall be wholly Yours.

X

Singulis manus imponens
Laying His hands on every one of them
(*Luke* iv. 40.)

HE cured them in days of old by this kindly and most merciful action. He cured them all . . . *sanabat omnes* . . . (*Luke* vi. 19) those who cried aloud to Him, and those who looked at Him without a word, those who came of their own accord and took their place by the way which He must pass, and those who were brought to Him from afar on stretchers and pallets, crippled with infirmities, or wasted by lingering illness; all those whose only claim on His love was their need and their misery.

Singulis; for each one of them He had some special attention, for each one He repeated His gesture of blessing. His actions are gospels: His movements are eternal lessons; that which He did in days gone by, He never ceases to do again, and His mission of redemption is continued unseen and mysterious in the hiding-places of the soul. He passes by again amongst us, He walks through the ranks of men who are ill, exhausted, paralysed. He passes laying His hands on *every one*.

I have never yet really understood this action of divine love, and yet to do so marks the beginnings of an interior life, both conscious and steady; it indicates the awakening of the soul to personal and deep devotion. It is under the hands of Christ that all must be born again; as it is into the hands of the Saviour that all must commit themselves when dying. *In manus tuas*. (*Luke* xxiii. 46.)

I must then understand that He has stood still before me, before me all alone, that He has taken notice of my particular misery, and that it is really on my head that He has placed His divine hands.

So long as we look on ourselves as lost in a nameless crowd of the faithful; so long as we imagine that the words of Christ are uttered in general to a chance audience; so long as we think that His promises, destined for all, are not to be applied to anyone in particular; so long as religion remains a vague and collective duty, *so long* the Christian soul is still asleep. Then a day comes when through the grace of Him "who has never hardened any heart" light breaks, suddenly it may be or gradually; an intimate realization, a purely spiritual thrill, a presence, felt and mysterious, warns us that it is to us personally that God is speaking. We perceive, as it were, His approach, we feel that two all-powerful eyes are fixed on our eyes; that a sign which is only for us calls us to attention. He comes, and

I am the term, the goal of this coming; He walks, and it is towards me that He directs His steps, He has marked me out in the crowd, He has recognized me, and through my whole soul there passes, as it were, a dread that is at once pleasant and purifying, mingled of desire, of transport, of fear and of suffering. He who advances towards me is He whom "man shall not see and live," and it is also He who gives life, and raises up into joy, even those who dwell in tombs: *qui habitant in sepulchris.* (*Mark* v. 3.)

Singulis manus imponens: When the consecrating Bishop imposes hands on those whom he ordains, at this simple contact the newly made priest realizes that all has been changed for him. A special calling has laid hold of him, one that will never again leave him free to dispose of himself as he pleases, but will stamp everyone of his actions and all his desires with an invisible seal. All in him must bear the mark of his priesthood.

When, O Christ, shall I at length understand that it is really with me that You have something to settle, when shall I realize practically that we have a great business to discuss between us, and when shall I value at its true worth, and love as I should, this touch of Your divine hands on my head, the head of a submissive and consecrated disciple? All in me should become Christian.

I am not one among millions; there are no "millions," there is only You and I, for it is in You, and through You, and not beside You or in spite of You, that I should see my neighbour. The words which You utter, the considerate encouragement, the thanks whispered in a low voice, all that is for me, as also the friendly reproaches and the sorrowful words of warning; *singulis manus imponens:* It is my turn . . . and You are wholly at my service; and since Your perfections never wane, what You are for me, You are always, and my whole life should pass under Your hands which bless. It is always "my turn," for You never abandon Your undertakings, and Your Spirit which sanctifies has not to begin again several times in order to complete His work.

May I then feel Your divine hands resting on me, may I abide before You for ever, and through Your grace, may that haze of unreality, that mist of convention and of mirage be dispersed, which has for so long hindered me from seeing You near to me, and has made me think that You only cared about me in general, with all the rest, and, as it were, *en bloc.*

Consecrate me to Your service. As You look down on my bowed head, that look will make my idols fall, and I shall no longer be able to keep within my soul all my false gods of selfishness, all my chosen bonds, all my crooked and tenacious desires, all that hinders me from being truly Yours, and which impedes Your holy work in my soul. *Manus imponens:* I have faith in Your all-powerful grace, and I believe that through You I can be made worthy of You.

Manus imponens: Yes, Lord, as on a sick person, as on one worn by a lingering illness, who, weighed down by a heavy and painful stupor, does not himself even know what he is suffering from, nor from what danger he must be rescued. I am before You as a paralytic, I, who am always so slow to follow You, and who no longer dare think of all my cowardly evasions. Long since I should have taken up my place . . . had myself carried . . . to waylay You as You passed, on the "paths pacific" where You are to be found, to petition of You alone the end of all my deep misery, those miseries unknown to man, and of which You alone—even better than myself—have divined the secrets. Cure me by Your divine touch, by the imposition of those redeeming hands, of those hands which hold the heavens and the earth, which grasp unseen the keys of hell and of the kingdom. Cure me of my fears and of my sleepiness, of my outbreaks of roughness, and of my dangerous whims, of my thoughtless impulses and of my calculated affections: yes cure me, You who can do everything and whose loving-kindness never draws back from any need. It is my turn, *singulis manus imponens,* I am one of Your own, one of those whom You have come to seek, and I need to be purified and made holy until that day when You Yourself will be my holiness and my justice, until the day when the power of Your redeeming work will have reached its fullness in me, and when eternity will seal my loyal surrender to Your will.

While awaiting this revelation of Your glory, let me look at You, O my God, let me see that You look at me: *sicut oculi servorum in manibus dominorum suorum!* (*Psalm* cxxii. 2.)

XI

Dum nescit ille

Whilst he knoweth not
(*Mark* iv. 27.)

I HAVE often been troubled, Lord, as to what I was worth in Your eyes. I have been worried about my progress in virtue; I have asked myself anxiously "Am I advancing, and at what rate? am I perhaps falling back, and how much? or can it be that I am merely marking time, and since when?" I have encumbered my soul with many useless cares, and the serene peace of an active faith has slipped out through thousands of invisible rents, and I have found myself as a land without water . . . *sicut terra sine aqua tibi.* (*Psalm* cxlii. 6.)

I beg of You to teach me how we can be unceasingly watchful to lose nothing of Your gift, without wearying our souls with blundering human anxiety, and without bringing in to the inner Cenacle any morbid clamorous desire, any troublesome guest who grumbles or is terror-stricken, who importunes or unnerves us. Between the carelessness which puts up with anything, even with what is mediocre or bad, and the too human anxiety which craves daily for reliable verifications and palpable results; between the listlessness which cares nothing for spiritual progress, and the pre-occupation which consumes and ruins itself with the enumeration of signs and symptoms, grant that Your calm strong wisdom may guide me in the paths of peace and light, *ad lucem quam inhabitas.* (*Hymns Matins C. Christi.*)

The kingdom of heaven is like unto a seed, which springs up in the field, where, by chance, a passer-by one day has thrown it. He who cast the seed seems to have no further anxiety about it. He rises and sleeps, he goes and comes, he slumbers and eats, leaving the seed and the earth to their patient and mysterious work. *Ultro enim terra fructificat* . . . (*Mark* iv. 28) "For the earth of itself bringeth forth fruit," first a green blade that quivers in the wind, a slender and shivering stem, *primum herbam* . . . (*Mark* iv. 28) then little by little the blade becomes a stalk, and on the top of the stalk an ear of corn swings to and fro: *deinde spicam* (*Mark* iv. 28) and in the ear finally, the closely set and savoury grains of wheat are seen to form and grow: *plenum frumentum in spica.* (*Mark* iv. 28.) And the almost fortuitous action of this chance wayfarer, who cast the seed into the earth, has ended in the harvest, and summons the reapers from afar: *statim mittit falcem quoniam adest messis.* (*Mark* iv. 29.)

If I had more confidence in the efficacity of Your supernatural ction, Lord, it seems to me that my co-operation in Your work within me would be free from anxiety, and that all impatience would vanish from my soul. May it suffice me to abide always very near to You, to work in union with Your grace and may all superfluous solicitude be banished from a life of which You are the strength, and of which You should be the end.

For long I thought that there were human and natural industries, which could do duty for Your grace, or hasten its action; I thought that by taxing my ingenuity, by splitting hairs, by urging myself on, I could do better than You Yourself could do, and surpass Your desires; I thought—it is always the same illusion—that the work of sanctity was an enterprise, before being an acceptance; that it was a personal initiative, before being a respectful answer, that it was for me to begin the great work first, whereas my first act should be to thank You for having already begun it in me, by Your grace forestalling all my desires.

And that which You have done in me, You continue to do. Father of the Family . . . it is You who lay up heavenly treasure for me; it is You who keep safe all my earnings, since it is through You and in You that I acquire them. What I am, I have no idea; what I am worth, You see; but I have one longing left, a longing which Your grace itself prevents me from renouncing, and which grows daily stronger with all the realization of my misery: the longing to respect You ever more as my Sovereign, and to love You ever more as my Saviour; the longing to possess nothing as my own —above all not my virtues—and to see You in all that I am, in all that I do, for You alone can make me bearable to myself, and prevent me from being disgusted with my virtues. I shall love them because I shall find in them a memorial of You, Your handwork, Your love, Your footprints. I shall love them because You have sown their seeds in me, and because being divine seeds—*desursum* (*James* i. 17)— they have found in my soul a soil which Your grace alone could make fruitful. I love them, all these blades of corn which are my merits, which go by the names of my mortifications, my sacrifices, my vows, my prayers, my repentance, my hopes; I love them because all these sheaves are in reality Your harvest, and because they proclaim Your glory—*Rex Christe, virtus fortium qui magna solus efficis.* (*Hymn Vesp. Com. Martyrs.*)

What need then for me to seek for reassurance by the verification of the growth of these virtues. Is it not enough for me to put all my strength into the effort of submission, trusting to Your love for the completion of my tasks, and postponing to the eternal vision all final valuation and restful certitude. *Dum nescit ille:* to measure virtue by the knowledge we have of it is a gross blunder, and would overthrow the peace of our soul at every moment. We must know how to leave things to Him, and watch only that we may work with Him as best we can; we must think of Him more than of ourselves, of His glory more than of our worth, of His favours rather than of our deserts, or better still, since our merits are His favours, and our worth makes His glory, and since *we* means really *He*, we must look on these realities in their divine bearing, with His eyes, in the true light of their beginning . . . *coronando nostra merita coronas Tua dona*. (*cf. St. Augustine, Sermon* clxx.)

Shall we not find in this uprightness of intention a beatitude of destitution? Will there not be a heavenly savour of spiritual poverty in this forgetfulness of self and this impossibility of thinking of ourselves and for ourselves, except in God and for God? It is not a question of remaining in darkness, but of being content with His light alone, as that heavenly Jerusalem of which He is the sole lamp. It is not a question of waiting in idleness, and of keeping our powers inactive, but of restraining our craving for independence, by subjecting all our activities to His rule, and working with Him to the utmost of our power. To be wholly a disciple; to be no longer anything but faithful: these two well-worn words should be enough to express us: *quod his abundantius est, a malo est*. (*Matt.* v. 37.) We shall only be in peace when we are what we should be; and we should only be *docility* in act and *surrender* without reserve. Peace without illusion, without flare, without false rest or earthly dreams, the peace of paradise which You prepare for me, *dum nescit ille*—without my suspecting it, and, as it were, unknown to me—give it to me. Lord, in purity, in truth and in justice.

XII

Unde et memores
Whence also, mindful of . . .
(*Liturgy, Mass.*)

MY soul, still so earthly-minded, is unaware of the sanctity of
remembrance. Too often I see in it nothing more than an agreeable
means of relieving the dull insipidity of the present, or of embroider-
ing exquisite designs on the monotonous background of everyday
life. When the sights that meet my eyes irritate or weary me, I take
refuge in my memories, and I unroll before my inner gaze, as a
consolation or a retort, the picture of all that is no more. Memories,
I use them for delight or for play, to stir up regrets or to distract
myself, to feed my sorrows or to strengthen my ambitions; I use
them to prop up my hopes or to barricade myself behind my pusillanimous distrust. I use them as some plastic material, as some mere
remnant, paltry or precious, which I may make the most of and
mould to my fancy, without being obliged to give an account to
anyone of the use to which I have put it. I treat my memories as
though they depended solely on me and as if their use concerned me
alone; I treat them as the fisherman treats the fish of the sea, casting
his nets to right or left, in front or behind, plunging at a venture
into the immense hunting-grounds of the ocean, caring only to
secure a plentiful haul.

All that is very pagan, and that rash seizure of God's treasure is
like a sacrilege. Does not my past belong to Him, as well as my
future? And my memories . . . penetrated with the fragrance of
His grace, steeped in His redeeming virtue, that "virtue which goes
out from Him," are not these memories holy things, relics of His
light and His love? And when I use them for my pleasure or my
folly, I imitate that puerile irreverence of the King of Babylon who
profaned the sacred vessels at his banquet, drinking to excess in the
golden chalices of the temple of Jehovah. Teach me, O my God,
"to remember" as I should, to use this holy power in a Christian
way, to treat the past which lives within me as a gift of love, and as
a touching pledge of Your partiality for me. *Accipe memoriam! (Sume
et suscipe.)*

Has not the Holy Spirit given Him, who is my Redeemer and my
sole Master, the name of "He that was" *qui erat? (Apoc.* i. 4.) All my
past has been seen by Him; all that has been good and beneficial in
it has been inspired by Him; He has endured it, and forgiven in it all
that my perversity or weakness has mingled there of guilt or sloven-
liness. I cannot then isolate a single instant of my former history, I

cannot separate from the action of the Eternal Word a single phase, no matter how small a one, of the development of humanity and of the universe. He stands at all beginnings. He is before all beginnings, before Abraham the father of the faithful, and before the first man, the father of sinners. When I endeavour to ramble through my memories, as through an immense and lonely park, as in "a garden enclosed" of which I alone have the key and in which I alone know the paths, I forget that He is the "Faithful witness" *testis fidelis* (*Apoc.* iii. 14), that He has seen all and knows all, that He has been the contemporary of my soul in all its failures and all its renewals. Memory is then a royal road, by which I should go to God, and down whose long way He himself comes towards me. Memory is a long-drawn-out colloquy, a hymn of thanksgiving, which consumes my past as incense: *sicut incensum in conspectu Tuo.* (*Liturgy, Mass.*)

Memory—full of Him—giving grave serenity to my thoughts, a pondered and deliberate nobility to my character, and a gentle and attractive dignity to all my ways! Is not all true greatness steeped in memory? Is not all tradition, all fidelity, all self-sacrifice; the qualities of race, of family, of country; is not all that supports us, all that makes us advance rooted in the memory of a past which rises up within us as the sap in the trees?

Alas—I am always a runaway, always transient, lost in the short present, without the calm of distant outlooks, without the horizons of eternity. I am always in a hurry, panting with wild desires—so foolishly ambitious are they, that I dare confide them to no one. Desires which the present never allows to blossom, and which fall in numbers on the soil of my soul, as disbanded soldiers whose courage is of no avail.

Memories! Recall my past, not as if it were something blotted out, not as an irreparable ruin, as a vanished dream, as a lost happiness, but rather as a reality that remains, as a treasure kept for me by a faithful friend and which has never ceased for a moment to be mine. Earthly and human memories are continually consumed by the moth and rust; the reality which these memories show us is worm-eaten and without brilliancy; *tinea corrumpit. Luke* xii. 33.) But if I keep within me Him who keeps by all the power of His word; if I dwell with Him, in whom dwells all fullness; if I see Him in all my past, see Him who is the eternal and unchangeable light of my life, what then could be lost to me as I pass from one day to another, and from birth to death?

Memores! Make for myself a consecrated memory, consecrated as a Church; divine and holy, penetrated with the breath of Grace, and living on favours received. Receive my memory, O my God, not in order to take it away from me—the meaning of sucha prayer could well be questioned—but so that it may be Yours and not mine; so that it may no longer speak to me of anything but You, and may educate me to fulfil my function of praise, my profession of a believer, and my role of eternal adorer. Be the sole object of my remembrance; You Yourself, and Your gentle attentions, and Your generous forgiveness. Memory thus understood would restore me to myself in easy recollectedness, and quite spontaneously I would close my eyes and join my hands. I would understand the deep meaning of "*Sicut erat in principio*" (*John* i. 2); I would know in a practical way that God surrounds me on all sides, and that nothing of all that rests on Him is lost. Recalling all that I have cost You, O my Saviour, I shall realize what divine outlay I represent, and it seems to me that in a boundless humility I shall rediscover a loftiness of spirit that knows no weakness. I shall be proud of You, and of Your work, and I shall do all "in memory of You".

Grant that I may remember well, so that I may also know what it is well to forget; my selfish interests, my stingy and cunning calculations, my false wisdom, and my immense stupidity. Grant me to people my memory with divine images, to keep there, as so many seeds of gratitude, the heavenly relics, the mysterious pledges of Your grace,—the remembrance of all that has descended "*a Patre ulminum.*" (*James* i. 17.) Make me understand that behind me there is still You; and that all the keys are in Your hands.

XIII

Rumor multitudinis

The confused noise of a tumult
(*cf. Ezechiel i.* 24.)

I HAVE sought to discover my true name, that which I deserve, that which defines me in Your eyes; and I have found it, Lord. I have found it in the answer of that unhappy man, from whom You drove the demons who held him captive from within. My name? I am also called legion, *quia multi sumus*, (*Mark* v. 9) because I am not alone, I am not one; I am many, I am a confused and restless multitude, a strange anarchy of contradictory tendencies, a senseless mob of persons who push each other about, drive each other out, and all aim at seizing hold of me.

I know it—and it is this perhaps that hinders me from penetrating to my own depths, and from making a serious examination of the subsoil of my being. I foresee that I shall not find anything simple there, nor calm nor clear and I shrink back from these disappointing investigations and these sorrowful examinations. I do not dare to search out the corners of my Jerusalem by the light of torches, for I know it is peopled by fantastic and ambiguous beings, whom I do not care to meet.

Legion; we are many; *multi sumus*. There is in the depths of my soul a machiavellian and crafty personality, coldly selfish, and quick to sacrifice everything to its personal well-being; a cunning and ungenerous being, the enemy of serene candour, and of uncalculating directness. It loves to evade, to cheat and to pretend; I know it; it is a being full of untruth, and I cannot say that it is a stranger to me. For it speaks at times by my lips, and each time that my speech has failed in sincerity, it has been uttered by this personality. My features are hidden under its mask *Omnis homo mendax.* (*Psalm* cxv. ii. Candour is not natural to me.

There is also in the depths of my soul a violent and irritable personage, who becomes exasperated in the face of obstacles, and cannot bear the slightest opposition, and who, beneath the exterior which courtesy imposes, boils inwardly at times with bad temper and anger; and who like an unjust and violent aggressor, throws himself upon his neighbour the moment the latter thwarts or contradicts him.

I cannot pretend, Lord, that this violent being is quite a stranger to me. Those rough gestures are too like my own, and I recognize the accent of my own voice in those harsh cries of smothered anger. Those acts of violence are my weaknesses, and they have injured me

too much not to be in reality my own. The confused and troubled
spirit of Your two Boanerges is restless and growls within me.

There is again in the depths of my soul a being made up of laziness
and enervating apathy, a being steeped in drowsiness and idleness,
who always finds reasons for putting off till later the accomplishment
of irksome drudgery, and finds means to throw all disagreeable
duties upon others; a being that desires nothing more than to let
itself live and be carried by others; that saunters along the surface
of all duties, filled with scepticism and contemptuous of all effort. I
know that personage, Lord, so like me that it can be none other
than myself. I recognize the lagging gait, the adroitness of the
strategical moves in the face of orders that are hard, and that way of
escaping from all that wounds. I have so often listened to those
complaints and those desires, and to give glory to God who has
redeemed me, I acknowledge that I am soft, indolent and sensual.

There is in the depths of my soul a being of grace and of good
desires, which loves to join its hands, to repent, to call to You, My
God, and to hear You. There is one in my deepest self, who has
sought You at all times, who has known no rest without You, and
who would gladly have sacrificed to You the hundred fold of all
that has been already offered—*quasi nihil despiciet eam. (Canticle* viii.
7.) I have never dared say that that being was I myself and myself
alone, for so many other sides of myself seemed to give it the lie, so
many others, commonplace and bad, supplant this better self, con-
sign it to the shade, and force it back until it becomes dim and
almost illusory. And yet, my God, You know that my deepmost
desire has always reached out after You, and if my faults have not
been as few as they should, my sorrow, at least, has ever striven to
be sincere, as sincere as my dull and groping conscience and the dim
light that burns within me have made possible. I have never wholly
given up the hope of belonging to You, and in the deep recesses of
my soul, I have always felt and always acknowledged that You were
necessary to me, above all else.

Who am I then, Lord? And by what name should I be baptized?
Shall I remain for ever in confusion and chaos? Can not Your Spirit
which "laid the measures of the earth . . . and the order of the
heavens" bring forth harmony and grace out of my anarchy and
disunion? Can not Your wisdom, which has regulated the rhythm
of the stars, direct the movements of my heart, and establish a
pacific equilibrium in the centre of my incoherence.

I hear Your answer. It has been given long ago, but the road is
long indeed, by which truth travels to the ears of men, and it is only
to-day that I begin to fathom Your eternal message. *Vocavi te nomine
tuo, Meus es tu. (Isaias* xliii. 1.) I have called you by your name, you

are Mine. *Mine.* No longer to belong to myself is then the only way
to possess myself. To go out entirely from myself and pass into You,
is the only way never to be separated from myself, to escape from
the inner disunion which is killing me, and to acquire a meaning
and a value. I am Yours, and together we shall make me overcome
myself. All freedom, of which I might dispose, I surrender to You,
so that with its help You may gradually penetrate all that dim,
untamed, deep zone of my being where I am not yet my own, and
where all my tyrants are restless.

In truth, I owe You all that I am, My Redeemer, and if later on in
Your Paradise, my happiness is to consist in no longer possessing
myself except in You, no longer knowing myself or loving myself
except in seeing and loving You, should not this future glory begin
even here below by Your grace, and should not my whole moral
being be mine only through You.

Exorcise all my evil spirits, You alone can speak to them with
power, and force them to take flight or to be silent. Give me back,
or rather, give me the peaceful serenity of those who having put
their sole hope in Your goodness, which has never deceived any one,
feel themselves for ever sheltered from all mishap. Grant that I may
be really Yours, for if I am Yours, You will be mine, and in that lies
the whole of life eternal.

XIV

Ut enarrent mirabilia Tua

That they may recount Your marvels
(*Psalm xxv.* 7.)

IT is sometimes said that holy souls are mirrors that reflect the perfection of Jesus Christ. This comparison is not quite accurate; if it is pressed a little its inadequateness becomes at once apparent. The soul of a saint is at the same time much less and infinitely more than a mirror; it is well to grasp this thoroughly so that we may not err as to the true direction to which our efforts should tend, nor as to the rules which should guide our moral appreciations.

The soul of a saint is far less than a mirror of Christ. For no creature can reproduce in itself the traits of infinite perfection. And yet a holy soul is infinitely more than a mirror; for a mirror explains nothing, develops nothing, and adds nothing; it restricts itself to a sterile reproduction of the image of the reality put before it, and which is no better known for being thus reflected.

But the soul of a saint should expand, develop and explain the perfection of Christ. How can it expand that which is perfect, and develop Him who is the consummation of all creation? How can it set forth in detail all the riches of the Incarnate Word?

The soul should be the mirror of Jesus Christ as flowers or, better still, as colours are the mirror of the sun.

Flowers do not directly reflect the sun; nevertheless there is not a single one of their hues which does not come from its sole light; from the sumptuous purple of the great flowering poppies to the ivory satin of the lilies in June, every corolla speaks of the sun, and the most humble flower of the field can teach us something of the star which has allowed one of its rays to fall on it.

It is the light of the sun that takes on all the colours of the rainbow in the hollow shells of mother of pearl, and it is this light that shines in the radiance of innocent eyes; it is it again which clothes the dripping autumn forests in sombre garb, and which glistens daintily on the little metallic corselets of insects. If therefore we wish to know what this simple white light holds within itself, if we wish to compose the history of the sun, it will not be enough to reproduce and multiply indefinitely its barren image in the mirror; we must rather question all that shines and all that is coloured here below; we must glean on every side the scattered hues of the ideal palette, we must display all the tints which the purity of its white light conceals within itself, unrevealed to our eyes.

Jesus Christ is King in the world of souls, as the sun is king in

58

the world of light; holy souls are the supernatural prisms through which His divine perfection passes that it may be broken up before our eyes into its infinite hues. Each of these souls should display one colour, in each should gleam forth one special tint, in isolation from the rest, and thus should they relate, unfold and develop the inner riches of the Son of Man.

For that which He could not realize in the limits of His mortal body, He realizes and will realize, till the end of time, in the fullness of His mystical Body; that which His human lips were not able to say, the grace of His Spirit will cause His Apostles to utter; the balm and wine which His hands have not been able to pour into wounds, will be poured in by the hands of His followers, good Samaritans as He was and through Him, who will pour them forth in His name to cure the unfortunate.

Coming as He did among us, desiring to be clothed in the reality of our human substance, He was forced to be but one individual in the crowd. He made Himself man, *one* man, and He accepted all the limitations that this Incarnation imposed upon Him. He was man and not woman; He died young and never knew old age; He was neither a soldier, nor sailor, nor public official, nor mason, nor field labourer; He had a certain height, a certain countenance, such and such a particular accent, the accent of the Galilean mountain-dwellers; He had His own manner of walking, by which He was recognized afar off; He had favourite expressions and words and thoughts which recurred frequently in His discourses . . . He was one among us, and He was called Jesus, as others were called Andrew or Pilate.

He was man not woman. He has never therefore, in His mortal body, known the passionate love of a mother for her children. And yet when we admire the self-devotion of Christian mothers bending over their cradles, it is something of Christ Himself that we find there, it is the work of His Spirit, the outcome of His grace. That which He could not realize in the limits of His material and sensitive body, that He realizes in His mystical Body—and holy souls explain, develop and show forth the inexhaustible richness of His perfection. Each one has his own peculiar shade—but all shades come from Him.

He never bore arms as a soldier, and when two swords were shown to Him, He made it clear that He did not wish to use them. In the moment of danger He bade them replace the sword in its sheath. And yet, when the Christian soldier slays in a holy cause, when he watches, when, in the fierce hurricane of the battle, he fights fearlessly and holds his own unyieldingly, it is something of Christ that we discover and admire in him. For that which the Lord of all flesh could not realize in the limits of His material and sensitive body, that He realizes in His mystical Body; it is His power which strengthens the arms of His crusaders, it is through them that He shows us His inexhaustible wealth.

He has never been old; "His own who received Him not" "immolated Him as a lamb" before the number of His days has been completed. And yet when Christian old age bends its brow towards the tomb, there is something of Christ that we all find and venerate in it. Old age shows forth one aspect of His fullness and tells of one part of His mystery. That which the Lord could not realize in the limits of His sensitive and material body, that He realizes in His mystical Body, in the crowd of those who belong to Him, and through whom He wills never to cease to act and to reveal Himself.

Ut enarrent mirabilia Tua. All our obligations are resumed in this one precept: imitate Christ in whom is found the fullness of all divine perfection. But what is it to imitate Christ? Does it merely mean to do again that which He has done, to reproduce His actions materially, and place our footprints within the marks of His? Are we merely to reflect the face of the Son of Man, as the mirror reflects an object?—No, far rather is it that we should do what He would have done if He had found Himself as we are, where we are; the meaning is that we should keep ourselves so close to Him, be so docile to His Spirit, that He, through us and in us, may complete His work, and His light may shine over our whole life. *Sic est omnis qui natus est ex spiritu.* (*John* iii. 8.)

XV

WE know Him in the measure in which we belong to Him; and
thus it is that life eternal, which consists in knowing Him, consists
just as much in being possessed by Him: *consortium Jesu Christi.* (*St.
Thomas.*) Those who choose to be wholly strangers to Him, condemn themselves to be incoherent when they speak of Him; and
that folly which drives them far from the Truth, makes them mistake
the Truth for Beelzebub. They call this a rational opinion, an
appreciation in harmony with their idea.

To know Our Lord as He is, and so to recognize Him wherever
He is found, is the seed and fruit of faith. To know by conviction,
by divine conviction that He is in the Holy, Catholic, Apostolic and
Roman Church, and that it is there alone that He is to be found;
that is to know Him here below as fully as our pilgrim state allows,
and to prepare in the hidden paths of faith, the visions of glory.
Merces erit videre quod credimus. (*St. Augustine on Psalm cix.*)

To know Him thus, we must belong to Him; and no one belongs
to Him who has not been chosen and desired—*electus*—(*Luke* xxiii.
35), no one belongs to Him who has not answered to this choice,
and to this all-powerful love by filial abandonment and reverent
submission. Faith is a gift of God, but no one is debarred from its
possession beforehand and absolutely: all are called to know divine
love through the Word made Flesh.

Faith is a gift which has been accepted; one which we all have the
power to shatter by a single blow within our souls as one breaks
an earthen vessel—*tanquam vas figuli.* (*Psalm* ii. 9), or to annihilate,
by slow degrees as a plant which perishes in a forgotten corner, as a
threshold that is worn by footsteps, as gratitude that is lost in
forgetfulness. One willed, brutal act is enough to shatter this gift
of God; a long continued carelessness, partly contemptuous and
partly lazy, may cause us to lose it gradually, almost without being
aware of it. God must protect Himself in us against ourselves, both
from sudden calamities and from stealthy invasions. That is the whole
work of His restoring grace, which hinders or neutralizes our folly.

Have I ever really understood that this divine faith, so readily
condemned by the pride of false wisdom, is in all its elements, a
heavenly gift coming down from the Father of light, an immediate
action of God upon us? Perhaps I imagine vaguely that faith is a kind
of natural conviction, more or less solidly established in the mind,

and on which an honest and self-sacrificing moral life can be built up
I am tempted to consider the whole matter with but a half attention
and practically to forget the role and nature of faith, just as we
willingly forego the examination of the foundations of our houses
and the excavation of the basements down to the lowest layer of
stones. Who among us thinks seriously of glorying in his faith, not
before men, and because of the practical consequences that the
profession of this faith entails, and which are often placarded forth;
but just simply because this conviction that Christ is God, that His
Church is true, is the work of the Holy Spirit and the seal of an
eternal love? Who dreams seriously of thanking God, not only for
all the providential circumstances which brought him to Baptism,
and to the "profession" of the Christian Faith, but just simply for
the very gift of faith itself? Who thanks God for having the certitude
that saves, and for knowing "that it is thus that the apostles taught".

And yet, this wholly interior faith, this purely theoretical faith,
apart from all the consequences which it introduces into our moral
life; this simple supernatural adhesion to the Truth of Christ, is
impossible except through Him; through Him who gives sight to
the blind, and whose secret no one knows unless He has Himself
confided it. It is His own sheep who recognize their true Shepherd
by the sound of His voice; it is the faithful servants, those who in the
night have kept lights burning in their doorways . . . it is to
watchful and faithful hearts that it is given to hear afar off . . .
coming down the paths of solitude, the stealthy, yet firm step of the
Divine Master who approaches. If we do not will to believe, we
shall not believe; but it is vain for us to try simply to will it; without
the grace of Christ we can never pass any judgment of truth and
justice upon Him; we cannot know Him. For God alone knows Himself in His own mystery, and angels and men only know something
of Him just in that measure in which they become one with God. No
created power can take hold of God. To become one with God, it is
necessary that God should win us and associate us with Himself;
there must be a wholly gratuitous initiative, an infinite condescension
coming down from above towards us, and this beginning of salvation is the grace of faith.

Thus it is that I have no longer the right to use my intellect as
though it were mine alone. It is consecrated by faith even as the
lamp of the sanctuary; and "to think as we should" of the things of
God is an act of homage and of worship. *Recta sapere*. (*Collect*,
Pentecost). Wholly steeped as we are in natural and earthly notions,
we often imagine that *the offering of worth* is that of our exterior
actions, that which goes under the name of our behaviour. We
think that our minds and our convictions belong wholly to the

order of nature, and it would seem strange to us, not only that God should claim them, but above all, He should direct them. We should accustom ourselves no longer to look on our intellect as a purely lay and secular faculty, but rather as the field of the parable, sown throughout with divine corn. There are attitudes of mind which are not catholic, there is a scorn or a weakness, a fear or a presumptuousness which are full of sin. To fear truth is to distrust God present in our mind; to enslave truth to our caprices and prejudices is to lead Christ captive in chains—*vinctum*—(*Matt.* xxvii. 2), to the mockery of the sordid cohorts. The Christian is at the same time very proud and very humble in his faith, as in his works, because he knows he is but an instrument and that nothing in him is derived from himself alone.

Since our whole life consists in searching for Christ, and our whole eternity consists in keeping Him, faith which, uniting us to Him, allows us to know Him and to recognize Him,—this faith is in reality the cause of all our good and the first of our virtues. *Fundamentum totius spiritualis ædificii.* (*Summa. De Fide.*) It suppresses nothing in us; it extinguishes none of our lights; it does not bind us down to childishness, it does not ask us to blindfold our eyes; but, supernaturally sharpening our faculties, making us see with God, and as God, it lays bare before us the Invisible.

XVI

Propter nos

For our sake (service)
(1 *Corinth.* ix. 10.)

I MUST find God! Is there an obstacle which hinders me from doing so, a barrier that stops me, an abyss between us? If there were any such thing I should have an excuse, and my apparent heedlessness would be the outcome of wisdom. But this obstacle, this unconditional obstacle is nothing but an illusion in the spiritual life. The first good tidings of salvation is just that heaven-sent message which teaches us, not only that an open road stretches between us and God, but that this open road is everywhere, we have but to walk on in all simplicity. Every creature that we meet will be the accomplice of our good desires, that is their only destiny. They cannot be our enemies, they exist *propter nos*.

This is the principle which Saint Ignatius has put, with such wisdom and simplicity—and as a matter of course—at the outset of our supernatural education; on the threshold of every generous impulse. It is the sum total of all lessons, the true and joy-bringing lesson which he calls the Foundation of the Spiritual exercises. This lesson is sometimes taken up in a narrowing and, as it were, niggardly sense. This truth, vast as life itself, and co-extensive with the universe, is crippled, turned into a convenient little receipt, a mild injunction to thrifty good management, a password of timorous and paralysing restraint. We say, and it is perfectly true, and always a necessary prelude: I must not become the slave of anything. But that is only one aspect of the matter, the negative aspect which prepares the way for true indifference. We should immediately add as a corollary to that remark: Nevertheless I am prepared to use all things. I claim nothing, I refuse nothing, my will makes itself as all-embracing as the Will of God, as pliant as His own immense work, of which no smallest portion can be cast off as useless. To true indifference belongs this energy that is ever serene, and a self-surrender that is stored with wealth. This *"propter nos"* goes its way stamping with the seal of brotherhood all realities here below; from my body and mind to the polypes of the deep seas; to the microbes of contagion, and even to death, calumny, neglect and incapacity.

Since "all the rest" *reliqua omnia—(Ex. S. Ignatius)* all that stretches out around us, beyond the visible horizon all this is a means to get to God it follows necessarily that the final and absolute obstacle, the being that is wholly stubborn, the thing that is simply evil and to be destroyed, has no existence, none that is to say unless

I will that it should be in me, unless my will itself becomes it, and that I maliciously refuse to use creatures, so that I may follow my own likes and extravagances. The obstacle is never really more than partial, temporary, apparent, since at the bottom and essentially, in spite of all the wounding roughness on the surface, the obstacle is a means.

Everything is a means, even opposition. Our virtues climb up over our faults as ivy climbs a rough wall. Difficulties, inward contradictions, the struggle of every day, these are the conditions of our progress, and through these alone we are taught to ponder while we grow to maturity. Our past is no more an obstacle to our advance than our present misery, for the obstacle as such is non-existent: *portas mortis et seras Salvator noster disrupit.* (*Holy Sat. Matins. Response to 6th Lesson.*)

What joy then to know that on our road to God no tree has been thrown across the path, no bridge destroyed. There is no impassable ford, no treacherous bog, no death-bringing desert to traverse. There are hindrances it is true, but only such as make for training, as the resistance of the steep banks of the river serve to control the flow of the waters; there are deeds of warfare too, at times, but only such as are serviceable to us, like the struggle of two hands which wash, while seeming to oppose and thwart each other. The paralysing thought of an all-powerful obstacle blocking our way to God, must then never be allowed to weigh upon the life of a Christian like a curse or a gnawing anguish. Evil has been conquered and its reign is over, and the first word and the last is the *"Confidite"* (*John* xvi. 33), of the Word made Flesh to all those whom He calls to follow Him.

An obvious conclusion forces itself upon us. The conclusion that we have always refused to draw: There is nothing to be destroyed in the work of God, all is to be used. Our past faults even are to be used as the curled shavings of wood which the action of the plane accumulates under the carpenter's bench. Destruction itself can only be apparent, temporary and make believe. The true and the eternal is the *"abundantius"*—the more abounding. The ultimate measure is the good measure pressed down and overflowing. That which is being prepared in each one of us is the full-flowering of all that we are, and to this development the devil himself must help.

How far away am I, my God, from Your calm unclouded wisdom! How little do I possess of Your spirit that orders all things sweetly! What secret force within me drives me to vandalism in the name of virtue? Why is my soul filled with childish and pagan irritation in the face of obstacles? What blindness is it that hinders me from seeing that both good days and evil bear a revelation for me—*propter nos?* How is it that I have not yet understood that health and sickness,

E

the foolish and the wise, troublesome people as well as friends are all, not only stepping stones to God, but heralds of the wealth which He, my God, destines for me, which He sends through them, through their hands, whether unseen or well known or even rough? All should help me to discover the treasure of the Kingdom. That impatience which has so long muttered within me; all the defects, which, unknowingly, I inherited at birth; my long years of study so inimical, naturally speaking, to childlike sincerity, so heavy to carry with their subleties of doubt and scepticism, their absorbing distraction and their spirit of pitiless criticism; the little I have, the little I am, the little I have done; my business and my handicraft hidden and profitless perhaps; all these things are means, and nothing but means, everything is a vein to be explored, a secret to be guessed, a spring of water to be made to gush forth in the desert . . . *in deserto aquæ*. (*Isaias* xxxv. 6.)

But, in reality, my God, I never think of these things, rather, like Your unfaithful people, I "murmur" and complain, and that is all. I spend my time regretting that things are as You have made them or allowed them to be. I have not yet learned that this power of regret must be done away with, or rather, since absolutely nothing is to be destroyed, it should be transformed, its face should be turned to the present and to the future. It should be turned into hope and love, instead of being allowed to remain as a mouldy growth, useless and ever-encroaching, at the very core of life. To change regret into clear-sighted love, to see our faults as so many lessons we have been taught, to make use of all that is, would not that be the true application of the words: *Funda nos in pace* (*Ave Maris stella*), and is not this foundation the only one? God does not begin by a warning, nor yet by a summons, but by a word of quietness and joy. All is ours: *omnia vestra sunt*, i *Corinth*. iii. 22), and we shall be what we will to be, since God is working with us. Nothing and nobody can hinder us, for there is nothing that is a stranger to our enterprise, nor is there any obstacle.

XVII

Communicantes

Being but one . . . all together
(*Liturgy—Canon of Mass.*)

THIS word is found in the Canon of the Liturgy at the moment when the Sacred Mystery nears the Consecration. And the thing which this word stands for, unfathomable and yet so consoling, is the cause of all my hopes and the beginning of my eternal life. *Communicantes*—the word conveys a complete meaning! No object is attached to it, it is final. It is indeed more than a word, it is a finished phrase.

I am not alone. I am rescued for ever from this curse of the isolated. Invisible links reach down from all the saints of God even to me, and I have a part, I share in all their riches. I am not an unknown person, a bit of wasted refuse, without support and without protection, but I am united, by my entire supernatural being, to the divine family *istorum et omnium sanctorum.* (*Liturgy—Mass.*)

Hence nothing belongs to me exclusively. I can lay claim to nothing as being wholly mine. That community of goods which is found in religious life is but an imperfect symbol of the unity of souls in the riches of grace, all the friends of God together making one.

Communicantes. I not only share the heritage of the dead. The friends of God people the world I dwell in; the friends of God and the instruments of God, all those that He has made use of to reach me and to whom without knowing it, I am beholden for my joys.

There is a commandment which obliges us to honour those who have given us life—a participation of their own, which we continue when they are no more. But where are the true fathers of my grace, to what unknown poor, to what suffering beggar shall I go to give thanks? Why is it that I am not a pagan? Who has earned for me the reception of baptism? I know of course that a priest has intervened, and that a father and mother have carried me to the font, but by what unseen influences were all these actions guided? Who is the old woman, or the youthful sufferer to whose unceasing recitation of the Rosary "for the intentions of God," I owe the grace of being a Christian? And in moments of difficulty, in the midst of unknown dangers, who was the invisible angel whose silent resignation, whose humility and courage won for me the grace of safety? Moment by moment I incur an immense and infinite debt to the whole Church. I am something, only because I am one with the one thing: the work of God. The lichen knows nothing of what it owes to the stone over which it spreads itself, and the ivy climbing up the trunks of trees is wholly unconscious that it is borrowing their strength.

The Communion of Saints would give me, if I cared to understand it, a glow of charity so purifying, that I would no longer live for myself but only to serve others. When I look at them, O my God, look at all those whom You have placed round me and before me on the earth, I see at a glance that they are all my creditors.

Priests, to whom do you owe the grace of your priesthood, where are your spiritual godparents? You know well that this grace has not come to you from yourself . . . In the shelter of the great doorway of the Church in your native town, some poor blind beggar stood selling matches, and praying with a simple heart for all those he could not see, one day this prayer laid hold of you as you passed by and marked you out for God. Apostle, to whom are you indebted for your reaper's hook and sheaves, for your boat and overflowing nets? You know well that the fruitfulness of your efforts is not due to you, and that even the courage to make that effort was grafted by grace on the selfish wild-stock of your nature. But one day a little girl, in the "Sister's school," joined her hands before the statue of Our Lady of Lourdes and prayed to God through His holy Mother to have pity on unhappy sinners. And the heart of God was touched by these hands of a child.

The threads of our supernatural destiny cross and recross as the threads of a web, and the cohesion of our lives and of our virtues rests on this oneness of interests. God does not tell us where our benefactors are to be found, so that we may look with grateful eyes on all those who surround us. *Communicantes.*

But if we may make a guess as to the methods by which our heavenly Father leads men, must we not believe that in the supernatural order He causes the wise to be carried by the ignorant, and the grown-ups by the children, and the leaders by those who are subject to them, and historical celebrities by despised sufferers? On what has He made the immense edifice of His Church rest, as a pyramid on its point? On a humble woman, Queen of the whole supernatural order, Our Lady, Mediatrix of all Grace. On the day of the Purification, in the Temple of Jerusalem, an old man carried a Child, but it was the Child who was leading the old man. *Senex puerum portabat, apuer utem senem regebat. (Gradual. Mass of Purification.)* The rich, says Saint Clement, are uplifted spiritually by the poor, as the vine is held up by young elms, so that rich and poor sharing all they have may mutually thank each other, and that each one may owe all to all.

My God, I believe that You sanctify parents by their children, and the learned by the illiterate, and those who labour with their minds by those who labour with their hands . . . I am filled with wonder when I think of all the power given over in Your Church into the hands of the baptized multitudes, and I shall no longer allow my soul to cherish feelings of spite or anger against those who have injured me, for I know not with what unknown blessings they have filled me.

The living helped by the dead; the civilized by savages who pray in their far-off lands to the eternal Master; sinners helped by virgins, the children of Eve by the Immaculate, man helped by God . . . *communicantes et venerantes*. (*Liturgy, Mass.*) I wish to keep alive within my soul all the gratitude of those who possessing nothing receive each day all that they are in need of. We become accustomed to be served, just as we become accustomed to the daily return of light, and plunged in gloomy routine, thoughtless and morose, we finish by believing that other people are parasites and that we are plundered by our neighbours. The Christian soul is broad, sound, grateful and loyal. It despises no one, not even sinners, it knows that hatred breeds darkness and that in detesting our adversaries we are failing, in reality, to recognize our brethren. *Sæpe fratrem odisti et nescis*. (*Wt. Aug. in Psalm* liv.)

XVIII

Sancta Dei Genitrix
Holy Mother of God
(*Liturgy, Ant. of Our Lady.*)

THOSE in the Church who have shown coldness or reserve towards Our Blessed Lady have always, rightly, been suspected of some error. Protestants find it hard to accept the "Marial exaggerations" of Catholics, though they acknowledge that they are found far back in history, so far indeed as to be met with almost at the beginnings.

Why is it that we need never be ashamed of tenderness towards Mary? What is the underlying principle of this inspired devotion? Is there really some "feminine weakness' in it? Does devotion to Mary impose and perpetuate childish ways that could not be suitable for a manly and strong soul? For want of clear vision in these questions people hesitate or go astray, and piety, no longer leaning upon truth, becomes quickly a morbid exaltation or a merely conventional performance.

Nothing is decrepit in the work of God; His grace never grows old and the virtues inspired by His grace know no decline. Thus it is that the Christian soul is the home of apparently incompatible qualities, it holds within it the prudent wisdom of experience and the fresh candour of an awakening mind. The Christian soul does not wither, the seasons succeed each other, and are merged one into another within her, without driving each other out as in the material universe. There is so much power in the heart of a child, all the power of the future; there is so much light in the soul of a wise man, all the light of the long past of experience. Could not these two treasures be kept together in a single life, could not ripe age bless God who always gives joy to youth? Why should this be impossible? The kingdom of heaven is for those who become like little children, and trustful goodness is so near akin to early simplicity. Protected by the grace of God, our souls can ripen without losing anything of value, and on our invisible tree the fruit does not develop to the detriment of the flower which it replaces. Eternity is not a continual flight before pursuing death, but the tranquil possession of all good, and of ourselves; our life of grace here is the beginning of this eternal life. We should then find in this life of justice the properties of glory in their early stages. Decay will not touch them. We grow rich without having to pay for our wealth by growing poorer, as those do who buy and sell and trade, clinging to all that flies from them.

To keep the freshness of childhood, this pure treasure in the deep places of a valiant soul, something within us must still be childlike. Shall we then curtail ourselves artificially and pretend to lisp? No, we need only understand ourselves in the light of truth to see that we still need a Mother.

For man is reborn many times; he is formed and perfected only through successive births, and if custom only keeps alive the memory of our physical and visible birth, yet thought shows us that it is but the first in a long series. The body lives, but the activity of the mind has not been yet born; the mind awakens, but our moral will still sleeps; the will is born, but the power of habit is not yet acquired . . . and thus we go from birth to birth till our eternal birth to that life which has no end. And in reality, in the order of grace—the only one that really counts, for it alone gives a meaning to the rest—in this order we are still unborn, we are infants not adults, *et nondum apparuit quid erimus.* (1 *Epist. St. John iii.* 2.)

Christian piety has understood this perfectly, and the faithful, by instinct, have had recourse to the Mother of the Word, because they are true and do not pretend, as presumptuous and illiterate scholars, that they have already passed the elementary stage in the life of Grace.

We need not therefore lie to ourselves in order to adopt towards our Lady the Mother of all those who believe, the attitude and gestures of childhood; it is only necessary to know ourselves and to silence within ourselves that evil arrogance of hollow pride.

This whole-hearted devotion to the Mother of Christ keeps the true family spirit alive in the Church. I do not know if I am a scholar, I do not know if I am virtuous, I do not know if I am strong or weak, or if I am worth being looked at. Round the hearth the children are but as one people, and the eyes of their mother have levelled them all in the same love: they are only "the children".

I thank Our Lady for having made all the faithful understand that, before her, there is neither Greek nor Scythian, neither man nor woman, neither learned nor foolish, but one same people, one same state, one same family, the family of those who must be born to light, and in whom grace moulds beforehand the ultimate traits.

We can never thank her enough for that spirit of calm and purity which she has poured into the Church. Only the wilfully blind can refuse to love her for all the spring-time freshness and the gentle thoughts that she has kept alive within the souls of old Christian warriors.

Our Lady of the dying, and Our Lady of the battle, Our Lady of consolation and Our Lady of good help, the Guardian Virgin whom the disciple of Christ invokes from his first prayer to the hour of his

death, how could any one imagine that devotion given to her hides
as with some non-transparent screen the Person of the One Media-
tor?

> *Splendour Patris*
> *Factor Matris*
> *Jesu, nostra gloria*
> *Da ut fiam*
> *Per Mariam*
> *Tua dignus gratia . . .*
> *Bernard of Morlas.*

Thus, O my God, Your monks sang of old, in formulas as clear
as they were touching, uniting piety and truth, sweetness and
strength, and knowing well that all grace has come to us through
You, and that You Yourself were given to us in the arms of Your
Mother, they knew that she could not be unheedful of Your work,
and that she took a share in all Your Redemption.

I ask but one favour of You, this evening, that of dwelling in
Your Church, not as a scholar nor as a philosopher, not as an athlete
nor yet as a hero, but just simply as a child of Mary Your Mother.

XIX

WHEN the mind refuses to pray, the lips can utter words, and something of us, by that alone, still belongs to God. And when disgust or weariness or powerlessness to speak takes hold of us, we can yet pray by our attitude, and offer our action to God.

A fantastic posture, it seems to be to some, with joined hands! Many blush at the idea of it, and shrink from doing as simple-minded pious people do! They have never asked themselves the meaning of this traditional gesture, they do not like it because they have never understood it. They seek far off for complicated methods, but the bread with which God feeds the soul is this bread they scorn, the Biblical bread which the patriarchs baked under the blackened cinders. To pray well, we need do no more than join our hands and bring our soul into harmony with this external attitude. The ascetics of Egypt asked nothing more of the sinner Thaïs, as a means of recovering her baptismal innocence than that she should turn towards the East at sunrise and say: *Tu qui plasmasti me, miserere mei.* (*Fathers of the Desert.*) Thou who createdst me, have mercy on me.

With joined hands, a fantastic attitude! Do the joined hands of little children mean nothing to us, and the joined hands of First Communicants under their white veils; the joined hands of the toilers of the world, and those of husband and wife, who side by side each day, in the face of the unknown morrows of God's Providence, ask of the Father a courage that will never fail. Are not the joined hands of our dead eloquent, lying there in the peace of the cemetery; those hands which we have ourselves perhaps composed in this last attitude, so that in the dreaded day of judgment the Angel of the Resurrection might recognize in them the dignity of the baptized! This time-honoured gesture is full of marvellous lessons, and it is ours to carry them on and make them known as good tidings of salvation, as a means of attaining peace and holiness.

Yes, what is it we want to say, when in order to pray to God we join our human hands, and add no single word to this action, like the cripple whose very misery speaks of itself for him and needs no commentary to support it?

Joined hands are the hands of prisoners, hands that will no longer resist, and no longer claim to be independent; they are the hands of those who surrender themselves, who yield, who assent, the hands of gentleness and obedience, they are then the hands of prayer.

Lord, when You behold the joined hands of Your disciples raised towards You on all sides, You alone know by what invisible bonds they are really fettered, and what evil spirits wish to keep them prisoners, You alone know that our revolts have never brought us freedom. You, who suffered from it before we did, alone know how closely we are riveted to our old slavery.

Behold then, my God, my hands of a captive; I shall make no more speeches, nor even think; I am weary and I long to find You in peace. Behold, my joined hands sum up the whole of my prayer, and I wait, like the bearer of a flag of truce who utters not a word.

Can we not then "in the secret of our chamber," for a few moments at nightfall, realize what we do in joining our hands, the hands of man, those hands which work out the designs of God, the hands which He has used in His work of to-day, used to bless, to help, to absolve, to raise up, to fight; our hands, which are bound and paralysed by so many secret faults, by so much pride, and by such ease-loving sloth.

Manibus junctis, I am not made to be independent, and, wishing to serve, I need some law, some duty, some reason higher than my caprice. My God, in joining my hands I wish to tell You that You will be my one Master. A prisoner, yes, I surrender myself. Why should I continue to lie and pretend to treat with You on terms of equality? Why should I not place my joined hands in Your everlasting hands? My life and all that I shall ever gain from it is held between them. Keep me, only thus can I escape from all that tyrannizes over me.

When the Church, in her Latin rite, confers the dignity of priesthood on her deacons; after she has conveyed to them the mighty powers of sacrificing, of absolving, and of blessing, after having initiated them into the Mysteries of the Body and Blood of the Eucharistic Sacrifice, as the ceremony approaches its conclusion, the Bishop, as though seized by one last anxiety, turns to the newly made priests and calls them back to him one by one. They mount the steps of the altar, and there as they kneel before the waiting prelate, he takes their joined hands within his own, and asks them, in the solemn tone which is befitting when eternal words are uttered, whether they will promise perpetual and entire obedience and reverence to their lawful superiors. *Promitto*, answers the priest. Then giving him the kiss of peace in the name of the whole Church the Bishop adds: And I promise thee that the peace of God will ever dwell within thee.

Each day Christ awaits His faithful, as one after one they come to Him. To-day it is your turn to mount the steps. The Bishop of your souls,—*episcopus animarum vestrarum*—(1 *Peter* ii, 25), asks you to place your joined hands with childlike trust within His wounded and redeeming hands. Let Him do as He pleases, offer no resistance, and if to be joined these hands must first be emptied, by one final act let fall all that the divine embrace refuses to accept and to bless. This is the ever pressing question which Christ puts to all His own: *Promittis?* Do you promise respect and obedience, without murmur or complaint, without weakness or gloomy sadness, the obedience of those who have surrendered from their hearts and to whom it is a joy to serve? It is impossible that the joined hands which are empty of all fleeting wealth, should not hold safe for us the invisible treasures of virtue and of peace without deception. . . . To find God again, it is enough to pray in secret—*manibus junctis.*

XX

THE eye that sees all things does not see itself; the eye that sees all things cannot manage to see the other eye that is its neighbour; and the right eye and the left live sixty years and die together without ever having looked at one another.

The truths most near to us are those we reflect upon least willingly and with the greatest difficulty. We pass over them without seeing them, and we go to seek afar off, in the depths of a desert that which God placed at the very door of our dwelling, and which in the impetuosity of our ways, we did not notice on our very threshold.

I know that God created me, and I think that I have seen to the bottom of this everyday truth. Its obviousness has become so familiar to me that meditation on it awakes no thrill within me. I know that I have been created, as I know the name by which I am called, and I hurry on at once to some less widely known considerations, to some more effective conclusions. God has created me, that is a story which is already old, an event which has been classified and dated, and from which every passing day removes me further. Once, in former days, I passed from nothingness to being; that is all. How could anything that would touch us be drawn from this rudimentary philosophy!

Too rudimentary in very truth! My creation is not an incident which took place once upon a time, it is a permanent fact. *I am being created* in the real meaning of the word, that is to say my being, as such, as God for its cause. Being cannot be made over to a subject, so that the latter shall keep it as one might an alms; for apart from its *being* the subject is nothing and creation is the perpetual law of existence, not merely the first getting under way. I need the creating hands not merely to begin to be, but just simply to be, and time alters nothing in this. The habit of being can never become stable in me. After the lapse of centuries my essence remains as incapable of existing by itself as it was on the eve of that day on which, through God, I began to be no longer *nothing*.

We imagine at times that existence has been given to us once for all as a gift, which therefore only calls for gratitude on our part towards a benefactor. One day, we think God made us a present of our being, and like a beggar loaded with treasure and thus made rich, we are the owners of the gifts of another. But creation is in reality an eternal dependence, and an always actual dependence. My being depends upon God as the echo depends on the voice and as the reflection depends on the light. Therefore the final law of my nature is pliant and absolute obedience towards the principle of my being. *Opis manuum Tuarum:* I am always between His fingers.

As in the hands of the potter who moulds the clay to his fancy, and as in the hands of the weaver who guides the thread according to his plans, and as in the hands of the gardener who shapes and cuts the impassive branches, and puts his own mind and ideas into the trees which he possesses.

There is in the innermost depths of my soul one particular point which I can always reach and which is in harmony with the whole divine work. My being is a being that has been received, and it knows this since it is a conscious being capable of self-knowledge. Thus docility is the very woof of all the virtues, and it is the breath of my supernatural life; there is in fact but one ill, which is to refuse to be dependent. For a creature to refuse to depend means that it throws itself into death with all the power at its command, just as an echo would annihilate itself at the very moment when, refusing to repeat the word that was shouted, it would give up being an echo and would itself cease to be.

Unhappily this simplicity which obeys and submits is not an habitual mode of mine. Over my created nature, like the accumulated debris on a mountain path, whole avalanches have passed, both evil-bearing and oppressive. And I have mingled my imperious desires and my exacting caprices with the sole necessity of serving God. The divine hands have seemed to me to be hard or too covetous, and I have fled before them like a senseless wild beast. I have let myself slip away between His fingers like worthless water. To recover my liberty! As if the condition of my liberty were not the submission of my being to its law; as if I could be really free by ceasing to be what I am, by introducing anarchy, chaos and discord into my nature?

Opus manuum Tuarum. How would it be if, instead of ruling myself according to my fleeting impressions, I should adopt as rule the first principle of supernatural life? Love the divine hands, those hands which make me, which create me without ceasing, and from which I can never more escape *de manu mea nemo est qui possit eruere.* (*Deut.* xxxii. 39.) And when an unseen Providence entreats me earnestly through events whether tiresome or pleasant, when it turns to the right or to the left, when it carries me in the night or in peril, *in hoc ego sperabo.* (*Psalm* xxvi, 3.) If only I do not leave the creating hands, if only my will dwells there where my nature cannot fail to be; if only I am with the whole strength of my desire that which I am by my whole essence, then my treasure, my security, my only good is in safety.

Our true glorying should have God for its object; for we are the work of God and it is His action in us that is worthy of admiration. The divine hands are rest-bringing, like a strong watchful guardian, and death itself is powerless against that which these hands protect and hold.

Give me, O my God, all that is wanting to me, all that I need: the taste for docility, and the hunger for dependence. This loyal and strong dependence has nothing in it that is trivial or lowering it is the condition of every kind of strength, as is the dependence of the root on the soil, and of the leaf towards the branch. It is at the very moment that the leaf separates itself from the branch that bears it and gives a meaning to its existence—at the moment that it is whirled away dancing like a creature that has been set free—at the moment when it is nothing more than itself alone, that it is called a dead leaf. I entreat of You, my God, to deliver me from sin which drives me far from You, and from pride which protests within me against the decrees of Your Providence, and the desires of Your grace, from all that insolent obstinacy, that discontent and complaining, those follies which a ray of heavenly light would slay as a nightmare; deliver me from them by making me understand that nothing is more beautiful, nothing more strong, and nothing more holy than to be the work of Your hands.

XXI

Always and everywhere
(*Preface of the Mass.*)

ALWAYS and everywhere! Of whom are we speaking? Of God, perhaps, of God eternal and omnipresent. No, the words are spoken of the deep and tranquil gratitude that the faithful soul sends back in unceasing echo to its Lord. *Semper et ubique gratias agere.*

We do not know how much we owe to God, we know still less what continual thanksgiving would add of light to our lives, and of wholeness to our action. We strive laboriously to shut ourselves up within our grievances, we mar the holy joy of the sons of God, and we cry like foolish children, not knowing with what treasures our hands have been filled.

And yet how often we have listened to the chant of the liturgical prefaces with their peremptory assertions! We do not deny that it is meet, just, right and salutary to give unceasing thanks, but we do not know the precise reason of this praise and the motives of that gratitude which never slumbers.

The motive is not far removed from the command: *nos tibi* (*Preface, Mass*), we and You; it is only necessary to grasp these two terms and from their relationship prayer will spring forth. How many souls wander through the world unconscious that God is loading them with favours, and without giving a thought to what He is.

He is the One who forgives and who cures, and I never could keep within my memory all that He has forgiven me. I only know that I need this mercy as the seaweed needs the ocean, and that without it I should have dried up beyond hope of recovery. And those silent pardons granted by God in the evenings of my days, when night casts on all things its pacifying shadow, that munificent and secret pardon hindered my soul from foundering in death, as a traveller whom a cruel shipwreck surprises in the darkness.

Frenum pullorum indocilium (*S. Cl. of Alex: Paedagogus*) My God— You Who have checked my untimely ardour, and restrained my restless folly, You who have prevented me from being inconsistent and meaningless, how often have I muttered in anger when some providential obstacle stopped short my presumptuous endeavours. *Gratias agere*, I thank You for having held me in, in spite of myself, as the bridle holds in the untamed foal, and for having made me feel that I had a Master and a law, and that, left to myself, I should destroy myself in anarchy.

79

Penna volucrum non errantium: (*Paedagogus*) You have co-operated actively in all my good deeds, and You have taken the lead in all my supernatural enterprises, as the sure wings of the bird which accompany it and uphold it as it flies off to the horizon towards unknown skies. When then I look at myself I always find You at the starting point of all in me that is of worth. It was You who spoke to me one day in that dim Church, when I was praying vaguely near the great entrance, penetrated by the silence and the freshness of the sanctuary; and that word, then spoken, makes it ever more impossible for me to pose as one who knows nothing of Your secrets. I know that You asked of me a service which no other could give, and that my life is the sole answer to Your special call. It was You who looked long on me in the calm of summer skies; and that almost religious serenity which brooded over my hours of study came down from Your hands. It was You who visited me—how gently? in hours of mourning and weariness, hinting that I should allow You to act as a physician, who causes suffering that he may cure our ill more speedily. On each cross that came to me I found Your name and Your command, and Your life-giving grace. And if I was unwilling to accept the whole of Your gift, it is my own fault: I have kept the bitterness without the strength, the poison without the balm, the sorrow without the light. In the depth of every trial, I knew well that there was, for me, a means of growing in goodness and of raising myself above myself.

Semper et ubique! I am always disappointed and disgusted when I look at myself; I prefer to thank You for all that You have accomplished in Your faithful ones. Your work is so beautiful, O my God, let others lament and sigh, I will admire You, and since You are labouring, I will encourage You. I am in admiration at You for having been able to draw such torrents of love from the hearts of Your disciples; yes, I wonder at You, watching You in the workshop of this Your world, always at Your trade, trying to make out of us (more or less reasonable animals) souls worthy of Yourself. I give You thanks that the whole world is not lost in paganism and ignorance, for we owe that fact to You.

I thank You that all those around me do not despise me and strive to injure me—for without Your grace, we do not know into what abyss our instincts would have driven us.

I give You thanks that at times souls have been compassionate, and have sacrificed themselves to lighten sorrow, for You were at the fountain head of these good impulses, and it was Your love that these acts of mercy expressed.

I give You thanks for having sent us Your Apostles, and for having first fashioned them, before putting them at our service. I give You thanks for the unknown marvels that Your power produces every day, and for the virtue which You keep guard over in the hearts of my unknown brethren. Why should I imagine, so falsely, that I alone count, and why should I not try to enlarge my soul and to become catholic—universal.

I give You thanks for all the Christian past, and for all the future which will be still more glorious; for the young and the children whom You are preparing in the shadow; for the light which, by means of our superiors, reaches down even to our "ignorances"; for all the secrets which Your Providence still holds in reserve, and for all that complex and pathetic story—story of our world being made ready for Your coming.

Semper et ubique faith, hope and charity, is not that enough to give food to my gratitude, and what human power can ever rob me of that? Therefore to my last day, and no matter what may be my moral weakness or my physical suffering, in distress or in triumph, and still more in that "creeping life I live," with its routine ways, without lustre and without heights, which forms the ordinary course of my days, everywhere, I shall strive to chant my preface, and the *Semper et ubique* will save me from all betrayals. We betray You when we cease to give You thanks; we forget who You are, and that is already like an apostasy. Thanksgiving turns our mere existence into a craft or calling, and this present life is the apprenticeship of that craft.

XXII

Vox Domini

The voice of the Master
(Psalm xxviii. 3, 4, *etc.*)

IT is only heard clearly in the desert, not because it is timorous, but because it is deep, and solitude recalls us to ourselves.

In our speechless prayer we listen, and we hear, not *one* voice but a multitude—*quasi vocem turbæ magnæ*—(*Apoc.* xix. 6): as the voice of a great tumult. The first lesson that solitude brings home to us is that we are not alone, far from it. We are being swept along in the immense current of the work of God.

The far-away voices of those who have gone before us which call to us in words of counsel and entreaty, whence do they come? *Vox Domini*, it is Christ who has borrowed the voices of our holy protectors. It is He who speaks in Peter and in all the missionaries of yore. *Rex Christe, virtus fortium*—(*Hymn Vespers, Com. Martyrs*): the King Christ, strength of the brave. It is enough to listen to the distant roar of past ages of Christianity to awake within us a great sense of our dignity. For we are the heirs of all those ages, nay more than heirs, through us the message of the past is to be carried on. All those voices without faces which murmur in our solitude, have deputed us to guard a sacred deposit . . . *Omnes sancti et sanctæ Dei* . . . (*Litany of Saints.*) All the saints of God . . . We are members of their company. We are the peers of those who lived for the interests of Christ, and who have no one but the Christians of to-day to carry on this, the one *real business* of the world.

Vox Domini, I hear it in the great crowd that calls: the children who ask for bread, the blind imploring for light, the deaf, who do not even hear the answer to their cry. The many orphans and the great crowd of all God's people, who suffer and are in captivity beneath the rule of the harsh Pharaohs whom they have chosen for their masters . . . All those who stand and wait . . . wait perhaps for me, and in whose lot we cannot allow ourselves to be unconcerned without incurring guilt.

They wait, they ask us to give them all that they need, that is to say that which we ourselves have not got, gentleness and energy, piety and self-sacrifice; peace-bringing light, and purifying love: all that feeds, and all that educates . . . *Vox Domini*, it is Christ in distress, Christ poor who entreats when they speak, and behold the hunger and thirst to be more just and more generous is born within me.

I must love, before I know them, all those whom God's Providence will place in my path: I must recognize them even before they speak, and my eyes must tell them that I am theirs. How is it possible that I should still live for myself and think that lost which I give away. On all the ways of my life, I shall recognize those needy ones for whom the voice of my God has cried out in distress in the night. Grant, O Lord, that I be not empty-handed before their prayers, nor deaf to their complaints. For it is hard at times to recognize the deserters from Your Cause, in their disguise of hardened sinners!

Vox Domini: In the solitude of my prayer voices call to me from afar, with prophetic warning at times, the voices of those who will do evil to me and succeed in injuring me, those who will be angry with me or hate me, or whose devouring zeal will one day or another bruise and wound me. And in them God asks me to grant, beforehand, a pardon so complete that hereafter the remembrance of their injuries or their blunders will call forth no resentment. I hear You, O my God, and using the words of Your own prayer, I beg of You to forgive them their offences because I have already forgiven them the injuries they have not yet done to me. The voice of Christ is a perpetual call to mercy, but hearts hardened by bitterness remain in their tombs, and His call does not restore them to life. They wish to be deaf, it will be done to them according to their desire.

Vox Domini, the voices of all who have helped me, fed me, trained me, and whose tutelary action still lives within me, as that of the unknown builder immortalized in the cemented masonry of the wall. It seems to me at times so natural, so simple to have been protected from my childhood by the services of unsalaried love. I no more dream of being enraptured at the sight of virtue, than I think of being astonished that the road beneath my feet does not give way. And yet all those who spent themselves in doing good to me were the messengers and the instruments of redeeming love; from every point of the horizon, love has converged towards my littleness, as the rays of light converge towards a microscopic centre. The voice of all my benefactors from the day of my birth rolls like a vast ocean over my life; and yet I dare to complain, at times, that I am not loved, and that I do not hold that place in the lives of others which my pretensions and my pride have marked out as mine.

What an ennobling responsibility to inherit, from the friends of God, the treasure of the theological virtues, and to be obliged to safeguard and increase it! What humble sweetness in the thought that we are the debtors of an immense though invisible multitude, and that we have but to look around us at the people who consent to put up with us, to discover that we have benefactors on all sides!

Vox Domini, the voice of the Lord above all within me, in the depths of my soul made holy by His grace, where He speaks, now as

Master and now as one entreating: humbly as one who petitions, and absolutely as one who commands. I have known it for long and like the child Samuel in the sanctuary of the chosen people, I have learnt to recognize the Voice of the Lord—*Sciebat (vocem) Domini.* (1 *Kings* iii. 7.) Each time that I have been surprised into hesitation, or have been troubled by some alluring delight, His voice has been heard, faithful and gentle; and through His law, through my leaders, through reason, He has told me what I should do, and what avoid.

And the Voice of the Shepherd calling His sheep at evening, that voice I shall still hear when all others are silent, and when, in the utter destitution of the final separation, He will come to relieve me of my watch, and to release me from all slaveries—*Nunc Dimittis.* (*Luke* ii. 29.) If I come to love the divine voice I shall not fear that final call, but as a watchman ever on the alert to answer the challenge, I shall pass across the ways of life, undistracted by the deceptive echo of my own voice, undisturbed by short-lived tumults. I shall be as one who listens—*auditor verbi*—(*James* i. 23)—and obeys—*obaudit.*

XXIII

COUNTLESS generations of men have repeated this little word which comes to us from the Patriarchs of old. It was resolutely reiterated by the Israelites at the time of the promises. It was with this little word that Christ opened His most significant discourses. It is the word which is found in the writings of the Apostles: the word which will resound in Heaven, summing up the adoration of the saints.

We have never pondered its meaning, nor learnt to love it. We have not tried to apply it as a lesson to our revolts, nor as a dressing to our wounds. We have not realized that it comes thus from afar, led by God to our prayer, and that it is enough for us to put our whole will into it, to find ourselves sheltered from all the attacks of our enemies and rescued from dissipation of strength, from regret and from death.

When the priest says Mass, he reads prayers in Latin from the Missal, which the faithful in the Church cannot hear, but the little server answers boldly in the name of all, "Amen. Yes, that is all that we desire, all that we ask for. We accept all beforehand, we ratify all. May God hear the prayer which this priest has murmured." Let the pagan-minded smile if they will, nothing, in reality, is more beautiful than this absolute confidence in the Church our Mother. Christ's disciples are so sure that the priest will ask nothing but what is good for them; it is so natural to them to leave the care of results in the hands of their heavenly Father; they have made their own the meaning of the Sermon on the Mount, and have understood that God is more solicitous for their needs than He is for the feeding of His sparrows; they believe so utterly in their Saviour that a simple Amen is enough to express their submissive trust and their foregone acceptance of all that Divine Wisdom has chosen for them.

Our life can be a resolute and all-embracing *Amen*. Perfection is not found in being *rare*, but in being straight, and to be straight we must not cling tenaciously to our own ideas, but rather suit ourselves to all the Will of God, and work only in union with the Master.

Unus est Magister vester. (*Matt.* xxiii. 8.)

An unbroken Amen, which like the weaver's thread turns back ten thousand times upon itself, crossing and recrossing in the loom, always pliant and always firm, becomes in time the marvellous tissue of the seamless garment—*inconsutilis*—(*John* xix. 23). There is not a knot in the whole, no resistance, no stiffness, but also no inconsistent weakness, no unexpected fancies. Nothing can be woven with grains of sand, ropes are not made with water.

How would it be if we should try to enclose our life in an Amen? We have uttered it so often, and it will be the final farewell of the Church militant placed on our tombstone after the *Requiescat in Pace*. This word which puts the last touch on all creatures as they are committed into the divine hands, might well serve as my distinctive seal. The Amen uttered from the heart, which dispels all grumbling, all exactions, and which fills the soul with luminous peace.

People have been known, at some given moment of their lives, to take, as it were, a large blank sheet of writing paper, and at the bottom of the page, in the guise of a signature they have written the one word, Amen. And after that, they have handed over their lives to God, and His Providence set to work and wrote above this preliminary Amen the long and sorrowful history of a human life. Sorrows were drawn up in line each under its gloomy date, but Amen had accepted them beforehand, and thus robbed them of their poisonous bitterness. And the mighty healing joys of life were there. God wrote each at its hour on the parchment page, like so many resting places on a journey, and far from avoiding them, or forgetting them, far from being caught by them or lulled to sleep among them, the submissive soul, having already uttered the word that delivers, rejoiced in them with God and for Him. Amen, then, beforehand to all the arrangements of God. Amen to the unexpected and sudden checks. Amen to the long-drawn-out troubles, to the unnerving disappointments of each day. Amen to the train that has gone too soon, or arrived too late. Amen to the rain and to the sun, to sleeplessness and to weariness, to tropical heat and to arctic winters. Amen to the sullen peevishness of the people with whom we work, to their bad habits and their little manias. Amen to the friends and relations whom old age makes selfish and crabbed. A joyous Amen if it is possible, but at least always a loyal and strong Amen. This little word will remove much sinful folly from our paths, it will hold us back from leaping into ditches, and from losing ourselves in the pursuit of our mad dreams.

And when prayer is difficult, when my treasury contains no hitherto unpublished formularies, when all seems dismal, uninspiring, devoid of beauty and tinged with grey, instead of setting out to see afar in the laboured pages of some mystic, for an inflaming theory or extravagant recipe; instead of bewildering ourselves with intoxicating words and vague sentiments, let us take our heads in our hands and try to utter, from the depths of our heart, one simple Amen.

Amen is peremptory like a conclusion, like a treaty that has been signed, a trial that has been ended, a dead man that has been buried. Amen is short as truth, which is but itself, and to which nevertheless there is no end to the telling. Amen is honest, clear and high-spirited, and the powers of darkness within us are afraid of its determined demeanour and of the light which it turns on the darkest corners. Ah! If only we could argue with Amen! Adepts as we are in all the arts of quibbling and contriving, we could easily find some compromise, and our clever casuistry would supply us with convenient solutions. We are past masters in the art of dodging—*rege quod est devium*—(*Seq. Mass, Pentecost*), and we cannot bear to surrender. But with Amen all resistance melts away and we cease to belong to ourselves. I shall say it then, this modest Amen, which is as humble and as eternal as the Son of God. I shall say it with the unknown and invisible crowd which ever unites itself with my prayer. The expression only of the word may differ, the meaning—never.

From the Amen of triumph to the sobbing cry that ends the *Pie Jesu*, (*Dies Irae*), they all can feed our daily prayer. This little word is enough to make missing virtues spring up in my soul. On the day of my baptism, when the priest pronounced the prescribed words "In the name of the Father . . ." he did not add Amen. May it not have been so arranged that I myself should have the chance of saying it? That my whole life might be, as it were, the complete yet simple answer to the grace which came to meet me before I knew that I existed and which can destroy all deaths within me. Amen.

XXIV

Ego vadam
I go away
(*John* vi. 7.)

WHEN Your disciples were grieving at the thought of losing You, You told them it was good for them that they should no longer see You, and that this departure should be a cause of joy to them.

Why? Should not the lawgiver remain in proximity to his laws to interpret them, and to insure their execution; should not the Master of Truth continue the education of those who have left all to hear Him? When You are no longer seen, Your words and actions will be forgotten and it will be as though You had never existed.

Expedit vobis. (*John* xvi. 7.) And yet divine wisdom is right; and if You went away, it was in order that the Spirit should be sent to us, and that everywhere and always, with the same facility and the same claim, all could become Your disciples.

When You spoke in Galilee, those only could hear who were not too far off from You, and on the outskirts of the crowd they caught but vaguely Your words of eternal life. They jostled each other at the door of the little house in Capernaum where You had taken refuge, and there as everywhere, the stronger drove back the weaker, who were gathered outside, disappointed to be able to see nothing. They had to tax their ingenuity, when they were ill, in order to get near to touch the fringe of Your cloak, and blind Bartimæus had to shout very loud, as he sat by the road-side, that his need might reach Your ears. You were in Galilee, and they sought You elsewhere; You crossed the lake of Tiberias, and the crowd ran the length of the coast to meet You at the moment of Your landing. Rome did not possess You, nor distant Spain, nor Gaul which had been opened out by the legions of Cæsar, nor beyond over the frontiers of the empire did that immense multitude, which was groping in the night. You were the privilege of a little number, prisoner of an hour and of a place. You the one thing necessary, and the life of all souls.

Expedit vobis. It was good that You should go, and that hiding Your visible and risen body in the clouds of Mount Olivet, You should leave us Your invisible presence and Your voice resounding *in fines orbis terræ* (*Romans* x. 18).

The Church which continues You is Catholic and universal, when she speaks all the world can hear, her sacraments are Your actions extended to the uttermost corners of the earth, bringing You quite close to each one of Your own.

For it is indeed You who remit sins, when Your priests absolve the sinners, whom Your grace has disposed to repentance; and to be cured of our infirmities there is no longer any need to take off the roof of the house where You are speaking. The cripples are always at Your feet, and Your eyes never lose sight of any one.

Each one to-day can be Your contemporary; no long distance need be traversed across the ridges of the centuries to find You are an appealing memory. Holiness is found in seeing You where You are, and in blessing Your redeeming hands: *Manus sanctæ vos amplector.* (*Arnulphus, Abbot of Villiers.*) You belong to the whole world, You speak to the whole world, You enlighten the whole world by means of the Spirit whom You have sent and through whom we know the Father and the Son.

> *Per Te sciamus da Patrem*
> *Noscamus atque Filium.*
> (*Veni Creator.*)

Is it not in that, O my God, that we have the beginning of all interior life, in knowing that You are present and working, You the eternal Shepherd in the midst of Your sheep-fold? And is not the beginning of Christian charity the knowledge that all, sharing in the same gifts, fashioned by the same grace, adopted by the same Spirit, are not many, but one, but You?

The Church was only really born at that moment when You withdrew Your visible presence, leaving to her the plenitude of power which was needed to carry on Your mission. But no, I speak amiss, and this lawyer-like mode of speech is not the most rich in truth. You have not been replaced on earth by any abstract powers; when leaving us, You did not leave a charter behind; and to speak correctly, it is not a mandate which Your Church fulfils under the guidance of the Holy Ghost, but it is You who continue to act, it is Your power that is being used, and Your living words that still resound through the voice of the infallible teacher. It is only the limitations of Your mortal body which have ceased to fence in and restrain Your visible action, and the most lowly of Your disciples, the dying, the poor have You with them in their homes, as long ago the Mother-in-law of Simon on the shores of Gennesareth.

Should I not then reverence this ineffable work of the Holy Spirit, as I would have reverenced the visible presence of the Incarnate Word, had I had the happiness of possessing it? Christ waits now, as of yore, for the answers of those who consent to bind themselves to the uttermost; and His eyes travel round the ranks of the crowd—*circumspiciens eos.* (*Mark* iii. 34.) All my brethren now are near to Him, as near as the disciples who could hear and touch

Him; and out of respect for this work of the unseen Christ in them,
I should behold in all of them some sacred thing.

Expedit vobis ut ego vadam. Grant me, O my God, to begin to love
Your Spirit and to divine its wonders. Your Spirit, the great bond
of Catholic unity—the Paraclete who consoles—consoles, not
exactly for Your absence, but for our misery, and who puts His
grace in our hearts, which have been saved by Him from being
nothingness; *quæ Tu creasti pectora.* (*Veni Creator.*) The Comforter,
who brings us into the presence of our Saviour and makes known
to us the infinite wealth of His message, and draws out its fullness
before us. The Comforter who suppresses the dead past and fills
up the gap of the intervening centuries, that we may begin now, in
the Church, the face to face vision of Paradise.

I understand why, in the Litany of the Saints, we implore Christ
"through His admirable Ascension"; I understand why the Angels
of Galilee warned the Apostles that they should no longer seek in
the clouds for Him who was to be met with, poured abroad over
the whole earth, for Him who had captivated their hearts and whom
they wrongly persisted in seeking here or there—*hic aut illic*—(*Matt.*
xxiv. 23), as though He were one of the false and passing messiahs.

Never could we have consoled ourselves for dwelling far off from
Him, had He not, in order to remain present with us, chosen to
withdraw from us His presence in the flesh, and to send His Spirit
to us.

XXV

I HAVE listened to Your friends and to Your enemies, my God, and I have been surprised to find that on certain points they are in agreement. The former concede to the latter that vocal prayer is an inferior form of prayer, a performance which is somewhat commonplace in its nature, an exercise for beginners which the perfect—those who adore in spirit—have the right and the duty to cut short or leave aside. To move our lips and to repeat words, in order to persuade God, appears to them to be a relic of those dim ages when our ancestors were still pagan. To recite a monotonous series of *Ave Maria* fifty times in succession in a quarter of an hour, is to be as those monks of Asia who murmur vocal prayers like unthinking machines.

Does this prayer of our lips really deserve this haughty condemnation? Is it true that the only prayer worthy of a man and of God is the meditation of a clear mind, which climbs to the battlements of its ivory tower, there to speculate on the infinite? What attractive lesson can be drawn from our vocal prayer, that prayer which the Church imposes on her priests as an imperative and binding obligation?

The lesson is a humble one, but it is true, true with all the actuality of our human state, and since it is true, it brings into our lives order and peace and justice.

I am very weary this evening. My mind succumbs and reels, I cannot speculate on Your Greatness, nor plunge into the abstractions of theodicy; I cannot even contemplate the scenes of the Bible story, nor read the beautiful inspired text. But there is one recourse left to me, to me the wearily stumbling pilgrim—I shall take my rosary and I shall say the words, like labourers of the eleventh hour, the pettiness of whose task did not dispense them from the obligation of performing it. I shall say the words and my lips shall move as they did when I prayed for the first time, and as they will doubtless move again, when in my agony I shall speak for the last time. Between these two prayers of our dulled perception, there are others to correspond to every degree of consciousness, to suit every physical condition, every state of soul, since the command to pray always was without exception, we must always be within reach of prayer. Instead of forcing myself into conventional attitudes, I acknowledge that I am

91

drowsy in the evenings of my long days of weary work, but my lips still watch as the sentry at the entrance of the sleeping garrison. And in moments of distraction, of bustling and of panic, on the bridge of a ship, on the top of a tram, at the window of the post office . . . I see that spontaneously, to keep in touch with You, the one Master, I murmur words, consecrated formulas, invocations, which stake out the paths of my thoughts and hinder me from losing myself in the solitude of illusion.

And You tell me to love vocal prayer, because it is lowly, that is to say suitable to my being, adapted to my weak nature, made for me, who as it were die a little every evening and am rarely wholly awake.

Christum tamen sub ipso
Meditabimur sopore. . . .

Is it not Your poet Prudentius who has already told us this in Your Name?

Prayer of the poor, prayer of the crowds, catholic prayer, in which I do not meet only with my own thoughts and phrases; eternal prayer which clothes my soul as in a uniform, by allowing me to speak as all my ancestors in the faith have spoken.

Ave Maria . . . I shall not invent a single word; I shall repeat this *Ave* as it has been repeated and sung for centuries in my Church, in Your Church, my God; I shall recite it as You inspired my fore-fathers to recite it, and as, in still more remote times, all Christendom of the Middle Ages recited it; I shall say it, as it was said, with bared head on the eve of great battles, and at the feet of Madonnas, in the cemeteries and by the cradles, at the family table and in the ship-wreck . . . all, all recited it as I recite it, and because I carry on this immortal tradition, I feel that I, too, am in the ranks, in the crowd, elbow to elbow with all the living and all the dead gathered round the Mother of the World.

A soldier in uniform seems noble, for in that dress, which he has not made himself according to his fancy, but which his country has imposed upon him, he is no longer of such a family or from such a village; he is neither rich nor poor, learned nor ignorant; he is not even strong or weak, fearful or victorious; but in his absolute resem-blance to all the defenders of the country, in the perfect regularity of his actions and movements, in the midst of the regiment on the march, he is nothing more than the soldier on duty. His whole people is seen in him. I have seen them pass thus, my God, returning from great battles, the helmet fastened by the chin-strap, the eyes fixed straight before them, as though impassible, all together, while a whole nation acclaimed them. They belong to all, they are for all and they are greater than themselves because they serve.

And when I pray moving my lips, when I recite the unchangeable Pater, the Psalms, the Gloria in Excelsis, the Magnificat . . . all Your prayers, preserved by Your Church, it seems to me that in the absolute resemblance of the formulas, in the material identity of the expressions, in the midst of the Church militant, I am no longer of such a family, nor of such a city, I am no longer of one century or of another, but, with all my brethren, with the Japanese and the Africans, with children and with the aged, with Saint Augustine and the old bell-ringers, it seems to me that, freed from all decrepit weakness, I become just simply "the Christian" the faithful one on duty.

And all my ostentation fades away, and my ideas and my phrases and my shadow recalling myself alone, appear then to me to be very narrow, and I begin to breathe freely, because I have escaped from myself and my soul has become catholic.

My God, when You come for me, grant that my piety may be clothed in this uniform, and that vocal prayer may have made me like all Your servants. Those who speak evil of this prayer know nothing of it, and those who blush for it or despise it do not know of what they should be proud *Labia mea aperies*. (*Liturgy, Matins.*)

XXVI

Omnia opera Domini Domino
All you who are His works, bless the Lord
(Daniel iii. 5, 7.)

FOR centuries, when praying, Christians have been harassed by distractions, as the Egyptians were tormented by mosquitoes—*ciniphes in omnibus finibus eorum. (Psalm* civ. 31.) They struggle against these parasites of prayer; they are right to do so, and their action is meritorious, even if the enemy appears to be microscopic. It is very difficult to free ourselves from these lesser slaveries; that indolence of the imagination, which follows every incitement from without, is one form of our servitude, and one symptom of our powerlessness. Perhaps it may even be said, that the more trifling the fault is, the less easy it is to correct. Tigers have been broken in, panthers have been tamed, but no one yet ever tamed a fly nor trained a dragon-fly. Failure discourages or grieves us, and Your disciples, O my God, think that their prayer is worthless because, during these holy hours, they find themselves pondering on other things than You alone.

And yet there must be a road which leads off in a straight line across all creatures to meet the Creator; there must be a way of looking at the most divergent and commonplace things, which will disclose Him who made them; there must be a way of questioning the work of the Word—*per quem omnia facta sunt*—(*Nicine Creed*), which will make us hear rising up from all that is, the voice of praise and the word of supernatural truth. Instead of slipping in and out between distractions, and of avoiding, now on the right, and now on the left, all that turns up, and all that chatters, would it not be better to look through all to the depths, with those clear-seeing eyes that pierce the heavens?

When the priest comes back from the altar, still wholly absorbed in the mystery of Communion, our Mother, the Church, bids him murmur the canticle *Benedicite*. And lo, at that hour of recollection, prayer flows over in an inundation of enthusiasm; kneeling at his *prie-Dieu* in a silent sacristy the priest speaks to himself of birds and fishes, of whales and sharks, of glaciers and tempests, of hail and frost, of the story of man and of the aspect of things, gathering together in his formula the whole divine work, with the power of that Spirit of the Word which still lives within him. That is in truth sacerdotal prayer, towards which all Christians should tend, a prayer that is open-armed and all-embracing, springing from one source, and which extends itself as the action of the apostle who baptizes, and of the officiating priest who blesses. There is no reserve and no restriction; only those escape the blessing who voluntarily exile themselves from it. From vault to pavement, from door to apse, the great divine blessing penetrates everything. Why should we make a distinction between the works of God and God Himself, as if between two antagonistic entities? Cannot our prayer interest itself in snails and weevils, since the words of Christ were concerned with the moth and rust, and oxen falling into wells, and scorpions and brooms, and oil that had to be put into lamps? Why should we persist in looking on those things which God has sanctified as commonplace or despicable or merely boring?—*Tu ne commune dixeris!*—(*Acts* x. 15.) The vision of Joppe has not yet come for us, that vision in which Peter understood, in spite of His Jewish prejudices, that God was no stranger to birds and beasts, and that a pure heart, a heart that was submissive and consequently free, could use things without being subject to them, and could draw from them a harmony of praise.

My God, at times I have had a presentiment that covetousness was only bad because it hindered us from going to the heart of reality; because it misused reality, that is to say, it turned things away from their real functions, and brought night out of light. But if in a prayer of happy rejoicing, or of simple trust, I should call together all Your creatures, if I should relate to You all that they say to me, as we go, at times, to read a message to the person who suggested it, and who smiles on recognizing it; if I should sanctify my very distractions by telling them to You, as I walk with You in that Eden of my life and of Your world, it seems to me that finding You thus everywhere, I should no longer be distracted by anything, and that You would have become my all.

Unhappily things beguile me, and that which is wrong in my distractions is, not that they terminate in Your work, but that they stop short at the surface of appearances, and do not press in to the heart of that which is. I see all that surrounds me as if I were myself its centre; if I saw all gravitating round the living Principle, round the Redeeming Word, that vision would be a prayer of admiration, and I would not be obliged to stop thinking of birds, or of looking at ants, in order to try to think of You alone, cut off, and, as it were, isolated from Your work. Is not a workman in his place in his workshop? Does the contemplation of a statue distract us from thinking of the sculptor? Teach me to look with clear eyes, and luminous perspicacity, and I shall no longer be forced to despise anything, but shall bring forth praise from all things; and since frogs are mentioned in that Apocalypse which was inspired by Your Spirit, I see no reason why their croaking, in the reeds by the ponds, should not delight my prayer.

My God, would not this be, even here, a little like a foretaste of Paradise? And if I should narrate all my long stories to You, if I should tell You all that fills my mind, and all that troubles me, if my prayer, instead of being by the side of my life or in my life, should become my life itself, conscious of being upheld and directed by You, I think that my old errors and my old terrors would fly away as ghosts, and that the dawn of a peaceful eternity would rise in the soul of Your vagrant disciple.

The final word of all is one of union with the divine work. Each one plays his part in the great game. Each one advances the one business of life . . . the glorious coming of the Son of Man; and the Earth, Your Holy Earth, the Earth that You loved, that You visited, that You formed in the geological millenaries, this Earth which is our dwelling, because You have placed us there, and which is furthermore our providential educator . . . this Earth . . . I love it, O my God, with a strong, jealous, upraising love, which makes me holy and enlightens me, because it comes from You and because in loving this holy Earth I meet You and I am like to You. *Benedicat terra Dominum* (*terræ*). (*Daniel* iii. 74.)

XXVII

Oculis clausis
With closed eyes
(*cf. Tob. xiv.* 15.)

IF we could bring ourselves to reflect for a few moments on what we are, it would not be long before we ascertained that the most decisive moments of our lives are not the hours in which we have spoken, nor even the hours in which we have worked before men. Our most important hours are, in reality, our most silent hours.

For it is in the silence of the soul that the seemingly most sudden resolutions have been worked out, it is in secret, too, that deterioration goes on, and that ruin is consummated, there, also is slowly tempered that fidelity which trial shows to be unalterable.

We know it well. We know that there is in the depths of every human soul a refuge that no love can unlock, and that no violence can force open. Advice, threats, orders, can indeed rain and strike upon this inner shelter; but never will anyone succeed in gliding cunningly within, nor in taking by storm that last retreat where we belong to no one but ourselves . . . No one can will for us, love in our place or live in our name. Whatever we do, our responsibilities are our own, and in spite of all appearances to the contrary, we live alone, we die alone, we sin alone, and alone we take the first steps to repentance.

And yet, no, this is not quite true. At the very moment that we penetrate into the desert of our inner self, we perceive that this solitude is peopled by an unseen presence; at the very moment that we shut ourselves up within our inner Cenacle, we find ourselves suddenly face to face with One whom no closed door can hinder from being everywhere at home; at the very moment that we believe we are alone, we realize that solitude is an impossibility, and that at the fountain-head of our consciousness, at the starting-point of our determinations, He who made us and re-made us, is busy about us, watches, directs and works with us. We have been invaded, we are an occupied fortress, we cannot escape from that God, whose true name is The Inevitable; and when we shut our eyes in order to see Him no longer, we do not banish Him any more than sleep puts an end to a storm.

The Christian who prays recollects himself, that is to say he re-discovers himself, gathers himself together, frees himself from all useless masters, from all unknown hands, from all fast-holding desires which tear him to pieces and so prevent him from being himself.

Oculis clausis. To recollect ourselves we shut our eyes. Is it in order to see nothing like a timid person or a hypocrite? No, but that we may see all without being dazzled by anything. We fancy that the real sky is that of bright day. No, the true sky is the sky of night, and the brightness conceals it as soon as the sun shines. Let us then shut our eyes that we may see, in the calm night, the sky of our soul, star-strewn with the lights of grace—*descendens a Patre luminum*. (*James* i. 17.)

The old traditional attitude of joined hands and closed eyes is full of deep meaning, a meaning which escapes the inattentive. With closed eyes! In order to pray do nothing else but this if words are too heavy for your lips and if you can find nothing to say to Him who is the Truth. With eyes fast shut, as those shut their eyes who receive a sudden intimation of unexpected joy, which submerges, in its abundance, even their highest hopes. With eyes tight shut, as of those who hear news of sorrow too deep for tears, and who see in the furthermost corner of their souls for some certainty to which they can cling. With eyes well closed like those of good servants, Your servants, my God, who sleep in the peace of their last sleep, enveloped in Your redeeming pardon . . . All these keep their eyes shut, because they have no use for the glaring light of the sun, and the glitter of things means nothing more to them.

Grant that I may live thus with closed eyes in a recollectedness which will not be due to ignorance or laziness, but to ardent concentration and interior light. For it is just what passes in the secret place of my soul, that is pre-eminently Your work. My silent hours are those in which we talk together looking each other in the face. I have never withdrawn within myself without finding You seated before my door, *sedisti lassus* (*Dies iræ*), and it is indeed within me that Your redemption must be wrought, if I am not to remain for ever a stranger to You.

Everything within me recalls You; everything speaks to me of You as soon as I consent to look upon my life as a conquest of my God, as soon as I seek within myself for the traces of Your love and the relics of Your Incarnation. See, I bear names which belong only to You, and I am a holy thing because of all that You have blessed and consecrated within me.

Why, alas! do foolish day dreams, pre-occupations, anger and regrets come so often to drive me forth from myself? Why is the greater part of my day spent in a kind of strange somnambulism, in which my actions are not really mine, and my speech has nothing in it but words?

I do not live in the deep places. My Cenacle has been profaned. I have brought the nomads into Your house, and the unbelievers have encamped in Sion. You alone can purify the sanctuary, and, driving out the intruders, restore me to myself in peaceful recollection.

Oculis clausis, should we not accustom ourselves to this act, which will be our last, and in our solicitude not to fail at the divine meeting-places should we not watch all the roads of our soul, and guide ourselves by the sole light of the Lamb: *lucerna ejus est agnus*. (*Apoc.* xxi. 23.) Recollectedness would teach me to value faith, and cure me of my ineffectual ravings, I would shut my eyes like all that relinquishes itself and all that entrusts itself, like all that ceases to dread and consents to die.

Hasten in me the moment of peace. It must come at its appointed hour, as the ears of corn which ripen all together on the same day in the immense expanse of the harvest fields. I shall not cease my restlessness until the hour comes when I shall have understood that nothing is wanting to me of all that I ought to have; the hour, when my desires shall be no more vast than Your Will, and when my treasures shall satisfy all my desires; the day when neither possessing nor seeing anything but You alone, I shall discover, *oculis clausis*, that it is very good to be Your child.

XXVIII

Surgam et ibo ad Patrem
I will arise and will go to the Father
(*Luke* xv. 18.)

I WOULD speak to You, this evening, O my God, of those who do not yet pray, or who pray without knowing that they do so; I want to ask You what You are, and what You do for the sheep—for Your sheep—who are not yet of Your fold. They interest me,—shall I say more than the others? No, for in Your work all is equally worthy of care, but their lot is more uncertain, and when one of these erring souls crosses the threshold of salvation, there is greater joy in heaven than for the perseverance of the ninety-nine just.

Tell me, Lord, what are You for those who seek, and what You do for those who do not find or who are mistaken, and for all those who have voluntarily abandoned the light. I want to be able to look at all things from Your point of view, and to impregnate my ideas with Your judgments, so that I may neither fall into the harsh severity of the pharisee, nor into the soft good-nature of the sceptic . . . I do not know with what feelings I should approach the incredulous or the perverse; I do not know how I should look on them and whether, perhaps, mistrust is not an obligation.

All these men have a supernatural vocation, that is to say that all, since their birth, have had but one sole destiny, to be united for ever to You. This call is not inactive within them; it is Your word which never returns empty . . . *non revertetur ad me vacuum*—(*Isaias* lv. 11), and therefore all, all these wandering ones, these careless and culpable ones, are being urged by You towards light and peace. It is You who are at work within them, like a workman working underground, who is not seen, and is scarcely heard, but who labours unceasingly in the depths. It is You who hinder their selfishness from congealing into a mass, like a sea that is frozen; it is You Who protect within them the spark beneath the cinders and Who incite the thrust of a new sap within these unfruitful trees. You are the Redeemer of unbelievers, the Father of the poor, the Friend of sinners, and those who have denied this, in their sour and rigid teaching, have been tranquilly excommunicated by Your Church, one after another.

Amator peccatorum (*Arnulf, Abb. of Villiers, Brabant*), *Pater pauperum* (*Seq. Pent.*), *Lumen ad revelationem Gentium* (*Luke* ii. 32) . . . If I adopt Your feelings I shall look on these wandering men as a great nation on the march, on the march towards an unknown destiny and towards a goal which is known to You. They shall attain this goal if they continue to advance, and to follow the star of the wise men: *lumen lumine quærunt.* (*Hymn, Epiphany.*) True light will lead them to Justice.

Surgam et ibo . . . I shall reverence, O my God, this first tremor that passes through a penitent soul, this first uneasiness in those who are searching.

For long ages mankind, the human nature that I share, and which is dearer to me than myself, for such long ages, from the depths of its misery has it dreamt of the one hope. To rise up and set out in search of an all-conquering love, which would give a meaning to effort and save suffering from being useless. My God, they have sought after You, Your apostle tells us so in Your name, and we may therefore repeat it, all these prodigals have sought for You, bearing the affliction of their own faults or of the fault of the race, but since they were seeking You, it was because Your grace was working with their effort, and You were less far off from them than they imagined. *Medius vestrum stetit quem vos nescitis.* (*John* i. 26.)

And in these days, too, may I not believe that You have prepared the savages of Africa, and the great peoples of Asia to know You fully some day, by putting them in the way towards horizons less gloomy than the senseless materialistic negation of all hope. May I not believe that in these strange religions something is yet being expressed of the *Surgam et ibo ad Patrem*, and that the movements of these prodigals, like those of cripples or of people awaking from sleep, show at least, in their awkwardness or their ardour, a real desire?

You have organized "economies" of salvation, progressive distributions of the whole truth, which You gave us at last when You came among us; and I do not think that I fail in reverence to the light when I seek for its first rays even in the night. Life has such deep beginnings, and man gains his experience so slowly. Since the fall he has been groping and calling for You, as a child who has suddenly become blind, and who cries out to some unknown piety.

Give me, my God, pity for souls, and grant that I may never despise sinners; grant that I may be keenly interested in Your great work out there, beyond the visible frontiers of the Church, and let me spare no trouble for the propagation of the Faith in our own countries and far off from our homes. I know people who devote themselves wholly, and quite lawfully, to the expansion of their national interests in foreign lands, and who burn with the desire to make others in some way like themselves; but to bring the orphans to the true Father, the sheep to the Good Shepherd, to co-operate with Christ who suffers and whose grace strives to overcome human weariness, that is a still more enviable lot, and one that prayer puts within our reach.

And then, my God, grant me also to banish from my conduct and from my thoughts all that harmful arrogance with which we so often crush the unbelieving among us, those whom we call our adversaries—the culpable and sinners. They are Your people, I shall speak no ill of them. They will be Your conquest of to-morrow, how then can I cry them down to-day? Wherever a soul is striving it calls for infinite reverence from us; every head turned towards the light bears its invisible aureole. And those who voluntarily do evil and who wickedly hate the light, these I shall not condemn until You have judged them. Since it would be Your triumph to bring all home—*noh perdidi ex eis quemquam*—(*John* xviii. 9), since You were merciful and full of care for Your fugitive and weak Apostles, I wish to work with You to increase Your victory, and I am determined never to hate my brethren, but only to hate the evil which I share in common with them.

Lord, I pass among men, I go round about in our great cities, I read the papers, I hear without listening, and I see without looking . . . We are all one on top of another in our civilized society, and I tell myself that each of these faces of men, each of those words heard, each of those actions seen by chance, can speak to me of You. When they are virtuous, it is because they depend directly on You, and when they are the deeds of a prodigal, they should make me think of the Father.

XXIX

In Ipso radicati
Being rooted in Him
(Col. ii. 7.)

LIKE the root which runs towards the centre of the earth, hiding itself that it may be more useful and be able to nourish better, drawn by the mysterious power which is its law, and becoming more strongly attached the longer it advances—thus it is that I should be; winning each day nearer to the deep of God, sinking more into Truth and Justice, attaching myself more and more, through all my actions and all my desires, without weakness and without wavering, to the Eternal which feeds us.

For the soil on which I am, is capable of making me live. The root does not choose its place, but utilizes it. The root is the plant itself underground. The soil in which God's Providence has placed me is full of juices which I know nothing of, or despise, and I refuse to take root in disagreeable occupations, in a sandy or morose environment, in an austere and stony duty; I have not yet learnt the art of fastening on to the roughnesses in the rock, of decorating ruins with flowers, and of causing an all-conquering docility and humble love to spring up everywhere in unfriendly crevices. I am a proud and haughty plant, and I go to pieces from lack of submission.

We lend ourselves temporarily to our work, as a root which drags itself along the surface of the ground and does not intend to fasten there; we dare not take that plunge into the soil, that decisive plunge, which would give strength to all our visible action, and would establish us *in Ipso*. We do not wish to entrust our stability, that is our progress, our future, our happiness, and our being to God alone, and because we reserve ourselves, we waste away.

Our environment, just because it is ours, should be loved by us—genuinely loved. The couch-grass springs up by the side of the roads, and the crocus pierces through an almost frozen earth, and water plantains grow in slimy, muddy ditches, and the fox-glove in the underwood—each plant peoples its own corner of the earth, and makes use of all that it finds there.

There where Providence has placed us is the place in which we should live. We are rooted in an immense and understanding goodness, and the grace of Christ mounts up within us through all the channels of our desires.

My God, I must acknowledge it, though it is utterly ridiculous, for a long time I strove to take root in myself. It is foolish, yet it was years before the absurdity of my effort became evident in my eyes, and even now, very often I find myself beginning it again. I wished to suffice to myself, and I thought that the determination to grow was the only condition necessary for growth; I thought that the firm resolve to feed myself was sufficient to appease my hunger and to preserve me from exhaustion from want of food; I thought that I was to myself alone my environment and my soil, and that I had no need of You nor of any one else to become what I wished to be. You appeared to me to be no more than a distant overseer, a gardener perhaps, but not the very earth in which my life was growing. I said to myself that others were only neighbours, models it might be, or rivals, but I did not realize that the soil in which I was planted was impregnated with their example and their virtues, and that growing within Your Church, it is through her that I have received all my powers and all the grace that makes me whole.

In Ipso radicati. Should I not attach myself to You, My God, with an unfaltering love, which would be quite another thing to a mere desire for You; which would be the claim, the call of my famished nature. For it hungers really, that root which goes its way and buries itself, and which must find what is wanting to it, under penalty of dying with all that it holds of promise within it. It seems to me that I have not yet understood that all that surrounds me is a means of uniting myself to You, and that I can grow each day by plunging myself more deeply into Truth.

In order to obtain visible results and to make the plant grow, I foolishly persist in pulling the ends of the leaves and the tips of the branches. I go the shortest way, as we say, when we want to dispense ourselves from thinking; I take hold of the duty, whatever it may be, by the most accessible side, and being very careful as to the exterior and legal correctness of my behaviour, I neglect to work at the root of my actions, and to fill my soul with total acquiescence.

In fine, I have never seriously undertaken this slow education, through the roots, and if You had not seen to it, there would have been no progress at all. To be just, to be sincere, to be good when no one sees us; to be deeply concerned as to the secret thought that leads us, the triviality of which is often so blame-worthy; to busy oneself, not so much with the plant which is seen and which is but passing, as with the underground plant, the principle and renewer of the other, would not all this mean to begin to grow through the roots and to work in union with the Divine Soil?

Events can carry me from one country to another, throw me out of all my usual occupations, bring me into a stifling or freezing atmosphere, blight my whole exterior life; but the eternal root, *in Ipso*, is unfailing faith and love, the cause of true virtue, and this root, my God, I beg of You to protect, for it is slender and weak:

it is at the mercy of the wild boar which roots in the earth—*singularis
ferus depastus est eam*—(*Psalm* lxxix. 14): the solitary wild beast preys
upon it—it is even endangered by the violent zeal of Your servants
who under pretence of tearing up the cockle, uproot Your wheat.
How often have I been shaken, bruised and wounded by the actions
—very meritorious actions in other respects—of Your friends?
  Even their virtues are a danger to my frail being.
  Thus it is that to You alone do I entrust the care of sheltering me
and making me grow. It is from You alone that I expect the grace
of being able to root myself in the environment Your Providence
has assigned to me, and of feeding myself on my duty even if it is
rough and unattractive in appearance. For if I dwell in the soil until
the end, if neither my faith nor my love allow themselves to be torn
up, I shall know that I was planted by the hands of the all-powerful
Father. *Omnis plantatio quam non plantavit Pater meus eradicabitur.*
(Matt. xv. 13.)
  And when I need more energy, more resignation, more gentleness
and a more active patience, I shall think all this surplus can be
acquired by penetrating deeper within You, and depending more
closely upon You. Between plant and soil there is a perpetual interchange. You will welcome my neediness and I shall take Your
strength. To be clothed in glory, as Solomon was, it will be enough
for me to be like the lilies of Galilee coming forth from their earth-
covered bulbs.

XXX

MEN do not easily love Truth for itself, but like savages and children they escape when they see it coming, not knowing if it will allow them to live as they like, and to continue their little affairs. They take shelter in the woods!

But behold, O my God, I am weary of fleeing before this patient, pursuing and inevitable Truth. I know quite well that one day it will overtake me, at the hour when blocked by death, and all retreat cut off, I shall see Truth gaining ground and seizing hold of me to demand a reckoning. I am weary of this childish strategy which rejects discipline and saving constraint, that it may keep its freedom of whim and of caprice. Like all those whom Your grace finally encompasses, behold I fall on my knees wearied out with my unceasing effort to hide or fly from You.

Positis genibus, it is in this attitude that Your faithful people wait for You in the Church, and it is thus also that a Christian prays to You in secret.

When words and phrases and ideas fail him to show clearly that he belongs to You, he offers You spontaneously the homage of bended knees. I have repeated this action thousands of times, without perhaps really understanding it—imitating others, or from routine, as we uncover our heads when greeting people, or shake hands or apologize. I have not reflected on the salutary lessons that are contained in this humble traditional action, since that evening in Gethsemani when Christ put Himself on His knees for us. If I had really understood it, if even to-day I could penetrate its meaning, I would never again say that prayer had abandoned me, and that the ways were barred between God and me.

Kneeling down, no longer wishing to escape, I allow myself to be taken by Him who has come up with me. Lord, my shoulders are too weighted, how could I dash off into the desert and again escape You; lo, the weight of my falsehood lies heavy upon my weakness. It is so painful to carry the errors which have been laboriously built up. It is so difficult to run when we are encumbered with idols, and when our arms are laden with false gods. It is, above all, so impossible to drag about a heavy heart,—*gravi corde*—(*Psalm* iv. 3), a soul overwhelmed by desires falling back upon it, and it is from myself that, on my knees, I entreat You to deliver me, O King Pacific . . . The beasts of burden in the East, the camels of the desert of which You spoke to Your disciples, kneel down when the moment comes to relieve them of their pack saddles. My weariness sinks under the weight of my errors, kneeling down, I surrender myself. Take pity on me.

Positis genibus. I shall go no further. Here Your grace will come in search of me. I shall not rise up until You have changed my name to unbeliever, and have restored Your light to me. *Non dimittam te donec benedixeris mihi.* (*Genesis* xxxii. 26.) Each time that I bend my knees, I put You under the necessity of granting my petitions. It is the only way I have of forcing Your hand; there is something which You cannot refuse me when, with all my brethren, I kneel upon the ground. This humble attitude is all-powerful, not because it is base, but because it is true. You have never crushed a man upon his knees; You have never spoken with severity to him; the *flagellum de funiculis* (*John* ii. 15), the biting sting of the scourge of little cords, has only been felt by the substantial tradesmen comfortably seated at their tables, and by the dealers absorbed in their good bargains. The man on his knees is protected by Your mercy and the look which You cast on him is a promise and a resurrection.

Yes, truly, *positis genibus*—he who is on his knees is almost Your Master, and the creature who silently appeals to You in order that he may become more true and less weak, will always triumph. The blessing which I ask of You upon my knees is not that of the sons of Jacob. I deserve no privileges, I do not know if wealth would not enslave me to a crowd of unfaithful longings: the Philistines would invade my soul and their shouts would profane Your sanctuary. I do not ask You to exempt me from the common burdens, to dispense me from the weary drudgery of man, to shorten my working day, to allow me to lounge about when others bleed and die. I do not ask You that I may not grow old, I do not ask You to abolish winter, to spare me from tempests and from ruin, to keep me from knowing that deep suffering of life poured out among the most trifling occupations, and of days swallowed up by legions of importunate people. I accept everything in this rough business of man, and I shall take my share in the common lot. I do not wish to shed fewer tears, or to receive fewer blows than my comrades in the journey and the fight. I accept to be jostled, I resign myself with all my heart to suffer, but, O my God, I beg of You, on my knees, to deliver me from that evil which is within me, *Libera nos a malo.* (*Matt.* vi. 13.) You would not Yourself have taught us this prayer had You not wished to answer it fully.

I know, indeed, that I must put myself on my knees each day, and therefore that each day, at each hour, You will deliver me from an evil which is ever multiplying. I know well that You will not suppress all my misery at one touch, as a tooth is extracted; I know that this misery is a condition of my virtue and that my supernatural energy increases and rises up on opposition.

Thus without asking You to change me by some instantaneous miracle, I entreat You to protect me from myself, to remember that the ill of my birth is, that I bear in my soul a wounded and foolish will, one which contradicts itself without saying why, and which runs away without saying where, and which changes without saying how. The ill I inherit from birth is that of being disgusted with good, and ever pining for the mediocre, it is of being, as children are, dazzled with all that shines, and absorbed in ridiculous amusements. My ill is that I am a poor sinner without stability and without worth.

And when You shall see me on my knees, silent, not daring to complete the inventory of my penury, nor to make the addition of my disasters; when, before You, with eyes shut and hands joined there will be nothing but myself, no phrases, no movement, my soul clothed in misery, say, O my God, that You will then deign to remember that You are my Saviour, and that if I were anything in myself, in that very same measure I should cease to have need of You.

XXXI

In finem
Unto the end
(*Opening words of Psalms.*)

THE Eucharist is not an accessory of my life as a Christian. It should be its centre: the centre to which all returns and from which all sets out. Perhaps I have not yet sufficiently explored the truth of His Sacrament.

In former days, at the time when protestant denials thrust themselves like a rough wedge into traditional dogma, Catholics, rightly anxious to protect the truths that were in peril, affirmed vigorously against the Calvinists and Zwinglians, the reality of Christ's presence in the Eucharist. They were right. But by dint of repeating that Christ was present, by dint, above all, of hearing it repeated, people ended by imagining that this presence was the ultimate end of the Sacrament; they thought that Christ was present for the mere sake of being present, and the second chapter of the Eucharistic doctrine faded as a star in the sunlight, in the augmented brightness of the first chapter.

From that time on Communion became more and more a kind of royal visit: Christ granting His presence to the faithful. But as a visit renewed daily would lose its distinction and even its value, so it was judged that Communions should be distanced from one another, and of rare occurrence, that their brightness might not be tarnished by placing them among ordinary everyday things. And as a princely visit demands laborious preparations the great anxiety became to know, above all, if the faithful were really worthy to receive the Eternal King. Questions of deportment, of etiquette, of cleanliness, of propriety, took the first places. The dwelling should be completely cleaned, adorned and perfumed, before the Divine Majesty could descend into it. And whole categories of Christians, considered too earthly to appear before the Prince of the Ages, were excluded from the benefit of frequent Communion. In a word, as a visit is above all a favour, and gives a good chance of obtaining others, it was said, that in accordance with the formularies of the courts of olden days, these decisive moments should be made use of to present—after the address—the sheet of requests, so that when the visit was over we should keep in our minds a grateful remembrance of it.

But the Eucharist is first of all the Sacrament of the work of Christ. He remains present there that He may work. The sacraments effect invisibly that which they visibly signify. The Eucharist is not a symbol of presence, as a flower might be, or a relic, or a precious pearl or a picture; it is a symbol of food, of spiritual food. *Panis vivus.* (*John* vi. 51.) Food must be received in order to be changed into the one who takes it, but here the food is divine and it changes into its substance the faithful who communicate.

Thus Communion can be frequent without any difficulty. Can food lose its value as long as it answers a need, and should we render our repasts more rare in order to prevent them from becoming commonplace events? Since the Eucharist is food, the first consideration of the Communicant should be, not to know how he stands as to worthiness, but how he stands as to need. Food is not, first of all, a reward, it is a remedy to that all-pervading death which consumes the organism; it is the reserve force, the rescue party, the ally from outside, that we call upon because without it we perish. The soul in the state of Grace can then communicate. Mortal sin deprives it of this right, for food is not given to the dead.

Finally, since Communion is not a spectacular visit, but the entrance into us of Christ working, the right way to communicate is to receive Christ not in order to present Him with a number of requests, but to offer Him, as it were, a vast timber-yard. He comes with His tools. *Faber et fabri filius.* (*Mark* vi. 3; *Matt.* xiii. 55.) A carpenter and the son of a carpenter. The compliments may be short, but the submissiveness must be absolute, and the prayer of the Communicant is just that supplication of Saint Thomas of Aquin: *Præsta meæ menti de Te vivere.* (*Adoro Te.*)

Christ comes into us to transform us from within. He is the Truth. Instead of losing ourselves in formulas of feelings that are to little purpose, let us love the Truth and accept that it should fashion us to its own likeness. Nothing is more terrible than Truth entering into a life. To receive it without resistance there is need of a lion's courage, for it dispossesses us at one blow, by one over-ruling act, and forces us to serve God.

Christ comes into us to transform us completely. He is love. And nothing is more inexorable than a true love, a real love, which we cannot throw off the scent nor put to sleep, and which clings to man as to its prey. *Attraxi te.* (*Jeremias* xxxi. 3.) Allow Love to enter, this ruling, jealous Love, strong as death, and see how He works the indomitable Workman! See what He will leave standing of our mediocrities and our selfishness, and what He thinks of our flagging laziness.

Christ comes into us to transform us completely. He is "the one who is to come" *qui venturus est.* (*Apoc.* i. 4.) Nothing is more compelling than a future, nothing is more exacting than that "which, must fall due". He will come and *omnes sancti cum eo* (*Zach.* xiv. 5), and He asks us to live in expectation, never fixing ourselves in the ephemeral as though it were something final, but desiring "always something beyond".

It would be easier to receive Christ as a guest, and to leave Him no other work than that of signing our requests. Majestic discourses and hyperbolical figures of speech are of infinitely less worth than the simple docility of the dying, who receiving Communion when their minds can no longer control their thoughts very closely, abandon themselves without resistance to the Workman of the last hour. *Domine, quid me vis facere?* (*Acts* ix. 6.) To work with Christ ever more and more fully is always possible, and it is the most desirable fruit which each Communion will ripen.

The Eucharist is food. To train souls for this Sacrament does not then mean that we should prepare little satin-lined oratories in the conscience, but that we should develop in these souls a hunger and thirst after justice, that we should give them a craving for divine things . . . *in invisibilium amorem rapiamur.* (*Preface for Christmas.*) A slow work as are all works of education. Time is not shoved on with the shoulder, and we should not go before the Holy Ghost. But we can ourselves hollow out in our souls that salutary void, which the plenitude of Christ will fill to the brim. *Tibi se cor meum totum subjicit.* (*Adore Te.*)

XXXII

THERE is no need to cease to be ourselves in order to begin to be pleasing to God. Man is an animal, endowed with reason. We know that since we learnt our first catechism. Why is it that the most immediate consequences of this simple truth so often appear to us to be very shocking? If we really understood what we are, we would never again say or think ill of the devotions of Christians. They are suitable to our nature. Man is an animal. The thing is true even if the expression of it is somewhat crude in its simplicity. And God has wished to be adored and loved by animals endowed with reason. There is the fact, in face of which our fastidiousness has no right to revolt. Men then, that is animals endowed with reason, will serve God in a way that is conformed to their nature. They will utter cries, in rhythm or not; they will weep; they will stretch forth their arms in silence; they will move about, run to the right or to the left, go backwards and forwards on the ground; they will gesticulate, and it will all be right, since they are acting according to their kind.

In honour of their God they will mix mortar, they will mould clay, they will make houses of baked earth; these will be the Churches. In olden days they raised a Shepherd's tent for Jehovah in the desert without water: *ambulabam in tabernaculo et tentorio.* (2 *Kings* vii. 6.)

Then they will make a noise, to show that they are in joy or sorrow; they will play music; they will engrave outlines on stone; they will light fire at the ends of sticks of wax; they will make resin give forth smoke from the bottom of a metal pot.

And with these movements, these songs, these rhythms, this smoke and these flames, they will compose the liturgy of men, that is the worship of animals endowed with reason, serving the Master of all things.

Where are those fools or pagans who will find in all this anything to be shocked at, or to laugh at! Have we not the right to be men when we *are* men? and being men have we not the right to act according to the nature of man? Whence then this disdain and scandal when a Christian people sets out on pilgrimage, when they sing or sigh, and when they enclose the Eucharist as a treasure in the Tabernacle?

My God, I love to find in Your Church this great respect for all that is corporal. The body is a holy thing since You have divinized

the nature of these rational animals, which we are, and since the
Word has taken Flesh and has come to dwell under our tents. How
I thank You for not having despised the body which labours and
suffers, and which is the instrument of thought and of virtue!
Without a brain, there would be no baptized soul, and without a
heart, within which Your love brings a quicker beat, who among
animals could fight in Your service? I love the iron-clad arms of
Your warriors of old, delivering the Holy Sepulchre at the cost of
great suffering to their bruised bodies. I love the hands of Your
Apostles, which raised up the wounded and poured water from
brimming shells on the heads of the infidels. I love and respect the
bodies of Your martyrs. The flames which burnt Saint Lawrence or
Saint Polycarp, the wild bull that tore Saint Perpetua, the sword
that gashed the neck of Saint Agnes would have all been powerless
against pure spirits; but the bodies of Your saints have suffered, and
You have been busy about them, just as long ago You went Yourself
to bury the body of Your prophet Moses in the Vale of Phogor.
Corpora sanctorum in pace sepulta sunt. (*Ecclesiasticus* xliv. 14.)

Was it not the mouth of Chrysostom which did homage to You;
and was it not the harsh voice of the Precursor which prepared
Your way? We admire the living breastwork of our soldiers serving
as a rampart to their threatened country; but have You not deified
our misery in a marvellous way since You have taken our whole
body into Your service?

Alas! Your wisdom is often misjudged, and man reels from one
delirium to another, from haughty contempt to coarse covetousness,
without being able to bring himself to rest in equilibrium. To love
the body means too often for him, unrestrained enjoyment, it means
to look upon the body as a last end, and to awaken in it a host of
destructive desires. But such love is contempt writ large. Love is
made up of esteem and of modest reserve; it fears to profane that
which it touches, as we fear to tarnish the limpidity of a crystal by
the marks of our fingers on it.

To love the body is to reverence it for all that it suffers and for all
that it prepares for us; for it is the labourer in every job and struggles
unceasingly under a stern command. To love it is to recognize that
it has been crippled since the first sin of the race, and that, in spite
of its wounds, it yet has the mission to reconquer painfully all that
it has lost, until it shall be re-clothed in glory and withdrawn from
all its enemies—*neque clamor, neqe dolor erit ultra.* (*Apoc.* xxi. 4.)

The liturgy of men, and their dumb prayer, *obsequium servitutis*,
the homage of service! Lord, we have not yet left Egypt and we
bear the yoke of slaves. We serve You, but we are still enslaved, and
we know not the liberty of pure spirits.

Therefore have pity on our weakness and on our little ways; on our paintings and our pictures, our stained windows and our clumsy buildings! Do not despise the hut where the missioner establishes his alter on two empty boxes; disdain not the hymn with which unskilful voices make the village Church resound after Benediction in the month of May; look with kindness on the battered censer which the little server swings at arm's length; and when your priest at the Altar intones an *Oremus*, think, O Lord, that it is Your people who pray, this people whom death holds fast and ravages, this people riveted to the body and to matter, this people, yes, this race of animals ever groping and uncertain, so often deceived by their dim conjectures, so often crushed under the blows of sorrow, and scarcely ever fully awakened from their long-drawn nightmares.

Populus Tuus (*Exodus* xxxiii. 16): they are Yours. They are a flock. You know it, You Yourself said it. It was to sheep that You spontaneously likened the multitude. They will serve You as they can, being quite sure, that if scornful people, ashamed of being men, judge them to be coarse and materialistic in their adoration, You who made them will never have anything but tenderness for all those bodies which have been redeemed by Your own.

XXXIII

Pretiosa Margarita
A rare pearl
(*Matt. xiii.* 46.)

THE holiness which only ripens on the wood of extraordinary occasions cannot be the daily bread of anyone. To seek the food of a people in what is rare, unheard of, unexpected, is to condemn them to die of starvation. And yet a Christian people should be fed on that exquisite and finished virtue which is called holiness. And the Kingdom of heaven is likened to a precious pearl which is found as a treasure.

Inventa margarita (*Matt.* xiii. 46), treasure, yes, but a treasure already discovered, and which is no longer to be sought for in the night. Sanctity does not lie in the extraordinary which is always a near neighbour to the extravagant and to the grotesque. The Friend of God is not only the leading actor. There are other friends in the roles, substitutes and even supernumeraries, all equally essential, and without whom the hero of the drama would not be able to deliver his speeches. To do very well, it is not in the least necessary to quit the ranks, nor to stand forward out of line. "Do not hide me, I wish to appear," said the Conqueror of Marignano in the heat of the battle. If everyone were extraordinary and if no one would accept to be eclipsed by another, the whole world would be levelled down to the ordinary and no one would be conspicuous. These truths are very old, but our foolish prejudices persist in turning their backs on them, and our pride has sworn to overlook them. We are immediately captivated, in the lives of Saints, by that which they themselves, or their biographers, show us of the marvellous. Their exploits fascinate us, not because they were just what truth required at the moment but because they are beyond the ordinary and attract the eye.

Even when we place our holiness in ordinary things, we again wish to do them "extraordinarily" well. "*Communia non communiter,*" said Saint John Berchmans. He was right, but there is a way of taking this splendid principle of supernatural motive, which quickly turns it into an error. We fancy we must give the same care to details as to essentials, that we must deposit a uniform layer of attention on little things and on great, and that to distinguish between the relative importance of objects is to cease to look on them in the right way. The soul then drowns itself in trifles. It maintains a uniform pace at all times, believing that peace and moderation consist in never changing anything. The soul becomes rigid and mechanical. Under the plea of doing everything with extraordinary care, it falls into an incurable error: that of accepting as of equal worth things which are not so, and for want of drawing a distinction between things all are confused.

Holiness does not lie in exaggeration, not even in pious exaggeration, but is is found in a very pliant adaptability to all duties. It does not treat all that presents itself in the same way. It attributes to details all the value of details and no more. It assigns to the essential all the value of an absolute, and nothing less. In its theoretical appreciations sanctity observes all faint gradations, and in the practical carrying out of the theories it observes all modes of the real. Playful or serious, sounding the fords or leaping over the obstacles, examining summarily or studying profoundly, sanctity adapts itself, that is to say it obeys and advances, not according to some personal rule, arbitrarily imposed on things, but by an intelligent and unreserved submission to the law which God Himself has given to them.

To be adaptable is to be detached, it is also to live, for life is only a continual adaptation . . . adaptation to the imperious but repelling duty; to refreshing recreation and to the marvels of art; to war, without, however, dreaming only of battles and being unable to understand anything else; adaptation to peace without being terrified and melting away when on a sudden the hour for combat sounds. To be adaptable is to carry our resources with us, by keeping ourselves always very near to God, who distributes these resources to us each day; to be adaptable is to do our own work without murmuring, but filled with a great, heartfelt and valiant submissiveness.

He who submits to being adaptable, submits to being dependent, and that is what we do not like. We arrange our lives for ourselves beforehand; there is a plan, a hermitage of our own, and we legislate as if we were the masters of our destiny, and the rulers of events. Our model is not Christ who subjected Himself to all, and who knew obedience by the things He suffered—*didicit, ex eis quæ passus est, obædientiam (Heb.* v. 8.)—but, unconsciously, our model is the one that formerly floated before the imaginations of the Greek Stoics, —Hercules of the mighty deeds and fabulous exploits—Hercules, a baptized Hercules no doubt, who walks through the world with his club in his hand making laws, and harsh towards everything.

My God, if I were adaptable to my duty and to Your will, I should never complain and You would have in me a docile instrument for all Your desires. If I were adaptable I should make use of all things and be a slave to none, I should keep a freshness of soul, a serene keen-sightedness, a living interest in Your work, all that, in fine, which anxiety about my own excellence dries up or destroys without any gain.

If I could but find my sanctity, O my God, there where You Yourself have placed it for me—in living without murmuring in this room, winter and summer, in doing my work, in smiling on those who are troublesome, in keeping my heart free from bitterness, and my soul free from anger, in sacrificing myself to the service of all, and in letting go that anxiety to judge myself and to weigh myself in accurate balances, as if the least of my little discomforts could disturb the equilibrium of the stars!

After all, it is never the work itself which is paltry or prosaic. It comes from You, it is divine, it is itself the rare, the unique pearl, *pretiosa margarita*, which is like to the Kingdom of Heaven. There *is* one thing which nothing and no one can replace, and that is myself, no matter how insignificant people may think me to be; there is one unique deed which no one can perform except myself, and that is the deed which I actually accomplish at this moment, praying to You in secret. To be rare, then, I need not copy any one whomsoever; it is enough that I do not cease to be myself, that I do not destroy myself in wild dreams, but that, wholly adaptable in the hands of Providence, without reserve, and without resistance, I am fully just what You wish that I should be.

SECOND
SERIES

FAC ME AUDIRE
VOCEM TUAM

PROLOGUE
TO THE SECOND SERIES

Quia sciunt vocem ejus
For His voice is known to them
(John x. 4.)

THE old antiphonal of Bangor contains some simple verse, dating from the seventh century, commemorating the ancient abbots of the convent. The first of these Irishmen was Comgall, of whom we know practically nothing but his name and this ingenuous and very complete couplet:

Amavit Deus Comgilum
Bene! et ipse Dominum.

The Lord God loved Comgall well, and Comgall well returned this love to Him.

We should be able to inscribe these two lines on every Christian life. Or rather, we may say, the first is already cut in the stone of each of our lives, it is the second that must be engraved unhesitatingly and without equivocation.

Since the moment of our Baptism, Christ has discharged His Office of Saviour, and He has accomplished to excess, His part in the work of our redemption.—*Amavit.*

It remains to frame our answer and to render to God through love all that we have received as a free gift, and first of all that love itself.

In the first volume of this "Prayer for All Times," while respecting the inevitable twists and turns of daily realities, an attempt was made to show how, at every moment, and in every situation, the road which leads to God is open to us.

Our call never fails to reach the Lord of all flesh, and is always welcomed; it wins home unceasingly, from the moment that, inspired by Him, it is in conformity to His desire. On our road to Him there can never be any other obstacle than that of our own perversity; no other screen is interposed than that of our culpable and selfish deceit.

Perhaps if the thirty-three meditations in that volume were gathered up under a single title, it would not have been inexact to say that, placing us in the presence of God, they had tried to show how we could attain to Him.—*Domine exaudi orationem meam.* . . .

How to reach God! The lesson is onesided, if it be not also shown, how He comes to take us, for we can only reach Him by His grace, and His grace is His own sovereign initiative, surpassing all our rights and preceding all our desires. We cannot attain to Him, unless, taking us in our misery, He cures us, in uniting us to Himself. And no one merits to possess God, but God Himself and those whom He desires, through His gratuitous adoption, to associate to His own nature. On the supposition that God and I are apart, I do not merit in proportion to the way in which I cast into the intervening space, many arduous and solid good works, to fill up the ditch and to lessen the abyss, but I merit only in the measure in which, through the ineffable mercy of the Supreme God, I become one with Him. My works are of value only if they have this union as their source and fountain-head.

How He comes to take us, by what roads He descends towards our weakness and our heedlessness, and what stupid obstacles our folly and our blindness throw across His peaceful paths—*semitæ pacificæ* (*Prov*. iii. 17)—all this is more specially the subject-matter of these thirty-three new meditations.

They do not aim at being rare, nor elegant, nor sublime. They only desire to express some of those divine claims, which are so often misrepresented through our prejudices and our ignorance, just as the thoughts of the Masters of antiquity suffer, in their passage through the minds of mediocre scholars.

We cannot then make a distinction between the way in which God comes to take us and that by which we succeed in reaching Him, as we distinguish between two different things. There are not two Jacob's ladders, but only one, which goes from heaven to earth and from earth to heaven. But we can distinguish, as it were, two movements, and two directions, and so speak of Grace that comes to meet us, or of the co-operation it calls for.

One word more to the unknown reader, to hinder any misunderstanding.

This little book is not designed to replace any existing works, it does not lessen the usefulness of collections of meditations for every day, from which, for many centuries, souls, with a true interior life, have drawn their waters each morning and each evening. It is to make this clear that these meditations have been called—"Prayer for All Times," and not for every day. Let no one be deceived by the word meditation. He indeed would have a soul more empty than a hollow nut, who would never meditate except at fixed hours and who would not strive to mingle holy thought with common work, as thought is mingled with words.

To prepare, as we should the only answer to the forestalling love of our Redeemer, the one method is to co-operate fully with this very love. But it would be a mistake to imagine that this collaboration consists merely in some exaltation of the feelings, or in a vague and mystic fervour, and that there is no need to plan it out with clear deliberation, nor that it runs no risks within us from our errors. It would be unheard of, if anyone in their devotion could be allowed to act as if the theology of Grace did not necessarily regulate all our collaboration with God, and it is impossible not to make mistakes in practice when we have gone wrong in theory. That occurs even in the exercise or ordinary relations, there where the control of experience rectifies so many principles which are in themselves erroneous: and it happens inevitably in our relations with God, as soon as true doctrine is excluded from them. That is why theology has been introduced even into the "Prayer for All Times".

XXXIV

Fracto alabastro

Having broken the vase

(Mark xiv. 3.)

I WISH that You would instruct me this evening, O My God, in the art of giving in the most perfect way. For throughout my whole life I have to give You what I am, to hand over to You my liberty, my time and my actions. And if I do not possess this art of giving perfectly, I run the risk of dying without having accomplished the whole of my act of love.

He who gives eight when he could give ten, has not yet surrendered the half to his God. He who gives grumblingly, with a sullen countenance and with a grudging heart, that which he could hand over by some generous deed, and part with by one act, is still far from perfection; he does not know how to enrich himself, nor how to despoil himself. In spite of his white hairs, he is a child, without its innocence.

Since repentant sinners will take precedence of us in heaven, it is but right that we should draw salutary lessons from their sorrow. The art of giving in the most perfect manner is taught to our pride of an old Scribe, by a public sinner. A despised creature will show us, by one single act, what it is we should do.

She came into the hall where the feast was being held, braving the stern looks or the mocking glances of those who, seeing her, would have wished to drive her out. She came in, in spite of shame, and there were tears in her eyes. She had recognized the Good Shepherd; she remembered that she was His poor sheep. That was all, but it was enough. She would offer more than her tears; she has taken, in both hands, the fragile vase of alabaster with its slender neck, full to the brim with a priceless perfume. She will, of course, pour it out drop by drop, and then again close up the delicately sculptured neck with a ball of wax! But no!—*fracto alabastro*—there is a sharp noise as of something broken; she has shattered her vase and in a moment all the perfume has been poured forth on the feet of the One Master. This is the action, the only action worthy of those who have made their own this science of the perfect gift.

Fracto alabastro.—When we consecrate ourselves by irrevocable vows, and thus deprive ourselves of the possibility of repossessing that which we have given, we are not yielding up, drop by drop, our moments of liberty, we are not giving our life to God little by little, but we are doing an irreparable deed. We have shattered something, and the *Voveo* of the formula, with the *perpetuam*, burst with a loud and sudden noise like the alabaster vase in the hands of Magdalen.

Alas! the greater number have no understanding of those absolute donations: they cannot see why we should give more than we must, nor why we give all at once, nor why we make it impossible to recover that which we have given and to refill the vase of our lives with some fresh aromatic and fragrant perfume. The immolation of the priesthood and of religious life appear to them to be an absurd prodigality, an unreasonable waste. *Et fremebant in eam (Mark* xiv. 5.)

Our false wiseacres have never had any difficulty in discovering bad arguments seemingly most prudent. They will tell you that God does not ask for so much, that by keeping the commandments we can attain with surety to salvation, that it is better to foresee the future, to keep the doors of escape wide open, and that it is a great exaggeration to push things so far. They have got hold of the idea that virtue is to be found in the absence of all excess, and so generosity, which surpasses the limits of our strict obligations, seems to them to be one of these regrettable excesses. Only think of it! this public sinner has just thrown the value of a whole year's work over the feet of the Master! More than three hundred pence has evaporated in perfume! Isn't it madness, and did the Master want this extravagance?

Bonum opus operata est (Mark xiv. 6). The action of the repentant sinner is approved of by this undying word, and this woman is given as an example to all the disciples. We are not to preserve our offerings parsimoniously or cunningly, nor to give to God, as we beg of Him to do to us, the daily bread of a beggar. The harvest and the store-house belong to Him, the oven and the flour and the one who kneads it. But ever grasping, we refuse to give up the resources of to-morrow with the wealth of to-day, and all forms of total donation appal us.

And yet, my God, I must understand and practise this complete donation. Slay within me the spirit of proprietorship, and all the errors that make me believe that I am what I possess, and that I lose that which I abandon to You.

Fracto alabastro.—The perfume which has been poured forth is not wasted, but used; it is not even confiscated by God, for God confiscates nothing; it is still mine if I consent to remain near the Master and not to leave His house.—*Impleta est domus tota ex odore unguenti (John* xii. 3),—for all the house was filled with the penetrating aroma, and I can re-find my gifts in Him to whom I have offered them all.

When we have made a vow to obey, do we not in reality, at each moment, accomplish our whole will in submitting it? It desires to be submitted; a voluntary captivity, a dependence which is loved and chosen cannot be a burdensome constraint. Is it not rather the highest liberty?

When we have decided to make the following of the counsels a law to ourselves, when we have irrevocably vowed ourselves to sacrifice, are we thereby left destitute and impoverished. Do we henceforth wander, haggard and mournful, among the people who are in enjoyment of their possessions? Every-day experience shows that it is to those who have nothing that the rich go to seek all that is wanting to them, and that joy is always living in hearts which have emptied themselves of disquietude, and seek the eternal everywhere.

Arm me, O Lord, with holy courage against all my hesitations and my pusillanimity, with that holy courage of which You gave the grace to the sinner in the Gospel. Do not allow my too eager desires to kill me, do not let me drag along with me, down here below, a divided soul, one that fears to belong to You without reserve. May the horror of all that is miserly purify me, and may I no longer be able to endure to carry, at the end of my arm, a hand which shuts tightly when there is question of giving, and opens out to the full when the moment comes to receive. And if in Your presence, I offer my life by a donation which I wish to be irrevocable, if I do more than my simple duty, if I go beyond the precepts, then in order to reassure myself as to the value of my action, and to be unconcerned at human blame, it will be enough for me to know that You praised the poor woman, who, by one single act, shattered her vase of perfume—*fracto alabastro.*

XXXV

THE very demons bore testimony to You! I do not see why, then O Lord, the pagans may not instruct me. Why should they be incapable of changing my pride of satisfied pharisee, and of enlightening me as to the nothingness of my works—*quia nihil est quod hactenus feci.* (*Imit.* i. 18.)

I am very much inclined to turn all comparisons to my advantage, and when I think of the pagans, I enumerate with haughty gratitude all that I have—through You—and that they appear not to possess. I imagine that they can and ought to serve as a set-off to my virtue, and I look on them from a height, as the civilized conqueror looks down upon the savages among whom he colonizes. I easily persuade myself that Your judgments, O my God, are to be measured by my miserable appreciations, and that You keep all Your Graces and all Your glory for those who serve You publicly, and bear Your Name in the world.

And yet, see how You set the pagans before us as examples, letting us understand how very little we are raised above them by our merits. Weighed in Your balance, it is not pretensions, but actions which count, and it is not in proportion to our personal conceit, that we have a right to Your attention. Among all tribes and in all races, Your Spirit, that makes holy, has chosen His own. The pagan rind covers, often perhaps, the fruit of some grace of choice, and the seed of the elect falls from Your hands over all the earth.

And so now I begin to think about them, about those who are my brethren by race, those of whom the Blessed Virgin is also the merciful Mother, those who struggle on by difficult paths and in nights filled with the fierce cries of wild beasts, those who stumble as they go, and grope their way, and whom I have despised in the foolish pride of youth.

I do not dare to say that they are better than I am, all those pagans; that would be to wrong my Baptism and to wrong the anxious love of my watchful Redeemer. But still less do I dare to say that I am better than they are, fearing lest Your thunders would fall and crush my lie, and remembering that You abandon those who raise themselves on high.

I shall then accept Your lesson without gloss or commentary, as our eyes receive the light and the desert accepts the rain.

Quid amplius? (*Matt.* v. 47.)—What *do you* more than these pagans?

Where is the surplus of your works? What is there in your life that
surpasses the limits of bounden duty, and goes beyond mere natural
virtue?—*Quid amplius?*—These two little words bury themselves
like spurs in the sides of all mediocrity and of all sloth; they can
pierce, so as to draw blood from the pride of the self-satisfied, and
their beneficent unreasonableness will not stop till the fullness of the
end is attained, when we shall at last have come home to You.

My patience! What a mockery! The very pagans would perhaps
have blushed for it. I am agreeable to people with whom I am in
sympathy, and I search in vain for a time in my life in which I really,
for a day, bore with my neighbour for the love of You. All my
virtue! Pitiful strategy! It consists in avoiding those who annoy me,
and because, not having seen them, I have said nothing disagreeable
to them, I consider that my conscience has nothing to reproach me
with, and that my behaviour is quite Christian—*Nonne et ethnici?*—
Seneca, Plutarch and Cicero both preached and practised these
reasonable virtues. If, Lord, You practised these reasonable virtues.
If, Lord, You seek in me what I have done more than they, I fear
You will return with empty hands—*Quid amplius?*

My piety! which is still but importunate begging, and which turns
its back on You, the moment Your Providence has filled its hands;
that prayer, which rouses itself a little only when there is a question
of soliciting privileges, or of escaping from common burdens; that
prayer recalls most vividly to my mind the self-interested petitions
of the old Romans, signing and sealing advantageous bargains with
their tutelary deities.—*Quid amplius?*—They took care of their own
affairs before dedicating themselves to You. Have I made much
advance on this artless egoism?

I am startled, at times to think that if Horace or Cæsar came back
among us, they could converse for long with me, at the same table,
without discovering that my valuation of things, and my appreciations were different to theirs, and that the wisdom of my Baptism
was wholly unlike their ambitious cunning. I would commend
success as they would, I would call that evil which resisted me, I
would laugh at simple people who sacrificed themselves without
gain, and allowed themselves to be exploited by the clever ones, and
I would myself engage in greater or lesser schemes to turn things
to my advantage, and to make good bargains, and these pagans and
I would mutually congratulate each other that we had brought our
common business to a successful issue, and triumphed by the same
means devoid of scruple, in the same cause of selfishness.—*Quid
amplius?*

But something must distinguish my behaviour and my thought,
and Your seal must remain visibly stamped on my life. I am not

aiming at anything extraordinary, and I do not wish to attract attention. But I desire to become worthy of You, and that the shame of my mediocrity should no longer be a burden on Your work. Help me to die to all that is not loyal and frank, to all that commercial vulgarity which I drag along with me in the clay of my earthly nature, and may faith and love at last pierce through my opaque envelope, so that seeing me, people may think of You, the Light.

I shall, at least, keep as a relic, a great esteem for all those who have loyally longed for You; and I shall no longer say, in my blind pride, that I am of greater worth than the ignorant, more deserving of reward than the savage, and that Your gifts give me the right to despise the pagans. Far from it, they but impose upon me the duty of spending myself in their service and that without bargaining.

XXXVI

Silentium . . . loquetur

My silence will speak to you

(*Imit. iii.* 21.

YOUR first word was spoken so deep within me, that my consciousness did not catch the murmur; it was Your forestalling Grace preparing my will even before it awoke to desire; it was Your love bending over me from the day of my baptism, watching for the moment when my eyes of a child should open. No, it is not I who have set out to meet You, it is not I who have cried out in the desert without water to a God unheeding and far off; it is not my word nor my call that have begun the work of grace within me, it is You who, in the silence, have deigned, in Your spontaneous mercy, to busy Yourself about me. *Ut diligeremus dilecti sumus* (St. Augustine on 1 John 4)—the love of God for us is the origin and the principle of the love which we have for Him.

Out of respect for this mysterious action of God, for this divine silence in which the roots of all my merits are steeped, I think I may be allowed, and that it will be of use to me, to answer silently and to offer You my dumb homage.

Silence is always more eloquent than speech, because it is far deeper and more complete. I shall keep silence before You, and my soul shall become like the calm, unclouded night, which is only inactive in appearance, and in which everything works to repair that which the dawn will enlighten.

My silence has waited long for You, and even now, in the depths of my soul, no word has ever been uttered, a wholly silent place exists, kept for the Amen of Life Eternal. I have waited long for You, knowing by faith that You were quite near to me, but respecting the tarrying of Your epiphanies, and the times which You have chosen in which to reveal Yourself to souls. My silence is perhaps a homage of deference, like the stillness of sentries at the gates of our palaces, and when I do nothing else but keep this interior quiet for You, this silence fills my prayer, as it fills the immensity of the heavens in the apocalypse.

It is no little matter to make silence rule within me, and I am astonished at those who, in all simplicity, take this interior silence as a starting point, and not as a goal to be attained with much labour. Silence in the pack when they have found the scent? silence among the swallows gathered under the cornices in the cool September mornings! silence in my passionate longings and in my frivolities, in my desires and in my feverish excitement, in my incoherences and in my obstinacy! the silence that follows when the hammer falls back upon the anvil, and when the file bites into the steel, when hard words and bitter deceptions cut into me, when the rude shock of a trial unarms me; it will not always be the placid and sweet silence of the sleeping child, it will at times, perhaps, be the heroic, poignant silence of the patient who is being operated upon without chloroform and of whom they cut the bone to the quick.

I believe, O my God, that it is this silence that gives most glory to You, as in a Church when at the moment of the consecration all keeps still beneath the vaulted roof. I have seen silent tears of which You have surely made eternal pearls: tears of resignation, without bitterness and without hatred, and which were good because they were so true. I have seen silences that were solemn acceptations, far more sincere than all eloquent formularies, silences in which souls wrapped themselves as in their last winding-sheet.

When You appear, what shall I be able to say to You? When You come to seek me on the last day of my life, shall I receive you with discourses?

The great silence of acceptation or of rapture will be my only answer, and I wish to prepare it to-day by saying nothing.

I was not baptized in my name, but in Yours, I am not asked to speak but to be; not to make phrases about virtue, but to let it grow within me, as roses coming to maturity, which open without noise in their flower-cups, now grown too narrow for them. All my actions should plunge their roots into interior silence, and a deepmost corner of my soul ought to be for ever free from all tumult and from all confusion.

To do better, to second Your supernatural operation with more docility, I must stifle my clamour. I offer You the humble fruit of my silence. And in this silence there is a victory over all my interior want of unity, over all that hungering multiplicity that thrusts me forth with so much noise outside the realm of peace. And in this silence there is an avowal, the avowal that outside of You there is no active peace, and that when Your fullness overflows my misery, I have only to allow myself to be thus invaded in order to escape from death. In this silence there is a great desire, quiet and tenacious, the desire to be fixed at length in the final and the eternal, and to bring forth calm truth from out the confused chaos of my many follies. My silence is Your victory.

Accept the oblation of it, Lord, and if the non-Christian is astonished and laughs at this microscopic offering, grant that this amazement may not shake my faith, and do not let me doubt Your love of silence.

I shall carry this silence into all my actions, but not as did the pagans of olden days in order merely to control myself, so that not a fold of my toga should be disarranged. I do not keep silence to think of myself, nor in order to contemplate the ideal splendour of an abstract law, nor in secret admiration of the qualities of the wise man, always master of himself and governing his action by the laws of reason. All this philosophy is too poor for your disciples, and when they keep silence it is to listen to You, to leave room for You, not to hinder Your action, and to allow you to model them according to Your divine idea. This silence is not a closed door, but an open way, and the sole means that we poor cripples have of working with You, the one Physician of our souls.

If my words never issue forth except from seeds of silence, if they are only the expression of Your thought in me and on all things, I may perhaps hope that in the day of retribution, You will not find many that were useless.

XXXVII

Jugum meum suave
My yoke is sweet
(*Matt. xi.* 30.)

IT seems to me, O Lord, that the day when You uttered this word many of those who heard You must have thought it a very rash, not to say preposterous statement. Your yoke easy to bear! With all the Commandments and all the duties of our state, and all its varying and encroaching obligations? Your yoke easy to carry! With forgiveness of injuries, and the campaign against selfishness, in spite of our natural indolence and the great anxiety with which we are obsessed of avoiding all wearisome effort?

I look round about me. It appears to me that all things unite to give the lie to Your tranquil affirmation. Those Christians who bear but the half or the third part of Your burden are very numerous, and with that alone they are already overwhelmed. Some have observed two or three Commandments out of ten; others give a few hours each year to You, the hours of Religious Services, if they have leisure to be present at them. . . . And Your yoke is easy!

But listen, Lord, to all that they are saying, or rather listen to what I myself have said so often: If You asked for less, You would perhaps obtain something; we are like ratepayers taxed beyond their resources, and Your exaggerated precepts kill our good will. "You desire too pure, the elect of Your choice."

So when I meet with this peremptory statement in the Gospels: My yoke is sweet to bear, I do not venture to allow my thoughts to dwell upon it, I fear to see them plunge immediately into objections. I pass on in haste, pretending not to have heard!

Can You have been mistaken, You the Infinite Wisdom? Or, perhaps, to entice timid souls, have You overrated, as merchants do, the merits of Your doctrine, and boasted to excess of the profit to be gained from being faithful to You. I wait for You to enlighten the night of my suspense, and to explain in silence, Your eternal words.

Your Law is a yoke. The rabbis had said that before You, speaking of the Tables of Sinai. Your Law is a yoke and You enjoin upon us to take it up courageously and to lay it upon our shoulders. . . . *tollite jugum meums super vos* (*Matt.* xi. 29).

There are two ways of carrying a yoke; one which appears quite reasonable and is wholly ridiculous, and one which appears very ridiculous and is completely reasonable.

I go to fetch water and I bring it back in two pails suspended at the extremities of a wooden yoke. Why should I place this yoke upon my two shoulders and thus imprison all my liberty of movement? Would it not be more reasonable to place it on one shoulder keeping the other for my own ends; I should then be only partially encumbered; I should carry but half the burden? Error! You would carry a double burden, that is to say you would feel yourself twice as powerless to raise the weight. Your wisdom has gone astray, and wishing to gain the upper hand over the divine Command, your arguments have turned into foolishness.

Other people, naïve and ingenuous souls, those that are simple and upright, accepting the Divine Command have placed the yoke of the Lord on their two shoulders, with their head well in the midst ready to accept the whole load and renouncing all personal independence. These may appear to carry a double burden, but watch them walk one would think that they were carrying but half the weight, for these burdens balance each other and the one on the right seems to lighten the one on the left.

When we carry the entire Law of God and when we even add the Counsels to the Commandments, the whole becomes lighter, just as the best way to give ourselves courage is to build up courage in others, and the most efficacious way of alleviating our own sufferings is to lessen those of others.

However, we wish to bargain! We say: I shall keep up the appearances of virtue; I shall preserve its propriety and decorum, but I cannot, in addition to that, watch over my interior, and regulate my secret desires. An impossible task! You are carrying the yoke on one shoulder only, and you will not carry it far; the proprieties are hard to observe when interior disorder renders these appearances a perpetual hypocrisy. If you watch over your thoughts, if your carriage and deportment is what it should be in your innermost soul, you will not have to preoccupy yourself with the exterior as an extra, any more than a happy man has to trouble himself to feign joyousness, or laboriously to set going those muscles which produce a smile.

We say: I shall not commit grievous faults, but I cannot bind myself to avoid slighter ones or to refuse trifling concessions; I cannot give up sentimental dreams, I love too much that which God forbids not to stay always quite near to it. An impossible undertaking! To preserve a half-chastity and to pass through the flame without being burnt, and without carrying away the smell of a thing which has been singed! But ask those unfeignedly honest people, who have given all their lives over to God by an irrevocable action, ask them if this sacrifice has been as an abyss of pain to them, and they will answer with a conviction devoid of all pretence, that they are unconscious of having even made a sacrifice, and that nothing is easier than not to count and haggle. He who has but two words in his vocabulary: *nothing* and *all*, is never puzzled to find a quotient, and he does not lose his time over multiplicands. Ask him what he gives: All. Ask him what he keeps: Nothing. With these two words we enter straight into the light of eternity, and the yoke of the Lord has not wounded the shoulders of His faithful ones, as formerly in the legend and as to-day in the world do the ridiculous amphora of the Danaides, human desire, that is to say, which is never quieted. Burdens added to burdens render bodies heavier but make souls lighter; as wings which weigh upon the bird, but upon which it can lay its own weight to rise up in the air. *Onus cuncta exonerans*. (St. Augustine.)—A weight which delivers from all others.

XXXVIII

Mirabilius reformasti
You have renewed it still more marvellously
(*Liturgy: The Mass.*)

MAN cannot resign himself peaceably to be no longer that which he should be. There is in him, by nature, a will which, spurred on here below by Grace, hinders him from finding complete rest at a lower level. Something cries out within him louder than all conventional discourses, louder than all fallacious rhetoric, something cries, as with the woman in labour, until the elect, willed by God has achieved its development. And since man cannot cease to desire to be that which he ought to be, it is impossible for him to become reconciled to the idea that he is a failure, and that in him the divine will can no longer realize the plan of love. Irremediable decadence is damnation. Here below man cannot believe that he is fallen irretrievably, nor can he believe that it is impossible for God to deliver him from all his many ills, even that of death itself. *Deus qui soli competit medicinam præstare post mortem* (*Liturgy: Prayer for the dead*).

He is right. The disastrous illusion of the irreparable, that sorrowful illusion which eats like a cancer, *ut cancer serpit* (2 Tim. ii. 17) into our whole-hearted repentance, must be taken from us, must be extirpated from our souls, out of respect for the merciful power of Our Redeemer.

We say I have spoilt my life. My infidelity has corrupted all my ways, I have gone astray among the Madianites. I long to return, to re-find myself, to be once more that fresh and limpid soul, that soul so many clouds of dust have stained and tarnished. I seek the road of return, and the house of My Father; I ask once again for work and for a tool, for an order and for my pardon. I know that He will forgive me; I almost fear lest He may forgive too quickly: thus showing me that I am of but little importance to Him, and that He has not paid much heed to my treachery. I know that He will cancel my weighted past, but can He remake my future for me? Am I not condemned, as those mutilated in the war, to be for ever impaired? Have I still the right to seek a place among the chosen ones? I who did not wait, in the night, for the crowing of the cock or the voice of the servants to deny Him without remorse? He owes nothing to me; I have no longer any claims; and in leaving me, these claims have carried off many of my hopes, and even some of my best desires. In days gone by I should have wished to offer Him ripe fruit in the freshness of its bloom; He will forgive me for having

137

allowed it all to rot, but my basket is now empty, and I behold with a sorrow that nothing can console, what I could have been and can now never be for Him; that which I could have done and which my hands now will never bring to pass. Forgiven but so lessened through my fault! I am like one of those porcelain vases knocked down by a clumsy person, which has been put together again by dint of patience. Cement, glue, varnish and clasps, all these may perhaps pass unseen from afar in the eyes of the uninitiated, and give the appearance of a piece of perfect china, but I myself know that the damage done cannot in reality be repaired, and that the integrity of my will, deflowered by my rebellion, exists no more.

Sion, noli flere.—O my people be consoled, for it is the irreparable that does not exist. It rests with you through repentance to ascend as high, higher perhaps than you would ever have ascended without the fault. God had made a plan for you, but not a blind and rigid plan, one rather that was supple as His Grace, and sinuous as your inconstancy. He still waits for you at the crossways of your road—*in medio semitarum* (*Prov.* viii. 20)—you can always mount with Him to the light of the Resurrection. You have given Him the slip! St. Paul did so too, he was at that time called Saul of Tarsus, but from his error and his fault the plan of mercy drew him forth a vessel of election, and it is through this apostle of the Gentiles that faith has come down to us. Is he really a diminished being in this plan of divine mercy?

You have sinned grievously, publicly and have become a source of scandal! The Latin Church believes that Magdalen was no less guilty, and yet for her alone—that which is done neither for Virgins nor for Popes! we recite the Creed at Mass on her Feast day, because her faith in Christ the Redeemer saved her, drawing admiration from the very heart of God. Is the plan of mercy for this repentant soul less good than that of the innocent?

Continue this litany. They are all marked with the divine seal: St. Peter, who only received the Fold after he had denied the Shepherd; Saint Augustine who tells of the Grace that came to meet him, and of the solicitude of the Shepherd for the lost sheep, and St. Francis of Assisi, and St. Ignatius of Loyola and all those who, like the prodigal, have returned, not to find themselves relegated to the rank of servants, but to receive the first robe of price—*stolam primam* (*Luke* xv. 22).

Those whom God raises up are not only cured of death but of the illness which made them die, and Lazarus coming forth from his tomb had nothing of the appearance nor of the odour of a corpse. He sat at table, he dined, and the Jews came in haste from Jerusalem to see this dead man, now restored to life, and more than to life, to health.

When God saw His first plan, that of the innocence of the world shattered through the original sin of the race; when the choice of the first free will, instead of directing itself towards Good and Order, left its orbit and turned towards decay and selfishness, was it in reality by invisible hooks and cement and uncertain methods that God, repairing His work, inaugurated His plan of Mercy? And can that word be a lie, which every Catholic priest pronounces in his morning Mass: Lord, who hadst marvellously created the world and still more marvellously restored it—*Mirabiliter condidisti . . . mirabilius reformasti?*

The illusion of the irreparable must be banished from our souls. The God Thief himself was the first to force open the gates of Paradise, and he fulfils an eternal function in the Church. The glow of repentance can be as strong as death. To know that we are among the pardoned is a conviction that is full of seeds of virtue. Those who have been preserved from falling and those who have been restored ought both equally to render thanks to God for having given them a Grace of choice.

XXXIX

MY GOD, I wish to meditate upon death in Your company, death which You have experienced for our sakes; I wish to meditate upon my death, on that death which is as a stranger to me, and which would frighten me if I did not know that it cannot interrupt our intercourse, nor change the attitude of my will, whole-heartedly turned towards You.

They have spoken at times of my last moments, in terms qualified to terrify me; they have described my end as pagans would have pictured it, insisting only on the destruction of the physical body, on the corruption of the coffin, on the solitariness of the cemetery, as if my consciousness as a dead person could ever find itself shut up in a wooden box six feet under the ground, and as if Your disciple after death should wander among the tombstones like the ghosts of stories.

Save me, O my God, from these incomplete and untrue thoughts; and do not, I beseech You, allow others to terrify me by making me doubt Your divine fidelity. For, sometimes, my last moments have been shown to me under such strange colours, that my trust in You was almost shaken and servile fears were born and multiplied within me.

I know indeed that those have everything to fear from Truth who have placed their hopes in a lie. I know that dissimulation is only for a time, and that death will roughly tear away all masks. I know that the covetous, and the lovers of that which passes will make acquaintance with the harsh abruptness of the midnight thief, snatching their imagined treasures from them. I love the lesson of death, for it is chaste and true, it puts each thing in its place and throws light on the background of our existence; I love its lesson, because it is serene and inevitable, and therefore solid and definitive; I love it for the certainty which it spreads abroad around itself, like an exact calculation, an algebraical formula, clarifying and solving problems in which the unskilful entangle themselves. Death sweeps aside all artificiality; it clears the ground of brushwood and makes us see what is.

But why should we make use of the physical fear which death inspires, to bring trouble into candid minds? Why should we, like the Turk, sow terror throughout Christendom and make the just man sorrowful, whose rest the Holy Spirit has bidden us not to trouble—*neque vastes requiem ejus* (*Prov.* xxiv. 15).

You are preparing no ambush *in extremis*, and You do not wait, as the wicked do, to warn true souls when it is too late, and when they can no longer have recourse to the Sacraments to repair the faults submerged in our weak omissions. You will not triumphantly exhibit forgotten liabilities to those who have implored You to remember no longer their former offences—*ne memineris iniquitatum nostrarum antiquarum*—(*Ps.* lxxviii. 8); to those above all who have begged You, on their knees, to make known to them their least debts, and whose will is bent on satisfying all demands *ad novissimum quadrantem* (*Matt.* v. 26); to those who have prayed to You without pretence and whose hearts, free from guile, desire to refuse You nothing.

My God, I can meditate on my death as a Christian, as a good disciple. It will do if I meditate upon it with You. Just as it is in You that I wish to end. *In manus tuas.*

I can meditate upon it each day, for I serve my apprenticeship to death at each hour and I die little by little as I entrust all my securities one by one to Your Divine hands. My days, You have taken them; my desires and my trials, my dull weariness and my sacrifices! You have taken my liberty, You have taken away even my remembrance of Your kindly corrections, and through faith, hope and charity I have already passed afar on the other side of the grave. Truly when my death comes I shall have but one last thing to render up to You, as the Christians in the days of old said in their simple language. I shall have nothing more to give back to You but my last sigh. To prepare my final passage, I should not surround myself with terrors as those do to whom You are a stranger; I should not fear You as the faithless people fear the vengeful rod of the Master, but I need only weave in peace the wedding garment of my soul, that which will clothe me at the decisive moment in which I shall appear before You. Appear before You! But my daily prayer has put me so often in Your presence, and my faith has assured me, for long ages past, that You are never far from me. Having worked together at our common work, can it be that we shall suddenly reverse our attitudes, and shall I see Your countenance, that of the Faithful Companion—*dedit socium* (*Verbum Supernum*)—change and become angry, because my soul, by Your own command, has ceased to be united to my body?

My death must be one of Your triumphs, how could I wish that it should not be a total one? It was said of the early Christians that they died with ease—*mori expeditum genus* (*Tertullian*), this sweetness was a testimony and a martyrdom, and won the pagans to believe in You. Yes, I accept beforehand, that You will come to seek me at the hour and in the manner that will please You. I do not know

what I am, I have not made a meticulous post-mortem examination
of my past, there are gaps in my memory and through them much
has escaped which would recall my weakness to me. But You know
me—You who know all—*qui cuncta scis*—and You can make me
worthy of You, *qui cuncta . . . vales* (*Lauda Sion*). I know how often
You have bent over my misery, and that all my existence has been
illuminated by Your Goodness. When therefore I shall find myself
abandoned to my native weakness, and when, no longer able to
bear the weight of my many ills, I shall descend slowly into death
like a sinking ship, I know that it will again be Your divine love
which will gather me up, and I am certain that You will not abandon
Your work at the decisive instant, at the critical moment, at the
moment when I shall assume my eternal form—*ib manus tuas*. I wish
to accustom myself each day to pass thus into You. To pray is to
give myself up; to pray is to unite myself to God and to detach
myself from all the rest; I can die by praying, and I must still pray in
dying.

XL

PERFECTION does not find its end in spoliation but in union; it does not make us poor but rich; the first beatitude is that of those who possess the Kingdom.

Thus it is that in face of all fanatical upholders of mutilation or abstention, Holy Church has always tranquilly declared that virtue is an enrichment, a development of our being, a way of becoming more completely ourselves and of imitating, by sharing in the fullness of the Divine act. Death is not the last end, not even if we think only of the death of the body, for resurrection awaits us. Death is never more than a bringing to birth, a passage; death and diminution are but the conditions of a subsequent and fuller life, of a growth more precious and more direct. We strip ourselves of our lower self, only to leave the true and higher self more entirely to the Divine work of Grace, that self with which alone we can be unfailingly content.

To lead souls to generosity is not then to mutilate them a little more each day, and any spiritual pedagogy may well be mistrusted which marks the stages of our progress by the more and more difficult acts accomplished, just as in contests of high jumping, where after each round the rope, that must be cleared at one bound, is raised higher. Advancement is not to be measured by the difficulty overcome, but by the love that is at work, and an easy action quite full of grace and coming forth from an undivided will, can be more worthy of God than some sensational and dramatic exploit. There are many ways of being martyrs, and those who bear the best testimony are not those who shout the loudest, but those who are most wholly one with the truth to which they testify.

Perfection culminates then in love, and love is quite another thing to a feeling of tenderness. It is a total, complete and active self-surrender to the Fatherly Masterhood of the One Lord. It is to that we must lead souls redeemed by Christ, that is the true Inn of Emmaus, and the House of Bethany, for eternal life begun here below by holiness, consists simply in being one with God.

What then should be the prayer of whole-hearted generosity, and at what moment in a retreat can it be said to the disciple: Go, now I have no more secrets to make known to you—*omnia quæcumque audivi a Patre nota feci tibi?* (*John* xv. 15.) What shall be the last word, and where shall we put the full stop?

The last word in this great school of renunciation is still a word of fullness and of satiety: *dives sum satis, nec aliud quidquam ultra posco* (*Apoc.* iii. 17)—I am rich enough, I ask no more, I am filled.— *Hæcmibi sufficit*—that which I possess is enough for me, and Your gift surpasses all my desire.

Your love and Your Grace! that is to say Your love in me, and my love in You, the question and the answer, the search and the discovery. In our roles thus mingled, O my Lord, am I the question or are You? Am I the treasure or is it You? You sought for me and found me, but Your Grace willed that I should seek for You, and I groped until the moment I seized hold of You—*tenui eum nec dimittam* (*Cant.* iii. 4). You question me, I answer You; but Your Spirit has made me call upon Your Name so often and I have scrutinized You throughout my days of weariness, as we scan the far-off horizons whence our one hope will rise.

Plenitude is the final end and that to which all upright hearts direct their steps. Progress is not found in giving ever more in order to have ever less, but in giving oneself ever more completely in order to become more and more the One to whom we give ourselves; as the hammer surrenders itself to the blacksmith to become one with him in lengthening his brawny arm, and as the mind surrenders itself to truth, so that truth may make it to its own image.

Sume et suscipe—the final prayer will then be a prayer of union. Take, O Lord, and make Your own my intellect, so that our thoughts may be one, and that I may judge according to Your wisdom, which will inspire all my counsels. My intellect will then be holy while remaining still itself; it is not necessary that it should be destroyed! that mind which contains my faith and which shows You to me always present. Take my memory, make it Your own, rule it so that it may also become a kind of divine memory, keeping only the recollection of Your mercies. It is not necessary that my memory should be destroyed within me, in order that my prayer should be heard! It is not necessary, in order to be perfect, that I should no onger recall my Baptism, nor Your Incarnation, that I should know nothing of Bethlehem nor of the Cross, and that in my unconscious delirium I should forget all, even this very prayer I speak of, and the retreat which has led up to it.

Take my will and make all my desire Your own. Your Grace worked for this before the awakening of my reason, and the spontaneous urgings of my instinct are mysteriously governed by Your supernatural Providence. Your inspirations must direct my impulses. Grant, O Lord, that our wills may be identical, and that I may separate myself from You in nothing. My faculties will then become divine and between You and me none will be able to distinguish different principles of action. Our harmony will be so deep that it will become eternal, and not to will as You do, will appear to me to be nothing less than suicide.

It is not necessary for this, that You should destroy within me the power of willing. And my aim is not that I may become will-less as I bring these days of laborious asceticism to a close. Of course, since I put myself completely into Your hands, I accept all, even that, if Your Providence has destined it for my good, but this catastrophe is not the precise and formal object of my prayer, and it is not even that on which I deliberately fix my eyes when I recite the *Suscipe*. Nor do I think that You have refused to hear my prayer and accept my offering, because I still keep some little intelligence, memory and will. I have not asked to become nothing, but through You, I wish to ask to become one with You.

XLI

In medio ecclesiæ
In the midst of Your Church
(Ps. xxi. 23.)

THERE is nothing better here below than prayer, and the best prayer is evidently that of the Church, since it is the infallible prayer of Christ, continued and always active. We can never boast too much of the excellence of this truly liturgical prayer, and of its great superiority over those devotions in which the Christian speaks in his own name and by his own authority.

But it is also desirable to know where to find this prayer of the Church, and by what signs it may be recognized. And even after we have acknowledged its excellence, we must be careful not to disdain or to suppress all that is not it. We must remember that the wisdom of the Creator has made many stars shine in the firmament. The least of them does not lose its right to exist in the presence of the greatest, and there is room for many a mansion in the immense house of the Father. To build a Church we use, along with the gold of the Tabernacle, the wood for the joists and the shapeless cement for the walls; the most excellent is not always and at all times, the most opportune.

The priest who, in the secrecy of the confessional, absolves an unknown penitent, having done nothing more than pass a narrow stole over his black soutane, accomplishes an act which is truly liturgical, whatever may be the narrow definitions of the theorists. It is indeed in the name and by the authority of the Church that he reinstates a lost sheep in the fold; his action does not derive its worth from his talents, or virtue, or experience; and this priest is at the service of God's people when he forgives; he is charismatic and divine.

To pray with the Church, to act in and through her it is not then necessary to appear in public, and it is not the external function which is the essence of the liturgy. The liturgy does not in itself presuppose pomp of ceremony, or presence of the crowd, or splendour of decoration, or dignity of movements, or beauty of melodies, and in a low Mass the Church does no less than in a High Mass. As the public function of Sacrifice, these two Masses are not of a different species, their value is essentially the same.

For the Church is not only the visible assemblage of the faithful assisting at Mass, or the choir of clerics singing the psalms together. The liturgy is not only made up of such demonstrations. The breviary recited quite alone by the curate of a parish, is just as

146

ecclesiastical as the Great Office sung in Choir, and the Vicar of Jesus Christ never recites his canonical hours in any other way.

For the bond which binds the Church together is stronger and more intimate than the mere jostling of assembled crowds. When the faithful are dispersed, they do not cease to belong to the fold. The bond of the Church is the Spirit of Christ, and to act in His Name it is not necessary to say so out loud. In the waterless deserts and in the cabins of our ships, at all seasons and in all times, those who have received the Spirit of Christ, His priests, His ministers, can act in His Name. It is enough if they perform the duties of their office. All the rest is accessory; which, however, does not mean negligible or valueless.

My God, grant that I may esteem ever more and more, even under the most humble appearances, Your action which is eternally being performed in Your hierarchical Church. Give me the grace to love the splendour of Your worship and to rejoice for Your sake, with pride, when on Easter Day, as if picturing to ourselves the heavenly Jerusalem, we adorn with stately decorations of song and light the simplicity of the Great Mystery, and when our united prayers are borne on high on the wings of glorious music—*in cymbalis benesonantibus, in chordis et organo (Ps.* cl. 5).

I desire to love all that recalls and is a relic of the worship of olden days, and I am not displeased, when out of respect for those who have gone before us, we keep or restore, even the very ways in which they gave You glory. Does not the celebrant on Holy Saturday still strike flints to try to force the new fire to spring from them? The kindly ritual, so full of Your Spirit, has not desired to change this archaic process, but so completely have we now lost this custom, that I know well the celebrant does not succeed in making the flints obedient to his will. Nothing comes but faint and useless sparks, and the flame of the lamp that burns before Your Tabernacle has not been kindled from these stones. No matter: the liturgy is not in this or that archaic action, and it does not seek its inspiration from the past but from the eternal. Your doctrine and Your Grace are alone unchangeable, for Your doctrine and Your Grace and You Yourself possessed by us.

I desire to love the memory and the past of Christianity. I wish also to love, O my God, the beautiful present of Catholicism; I wish to love the worship of to-day, adapted in so motherly a way to the hard necessities which our lives impose upon us; I desire to love Devotion to the Sacred Heart, to the grotto of Lourdes, to love Benediction of the Blessed Sacrament in presence of the crowds who gather in the evenings in our great towns. While outside the Church all is in disquiet, moving to the frantic measure which is killing us,

Your people, separated from the tumult which whirls amidst the scintillating lights and the roar of heavy vehicles, have come this evening to this little Chapel in a suburb, where the Children of Mary chant their simple hymns, such as they sing in their homes. Grant that I may despise nothing of this devotion, which is inspired by Your love and encouraged by Your Church. Give me a large, a very large heart, neither eclectic nor fanatical, but ready to bless even that which it cannot understand, so long as Your Church has not condemned.

You are the eternal present. When I confess my sins, it is in the presence of the whole assembly of the faithful, invisible but operating, that I accuse myself and that I entreat *omnibus sanctis et tibi, Pater.* . . . Grant that I may understand ever more fully how intimately dependent I am on all this enduring liturgy through which my real treasures have come to me. From my Baptism to the Requiem of the grave, it is the public prayer of the Church which have saved me, even when in fact it has not been said in public, for You are in all places where we work in Your Name, and not only there where that Name resounds. It is not in tombs that we should go to seek for You, who have preceded us into the eternal Galilee.

XLII

Domus negotiationis

A bazaar in which we traffic

(*John ii.* 16.)

THE spirit of Prayer encounters resistance within us. Like the slackened strings of a violin, we give forth confused and mournful sounds under the impact of events, and no clear, throbbing music.

When God enters into us to speak to us, when His reproaches or His words of advice appear to be about to penetrate into our temple the mob of buyers and sellers established under its porticoes rises up to bar the way.

For my soul is a building in which one buys and sells and in which the law that regulates all is the profit to be gained. I bargain and I calculate, and I call this mediocre cleverness, wise experience, robust commonsense, shrewd prudence. Let me see now, if by any chance, God wishes to take me in! let me see if His proposals do not hide some snare, and if he is not seeking to gain some profit to my disadvantage! I must really examine His desires to see if they are in accordance with my interests; it is necessary that I should negotiate a little *modus vivendi* with His unreasonable claims, and that I should make arrangements to obtain reduction of rents and delays in payment.

But all that negotiates with God is idolatrous, and that abject paganism which I have not yet got rid of, makes me see everything from the point of view of my earthly profit, like the icterus which turns the pupils of the jaundiced yellow. Looking at things in my conventional perspective and through the mirage of my infirmity, I begin to believe that we, that is to say God and I, can, each on our own side of my table of money-changer, discuss the conditions of our transactions.

I listen to one who speaks within me. In presence of a painful sacrifice he goes off at a tangent murmuring: Bah! others would do as I do! Run after the one who speaks thus; stop him, bring him to the light and look him full in the face. He is a pagan. Most assuredly he has never been baptized. There are then within you, in the domain of your thoughts whole savage zones where the virtue of the Cross of Christ has not yet penetrated. For it is not a matter of knowing what others will do, nor even what they have done; there is no question here of ruling our conduct on the doings of our neighbour, but of obeying God who asks of each one according to his measure, and who judges each according to His gift.

A God who can be argued with, a God contended with, is no

149

God but an idol; for He is God just because He is the Supreme and Only One.

Domus negotiationis.—I listen to one who speaks within me. He has just refused an act of self-sacrifice, and justifies himself by saying: What would become of us if we had always to say yes? He does not dare to add to his phrase the accusing words which would give them their true sense: What would become of us if we had always to say yes to God? Run after the one who has spoken thus, stop him, look at him in the light: he who speaks thus within you is a pagan! He has never been baptized in the Name of Christ Who died for us and who loved us to the end. What would become of us? There are then frontiers, barriers, ditches, which God has no right to cross! This place here is mine, that down there is His. And when He trespasses, and when He usurps, I have the right to reconduct Him respectfully to His domain. But that is not God but an idol, an old deity of some town, the genie of some forest or some spring; it is not the true God, Master everywhere and in His own in all places. When I dispute with Him, and draw frontier lines, I talk nonsense and I blaspheme. It is I who belong to Him, and He never usurps when He breaks the boundaries of my closed garden.

Domus negotiationis.—Again I listen to the one who speaks; he has knelt down, he has every appearance of submissiveness, and on the altar I see his offering, large and magnificent. He has given all. . . . Yes, he has given almost all, and he murmurs between his teeth: All, yes, I will give all except . . . this or that. He has a hidden treasure in his napkin, a worthless thing, a mere nothing which has no value except that of his affection for it. And yet see, in the scales of generosity, this empty place, this lacking gift, this thing held back weighs more than that which has been offered as its ransom; and see how, from all this offering the eyes of the true God turn away. He has no wish to enrich Himself with our cast-off things, but to fill our poverty. The one who offers thus is not a poor man, since he is as grasping as any proprietor, and even more so. I will give all except that which I keep. Illusion! pagan error! The one who speaks thus is a savage, a simpleton. He has never been baptized in the Spirit and in fire. He does not know what is God's due.

The misery of a divided will! In our confusion, we can hear nothing but our interior wranglings, and their clamour will for ever deprive us of true rest, which is ever active and so full of joy.

Our soul is not a bazaar where one should trade, it is by vocation a sanctuary in which to adore. Why have we cumbered its porches with our "ifs" and our "buts", our reserves, our delays, our backslidings. Why do we not help Our Lord to overthrow all the tables of the money-changers, who merely barter mortal goods for others and only enrich themselves with that which slays? Why do we not allow Christ to enter into His own place, as Lord and as the unquestioned God, whom we receive on our knees in the adoration of unfeigned humility. Complaints, recriminations, ill-feeling, sullen temper, all this race of Jebusites and Amorrheans who cumber my holy land! May all that be dismissed, O Lord, so that You alone may reign in me in peace and for ever.

Domus negotiationis.—Prayer can penetrate to the very roots of my actions; it can saturate everything in my life, if I make up my mind to suppress my paganism, no longer to take refuge behind foolish principles of a false wisdom, and if, putting everything into its right place, I understand that Your place, O my God, is not the first but the only one. For all the rest is nothing except in You, and You are not the First of a series. We do not end with You in order to pass on to something else, but You are the absolute and therefore without compare.

XLIII

In laudem Dei

In praise of God

(*Philippians i.* 11.)

I HAVE often been told that I was created to praise God, that the glory of God was the sole end of my being, and each time that I went into retreat to meditate on my obligations, I met with this first and most solemn declaration.

It is indisputable, and the Church has often approved it; She has even defined it in the Vatican Council; the world to which I belong, and I myself with it, have come forth from nothingness, only for the glory of God—*ad Dei gloriam*—to deny this is to be anathema.

Since this is the truth, we ought to be able to feed ourselves upon it, and it should have the power to keep all our actions in the poise of perfect balance. All we need is to understand it aright. What is this glory of God which is here spoken of? If we consider it from the purely human and finite point of view, we shall easily come to think that the honour of God is all that He receives from creatures, all the blare of trumpets that rend the air around His Name, His work, and His attributes. And we shall arrive at the practical conclusion that the most perfect act of all is to *give* to The Almighty, to hand ourselves over to Him, to magnify His Being through our action, and to sing unwearying *Sanctus* all the world over.

For long, O my God, I have lived in this illusion, in this incomplete truth; I thought You were a kind of potentate who created creatures to draw some profit from them; I thought that to serve You was, as it were, an obligation imposed from without upon my nature, which by its spontaneous law would have tended towards its own good; and thus I seemed to discover some antagonism between Your requirements and mine, between Your service and my greatness, between Your glory and my profit. I acknowledged indeed that You had the right to treat us as You pleased, but this right appeared to me to be harsh in its application, and I did not succeed in reconciling in my prayer, the God of philosophy who had created all for Himself and His glory, and the God of my Creed who became incarnate and died for us and for our salvation—*propter nos et propter nostram salutem* (1 *Cor.* ix. 10).

And yet Your inspired Church has given me words full of light, and doctrines without confusion, and I have only to take up again this teaching of the Council in order to escape from the morose theories of the Jansenists and from the fickle dreams of the adorers of humanity. Yes, You made us for Your own glory and that is what explains us all, and what we must understand and assent to with all the energy of our free will. Yes, from the least of our actions to the most formidable of our decisions, it is the glory of God alone which should be our end, but this end does not lead us to annihilation and in no way suppresses our worth. The question for us is, not how can we destroy ourselves, but how can we perfect ourselves; we have not to seek to grow less but to expand, to open out and to become fully that which we are.

For the glory of God does not consist in receiving something from us which will make Him richer! It consists rather in giving us the means of being no longer nothing. The glory of God is not make up of our offerings, but of His gifts, that is of our offerings in the exact measure in which these offerings are His own gifts. *Coronas tua dona* (*cf. St. Augustine, Sermon* clxx.). The glory of the sun is nothing else than to enlighten the darkness, to melt the snow, and to ripen the harvest; the glory of truth is to communicate itself to minds in making them like to itself; the glory of the tempest is to pass on its frenzy to the forest or to the sea; the glory of God is to make all things divine by imparting to them being and Grace. God did not want to increase His own happiness, nor to acquire new perfections —all these are but absurd and blasphemous thoughts; but His glory was to make known His perfection in filling His creatures with blessings. To receive Him is then the perfect act, and the one which at the same time realizes the deepest desire of my being. So much so, that His glory and my happiness are not two distinct terms between which a death-bearing choice is forced upon us, but they are rather the cause and effect, the principle and its consequence, the origin and the result in a work which is one and indivisible. It is impossible that my happiness could be found in any other thing but in receiving God in fullness, and in possessing myself through and in Him; and it is impossible also that the glory of God in His creation could be found in anything else but in giving Himself. For if God does not give Himself, nothing and no one can force Him; and I exist only because He has given Himself as the First Cause of my being. I am unceasingly the end of a divine action and I am nothing else.

Not to give glory to God is then to refuse Him admittance into myself, it is to barricade myself in selfishness, and like the darkness, to refuse to understand the light.

In laudem Dei.—Exterior praise has no meaning unless it is the expression of total surrender to an invading God. I knew indeed that in the depths of my being His idea and my desire could but be one, since my nature is His divine idea realized, and my most fundamental desire is the desire springing from this very nature.

I have not got to choose between God and myself, since I can only find myself in Him; I have to choose between the docile and true self which freely is at one with all my nature, and thus gives glory to God, and the paltry self, ridiculous and contradictory, which is divided against itself and destroys itself to the utmost of its power by refusing to receive God.

My being is a holy thing; I shall speak no ill of it, as do those quietists who imagine that self-annihilation is the splendour of homage. I shall understand that nothing is greater than to receive God, and that there is no selfishness in my happiness, when this happiness, being in conformity with my nature, is the very expression of the divine will and glory in me. My God, we are far more one than I thought, since I am nothing by myself but only through You.

XLIV

THOSE who move about here below are numerous enough; but those who live are, perhaps, rather rare. Those who live, keeping the health of their souls are, perhaps, but a chosen few. Beneath them is the immense army of the mediocre and the cowardly; all those who, since the Apocalypse was written, have been called, in spiritual language, the tepid.

When man seeks to free himself from the divine control, he falls among robbers who beat him unmercifully, overpower him, rob him, and make off. His foolish desires and his ridiculous tendencies lie in ambush for him on the road to Jericho, and leave him half dead, wounded by their blows. My God, I wish to understand clearly what this tepidity is, of which they often speak so threateningly to me; I wish to know really if I, weak and feeble as I am, find myself among those tepid people who disgust You, among that common herd of wounded men, who are the victims of petty brawls, or of obscure affrays in our alleys and our public streets.

When they tell me that tepidity is a weariness, a satiety, a languor of the soul, I recall that I have known all these states and I am filled with anxiety. Can it be that wearied as I am to utter boredom, without spring, without fire or vigour; can it be that when I am in a dejected mood the severe condemnations uttered against all the tepid shall ring out once more against me: must I be classed among them because I am dejected and disappointed?

Tepidity, first of all, is not a feeling, and it is badly explained when it is spoken of as being an emotional state. Tepidity is primarily an attitude of the will, a conscious determination, a deliberate state. It does not consist in gloomy weariness, but in a deliberate refusal to follow the will of the One Master to the end. It is to be met with in all souls who accept beforehand to commit venial sin, and who thus make as it were a habit of it.

To know whether I am tepid or not, it is not then of primary importance to discover the number of my faults. This number can increase or diminish without changing my interior dispositions. It is enough that circumstances change. The most impatient man will have fewer fits of anger if he is transported to the heart of "Sion the pacific," and if he is surrounded by obliging docility. His impatience which shows itself less often, is not lessened in the same degree, and the eye that sounds the depths of hearts sees, perhaps, no progress.

We can even say that the gravity of faults is not absolutely and immediately a sure indication of tepidity. Saint Peter was not tepid that evening he denied Our Lord, and there are deep and sudden falls which the fervent have to fear just as much as other souls should do.

But the ease with which one sins reveals some antecedent collusion with the enemy of souls, and when evil enters in without disturbing us, it is a sign that our will has secretly accepted it beforehand. He who can say truly to God: Lord, I am determined to refuse nothing to You; I wish to accomplish my whole duty and Your whole will; I keep nothing back, I conceal nothing, I make over to You all the power of my will; that person is a good servant and a faithful disciple. He is not and he could not be tepid; and yet he will fall again! His falls will be localized incidents, sudden breaks with his former good dispositions, and to repair them he need only, with the Grace of God, restore within himself that initial goodwill, and thus close the parenthesis that the fall had opened in his life.

The tepid person on the contrary is unwilling to utter, in sincerity, the word of total surrender. He will give, but just so far; he will submit except in such a case; he foresees and accepts his spiritual deficit, and he decides that he will not give up such and such a thing —not a thing of grievous moment, but one which the divine precept commands him to let alone. The attachment may in itself be of very minor importance: accepted laziness, a bitterness kept up, irregularities becoming permanent institutions, it matters little what the precise thing is; that which makes the soul of a Christian a tepid soul is voluntary enslavement in the hands of some earthly tyrant.

Two men are travelling on a road. The first walks erect and straight, but he strikes his foot against an obstacle and falls. Once up again he continues to walk as before, the mainspring of his walking power is not vitiated. The other man is lame, he does not stumble over any stone, he does not fall heavily, but not one of his steps is as it should be; the mainspring of his walking power is defective. The mainspring of our moral actions is our free will. When this will is right, it obeys its own supreme law and submits itself deliberately and totally to God alone. This submission does not do away with faults but it disowns them all; it does not make falls impossible, but it makes them all illogical. The man may fall, but he will not limp, and when he rises he will again walk straight.

When on the contrary the will is wrong and deliberately refuses this total submission to God, no matter what the partial surrenders may be, this will is that of a limping soul, and the evil actions that come forth from it are logical results of its state. The fault is not destroyed, it is not even disowned.

Then, O my God, I look to myself. Perhaps I am one of those slumbering souls who have never thought of taking a side in respect to Your will! perhaps my conscience is drowsy and heavy—*gravi corde* (Ps. iv. 3)—incapable of pulling itself up unless Your thunder wakens it. *Vox Domini confringentis cedros* (Ps. xxviii. 5). Bring me forth from my tomb! But perhaps, too, quite knowingly, I have, like Ananias and Saphira made two portions of my possessions, and keeping, in the hollow of my avaricious hand, a part of my will, I have only consented to give you a false submission. Perhaps I have said to You: All except this; imagining to myself that I had rights to assert and personal possessions to defend, and fearing to be too much despoiled by God. Yes, then truly I am among the tepid, whose foolish cowardice disgusts You, and I have not understood that I have sown nothing in my furrows.

XLV

Obviam ei

Going to meet Him
(*Matt. xxv.* 6.)

THERE are many ways of going to meet Him, and if we were to count His disciples on the day of the Palms, His sheepfold would be over-flowing! But He is rich in His many-sidedness, disconcerting to our base-born wisdom. We never really know, when we are told to betake ourselves to Him, under what form He will appear to us.

To go to meet death, to meet an enemy, to meet bad news, to go, as the sailor, to meet the wrathful ocean and the wild tempest, to go to meet the Master coming in the night watch, and the midnight bridegroom, to go to meet Judas and his cohort—*processit et dixit eis* (*John* xviii. 4)—to meet justice or calumny, all these are so many different courses, and they will perhaps be imposed upon me. On the horizon of my life which mounts upwards, on the road that my unknown days will follow, what is that meeting which is being prepared?

Lord, I cannot lie to You, I cannot say that my path is clear and that before me there is nothing but my own shadow. I see You barring my road, and I know that to-day, as yesterday, and to-morrow, I shall come up against Your daily demands. I know that You are there, inevitable, and that since You came to earth You are the end to which all steps of men must lead.

I see You. Your lips have not yet opened to speak and I already question You, for my slothful cowardice grows troubled at Your approach, and as all my faults rise up in confusion, prepared to defend themselves, as an outpost that has been roused in the middle of the night. Your arrival is light-bringing, and my soul, like the bat, naturally prefers the soft shades of twilight.

Obviam ei.—Behold how I am drawn towards You by the weight of my being and by the power of Your Grace. We are about to meet What will You be for me, under what terrible appearances are You about to show Yourself? Shall I not be swamped in my miseries, as Your Apostle in the waves of Gennezareth when he walked on them towards You?

Now we are face to face, and I feel Your immutable and all-powerful gaze fixed steadily upon my eyes. The lot of my life will perhaps be decided for ever in this supreme moment, in which I should understand You, and in which through purity of heart I should see what God is.

He who comes to meet me is not a triumphant and ostentatious sovereign, a kind of peaceful potentate, whom I can honour by ritual prayers, by brilliant ceremonies, by salutations and phrases.

Nor is He a hard and indisputable Master, imposing on each one a share in the forced labour, claiming interest on the money He has lent, and reaping and harvesting where He has neither sown nor planted; a master whom one serves through necessity and by constraint, and towards whom one would feel a kind of haughty pride in discharging all one's due.

He is not even a pitiable victim who asks only to be consoled and comforted, and to whom it will be enough to give compassion and tears of tender sympathy.

No, He who comes to me is not only a master one serves, nor a king one honours, nor a victim one compassionates, He is the One all-invading Christ, Christ in His role of the Redeemer at work.

A Redeemer at work—who asks dumbly for a collaboration without reserve, for the gift of a loyal heart, the sacrifice of a life to a cause which is greater than itself, and therefore worthy of absorbing all its energies; a Redeemer at work—who is weary and endures, and who begins again each day in the hearts of forgetful and perfidious men His labour which is perpetually undone.

Obviam ei.—It is truly He who now speaks and asks me for a manly and simple answer. He does not tell me that I am invited to a triumph, but rather that in His work nothing is finished except His own part and that it is therefore an immense burden which He entreats me to take upon myself. No, nothing is finished! Look round about. Has the world taken on the likeness of Christ? Is the form of this century the form willed by the Holy Spirit? Has man come back from his dispersion bearing in his hands the whole world to do homage to the Creative Word? Nothing is finished, all is but just begun, and it is the painful begetting of holiness which is being prepared—*initia sunt dolorum* (*Matt.* xxiv. 8). Nothing is finished and all is most difficult! Evil cannot be extirpated unless the workmen bleed. If you are determined to answer the call of Christ whom you meet upon the road, you must surrender yourself without reserve and enter wholeheartedly into the ungrateful labour, into the obscure crusade against the powers of darkness, more cruel than Saladin of old. You must consent to live by faith, without salary, without seeing the dawn of your harvest or the glimmer of your victory. Nothing is finished and all is most difficult! We can avoid the work, we can escape from the toil without even losing our eternal salvation. For God has not shut His Paradise irrevocably against those who calculate selfishly and who are satisfied if they can avoid grievous sin here below. To rouse us to give all, to cast in our lot with His, to be dissatisfied with the mere observance of the greater Commandments; to win us to follow Him to the end without reserve, He has willed but to put His grace in our hearts and His need in our neighbour. He has undertaken to put His desire within us, and to prepare in secret the answer that we will make to Him when we meet Him on our road as the Redeemer at work. *Obviam ei.*—It is wholly useless to put off this meeting, it is very hypocritical to hide it from myself, and to pass by the desire of the begging Christ, pretending to see nothing and wishing to hear nothing.

The generous people are not those who take part in the triumphal procession, and who wave palms while all the world sings Hosannah. They are those true people, who, without any illusion as to the wounding obstacles, and knowing full well that the pebbles on the road will cause their feet to bleed, have yet deliberately answered their Redeemer: Everywhere, for everything and for always.

XLVI

Semper orare
Pray always
(*Luke xviii.* 1.)

WE must come back upon this, for useful lessons do not find an easy entrance into our crowded heads, and our ever wandering eyes seek elsewhere than in the unchangeable for that which attracts and completes us.

Pray always. In presence of this command, I feel that I am at once enraptured and disconcerted, for I foresee clearly how much unity and peace continual prayer would bring into my life; but I also see very well, or so it seems to me, that between my external activities and my internal prayer, harmony cannot be attained in a moment, if it is attainable at all! To contemplate should I not give up my work? To work and to attend to my calculations and to my researches, to the technique of my business, must I not stop my prayer and give myself to my employment.

For so long a time, O Lord, I have sought to balance these two claims, and I have tried so many solutions of the difficulty! I have attempted to do away with the problem by disregarding one of the two terms, and I sacrificed my prayer, saying, to quiet my conscience, that in this way I worked more. Paltry excuse! for the work of the Apostolate does not make up for the absence of prayer and nothing can in fact replace it, not even the self-sacrifice of the fishers-of-men, not even the conquests of the Crusaders. Where prayer is missing there is a deep cleft in the divine work, a yawning chasm, no matter what may be the adornments with which we surround the fissure. Health cannot be replaced by wealth; ignorance cannot be supplied for by strength of muscle; the eyes cannot do the business or the hand and tear out the grappling-irons from the walls. Prayer is a special and necessary function. The whole question is to know how to acquit ourselves of it.

My God, in old days, I have tried to reconcile action and prayer as an ingenious system of rotation. I was on the watch not to allow myself to become absorbed in my work, and as soon as I felt that I was burying myself in it, I raised my head and my mind towards You, and I prayed, adjusting my intention, petitioning for light or entreating mercy. Then, from prayer, I went back to work, somewhat as an imprisoned bird, jumping from bar to bar of the scanty perches in the aviaries; or as the feet of those who walk, which are only put upon the ground in order to seek the means of not remaining there. I said to myself that my life, in the manner of an alternating

current, would find a sort of continuity as soon as the frequency of
these interruptions would be sufficiently great, and the rapid oscilla-
tion of my will appeared to me to be the only means of not failing
in due reverence to You, without withdrawing myself from work.
Our converse was like those dialogues cut short by the ringing of
the telephone, or by a succession of visitors, and I watched over the
double lines of my work and of my prayer, while trying to keep
them exactly parallel.

Lord, all that was useful to me and very laborious, and I learnt,
thanks to You, in this perpetual coming and going, to free myself
from more than one foolish slavery. This harsh asceticism shook to
their very roots parasitical attachments and intruding desires, and
like teeth that should be drawn out, I felt that many of my old
established faults began to loosen in the depths of their sockets.

And yet it cannot be that this system of rotation is the only way of
reconciling work and prayer in my life. Prayer should not distract
me from my work; my work should not withdraw me from my converse with You. It is not enough that I should periodically rise up
from what I am doing, in order to look towards You, and it is not
recommendable to cease to look to You in order to return eagerly
to my business. There is danger that we do nothing thoroughly and
whole-heartedly in jumping thus from side to side; there is danger
that we shall be able to see nothing correctly by squinting thus in
two opposite directions. And then, my most important actions do
not allow me to withdraw my attention from them even momen-
tarily. When I am speaking in public, I must remain with my mind
bent upon my phrases as a rider on the neck of his galloping steed;
when any one asks counsel of me on some perplexing point, I must
listen with my whole soul, like a doctor who probes and sounds.
To divert any part of my attention would be to run the risk of
understanding nothing, and of answering at cross purposes. I have
no right to do this and You do not desire it.

I shall try then to put my prayer, not alongside of my work, as a
sister by a brother; but I shall put it into my work as a soul in a body.
The connexion between prayer and action is not one of neighbour-
hood, nor even of very close contact. The meaning of a sentence is
not in proximity to the words, it is in the very grouping of the words
and rules them all. And it is not necessary to cease to hear words in
order to think of their sense, or to cease to know what they mean,
in order to listen better to them. Prayer and action are like the feeling
of mercy, and the gesture of our outstretched arms, like the determination to fight and the hand that tingles on the weapon; action
should be nothing more than the visible manifestation of the spirit
of faith by which we live.

Since God works with me and since His call precedes my salutary decisions and directs them, I need not divert myself from work to find Him; prayer should enter into my life as water which falls upon the dust, or as leaven which does not place itself beside, but mixes itself with the dough.

My God, all this is very easy to determine, but experience has convinced me that the carrying out of it is arduous. I am attracted by the charm of appearances; I love to lull my secret dreams with softest music, and to plunge myself into things as if they were my true element. I am like those insects which are caught by the sticky and treacherous drops secreted by the marsh plants, and because I am weighted down by desires which are not approved of by You, and which I have never even thought of submitting to Your censorship, I can no longer rejoin You easily, and I drag myself along like a reptile. My soul should one day communicate to my body the agility and subtlety that belong to the risen and glorified. Prayer can begin this work down here below, by suppressing all my slaveries.

XLVII

WHERE can we find a shelter for our hopes? He who no longer hopes is worse than a dead man; and all our life strains forward. Hope is as necessary to us as bread. Where can we place it? In what element can it be safely kept, as fire is kept alive under ashes, fresh water in amphora, and snow-drifts in the mountainous ravines. Where shall I place all the desire that is within me, so that I may lose nothing, that nothing may be quenched, and that passing years may take from me nothing of my worth nor of the splendour of the destiny that awaits me?

We place our desires everywhere at random, like people in a hurry, who throw their heteroclite possessions pell-mell into boxes and drawers and can never find them again when they are wanted. We waste our future in entrusting ourselves, in order to assure it, to the powers of deceit, to broken-down and faithless deities. And for want of something better, we end by longing for the common husks on which the herd kept by the prodigal feeds itself each day; we end by resigning ourselves to our falls, and weary of disappointment we aim at nothing more than a repose that is steeped in apathy.

Is it not strange to see, in so many Christians, the disillusioned, bitter smile of the undeceived, replacing the initial candour of Faith? Has experience as they say, taught them nothing but to distrust everything, and everybody, so that they may grow old in a gloomy wisdom that is empty of all joy and utterly pagan?

It is not an easy thing to keep the youth of our souls and the vigour of our supernatural desires. Most people round about us are unstrung, and like slackened bow strings they are unable to transfer energy to the arrows. They no longer desire anything more but to live in a quiet routine; machines which necessity winds up and which are unaware of their own existence. They have no other wish than to glide down the slopes with all that dies and is crushed among the debris.

They declare they have had too many desires. But these words are full of error. We cannot desire too much, when we have the obligation of loving with all our heart and our strength. They have desired badly, too little and too low; they have longed for things they thought to be sublime, and which were only pretentious and out of place. To desire to be sublime is often the worst of vulgarities. They have desired impatiently a thousand little nothings, in which in turn they have placed their hopes, as children who gather up all along the avenue the mahogany coloured horse-chestnuts which are of no use to any one. It is the dispersion of their desires which has ruined them. They have swooned amid the multitude of their instincts and impressions.

I know it too well, my God, I know it and yet I begin again each day, and I hide my little hopes in my pockets; I carry my future on myself as a fortune, and I expect this future from myself.

To place my hopes in my will, in my resolutions, in the solidity of my building, in my judgment, in my desires and even alas in my past! to hope in all these dead things and in all these dying ones is madness, but madness is tenacious. It has penetrated to the very depths of my wisdom, and You know well, O Lord, that it is not easy to go out from oneself and to free oneself from what one is.

All that I thus slip into my pockets, my little joys and my great desires, all this is put *in sacculum pertusum* (*Agg.* i. 6), into a bag with a hole in it, which is a thief and false as an unfaithful person.

I have been told to hope in You, and in You alone. I can imagine that this would be my salvation, but I do not yet really know what this formula means, nor by what manœuvres I can place the desires which daily cross my path in You who are, it seems, so far off and so invisible. And when I meet those weary and dejected Christians, who complain that they have always been deceived, I do not dare pour the lesson of this primordial truth over their discontent. I do not dare to tell them to hope in God alone. They would think this advice ironical, and would fancy they were being decoyed by some empty dream; it would seem to them as if they were being sent out into the desert in search of men clothed in soft garments.

What does it mean then—to hope in You alone? Would it not first of all be to concentrate and control all our centrifugal desires, to bring them back to the one thing necessary and to judge all in the unchanging light? If we go astray it is too often because our vision is at fault and deceives us as to the right road. Faith should be strong enough within us to show us things in their true relationships and to show us the Invisible dominating all.

To detach and tear ourselves away from anything is a most painful business. Mortification of our desires does not mean that we kill within us all that hopes, but that we tame our wild wills and domesticate our ardent or indolent instincts. Those who flatter themselves that they will attain to interior harmony by means of poetical songs and allurements run great risk of finding within them nothing less than a masqued anarchy, covered, as a festering sore is covered, with a bandage.

What then should we do? We should *not* pour ourselves out on things, nor allow ourselves to be taken captive, for a captive is one who is worked and pushed here and there by others. We should not remain in a state of contemning the present, that would be but a dismal wisdom, but we should rather live persuaded that the future is rich with an infinite value, and that our God works, unknown to us, for our eternal plenitude. We should hope, not for some elementary and common happiness, but for the part of the inheritance promised to those of good will. We should know, in fine, that the invisible does not mean the absent, that Christ is quite near, near so as to touch us, to draw us, to speak to us and to uphold us. We should not shut ourselves up in any attitude of resentment or of regret, but we should await, not the gift of God but God Himself, as the ultimate term of our efforts and the cause of all merit; *Sperantes in te*. May it so be done.

XLVIII

Adaperire!
Open!
(*Mark vii.* 34.)

I KNOW people who, in order to explain their inertia, declare that they are timid, and who think that they are excused when they say this. As if timidity were an irremediable defect, as if we could justify our harshness by alleging that we were cruel. Cruel, timorous, fanciful or cowardly, we have all to transform ourselves by Grace and not to sanction our natural mediocrity.

We should also turn our talent to account. This very word has come down to us from the Gospel, it is a word laden with difficult lessons for us. Too often we are satisfied with merely negative virtues; and having done no harm to anyone, we consider that we are righteous. We have not sufficiently grasped in what the crime of that servant consisted, who kept the talent he had been entrusted with in a handkerchief, and who contented himself with returning exactly what he had received.

One of the most harmful illusions of the spiritual life is that of finished growth, that of self-satisfaction in acquired virtue, the illusion of the *parvenu*. *Parvenu* without much trouble or after years of struggle, it matters little which, they are worth nothing the moment they stop short, and seeking no more to fathom their possibilities entrench themselves on the spot. There can be no such thing for a Christian as finished growth here below, any more than in the course of a voyage we can have absolute rest.

When a plant is shooting up, the beginnings of its growth are rapid; all the energy that dwells within it is plastic and turns wholly towards the future. But as the organism develops, this energy becomes as it were divided: a part, which grows ever greater is absorbed by the way, to maintain, conserve and repair that which already exists; and it is an ever dwindling part which is still used to spread abroad the branches, and to bring forth leaves at all their tips; just as an army advancing into enemy territory, detaches regiments all along the route to secure its communications and to garrison the conquered towns. And the moment comes when the plant grows no more, all its energy being employed in maintaining itself as it is. Trees do not reach to heaven. When their upward growth stops short, it is not because they have met with some external obstacle, but it is that they have no longer the necessary vitality within.

Many Christians are like these trees. They have stopped short in an agreeable equilibrium, and satisfied with themselves, they limit their ambitions to remaining as they are. Virtue does not appear to them to be a habit of ever tending towards the better, but an honest routine in a sobered-down existence. They have conceived of perfection as modelled on the type of annuities, retiring pensions, superannuation doles. As soon as they have so arranged matters that gross exterior faults no longer cause much trouble; as soon as they have reached the point of avoiding the unpleasantness which always follows our sallies of impatience and the variations of our caprices; as soon as they can live in peace with those around them they gently fall asleep, and desire only to remain as they are.

But this rest is deceptive, and the spur should prevent us from becoming drowsy even up to our last day. The spur of divine Grace, the terrible invitation, which is more than a wish, it is an order: Be perfect as Your Father is, and surpass all records, the very day you have attained them.

The seed that has been sown within us is not a seed of finite energy; He who makes us grow is the Infinite, the All powerful, and Grace which begins the work within us, is rich in all we stand in need of for salvation.

Grant, O my God, that I may abhor this evil satisfaction with myself. It is as harmful as opium and as flattery. Give me a virile soul which will like to judge itself without complacency, and in Your light alone. Let me never expatiate upon my past; upon the services I have rendered, upon my prowess and my exploits in order to dispense myself from hard work at times of general drudgery, or to lay claim to favours and alleviations.

Contempt of self then means, not a diminution, but a growth. Contempt of myself and of all that I have done, as a soldier contemns all battles he has fought so long as the campaign is not ended; as the sick person scorns all treatments he has followed so long as no cure has supervened, and as we despise all the phrases of our discourse as we utter them so long as they fail to obtain from our audience the resolution or the conviction that we were trying to call forth.

If I lived thus, I should remain always full of energy, always active in Your service, and above all I should never fail to welcome whatever urged me to greater effort and called for more self-devotion.

It is difficult to be satisfied with this happiness, never to turn our heads, and to develop through all these powers of light and goodness.—*Adaperire!*—Each day I should hearken to the command, and instead of becoming absorbed in my wealth, and coiling up in myself, in my works, in my merits, as animals roll themselves up to sleep I should each day note some progress in the understanding of Your Mystery, and in the transformation of my being.

If You do not intervene, dear Lord, I shall inevitably crystallize myself in mediocrity; if You are not exacting with me, I shall be so quickly and so meanly satisfied with my attainments; I shall encrust myself in the literal sense of the word and I shall imagine I am quite secure beneath my crust. I shall not move again, my life will consume itself in and for self alone.

A Church ought to stand open, my soul should be this Church; the hand that gives should be an open hand, the granaries should stand wide when famine makes the hungry turn to them; so too the house of the Father of the family when the prodigal wishes to re-enter it. . . . Could I not be for all Your own, the one whom no toil wearies, and in whom You overflow beyond all measure?

XLIX

Congregavit pereuntes
He gathered them that were perishing
(1. Mac. iii. 9.)

THIS is the work of the strong and of the merciful who are always a bond of union and who give to the scattered crowds that which is wanting to them: the principle of unity without which they must perish.

Pereuntes.—Each moment as it falls upon us scatters us, as it were, in all directions, as the blow of a hammer struck upon glass beads, and our life flies off in transient splinters. Our unattained and shattered desires strew the ground as do the window panes in a city that has been bombarded. Our unsuccessful projects are so numerous that our memory gives up all effort to recall them. We have not been able to plan out anything in our lives clearly and precisely, and those who admire us and who think we are hard-working do not know from what a heap of rubbish our rare achievements have merged. Everything is perpetually dropping off from us, and everything within us breaks to pieces; we are scarcely ever coherent; a secret anarchy lays waste our efforts and our harvests are but wild oats.— *Fenum tectorum (Ps.* cxxviii. 6.)

I am as those damask roses, which spread themselves along the stalks; when those at the top open, all those below are already faded. At times a keen sense of bitterness fills me when I think how my life only lengthens in perishing. Who then will redeem me, who will save me at each moment, from this death?

Congregavit.—He who gathers all together. It is His work. Overshadowing all that falls asunder, He will be the great uniting force, and if He brings the sword with Him, it is not to separate that which God has united, but to undo all those temporary associations which careless and covetous men dream of guarding jealously. He strikes hard and for long—*tunsione plurima*—(*Cœlestic Urbs*) but it is that He may build harmoniously and put back each thing in its place in the poise and balance of the whole. His final act is to gather together the vagrants and the wanderers; it is to reunite all those who have missed their road, and to bring back the never ending lost sheep upon His shoulders.

He has realized this wonder, for which we, alas! are not grateful, and which we blunderingly persist in destroying. He has reconciled man with his neighbour, and over all frontiers of countries, He has thrown the bridges of His command, "like unto the first"; and He has made His Church more glorious and more beautiful than all transitory "fatherlands". He knew well that neither individuals nor nations could become better or stronger by isolating themselves from others, and He did not wish that our prayers should furnish restrictions and place limits there where His love, the love of the Good Shepherd, gathers all in one embrace, all those whom the Father has given Him. We who are at work with Him should interest ourselves in all sinners, implore deliverance from all evil, and make up for all the weak and for all the afflicted.—*Congregavit*. His Church is the great assembly. Hatred and self-interest, party-feeling and bitterness are but surface disturbances, and unworthy of a truly Christian heart.

If I entered into His views and if I helped with His plans, I should be more truly His disciple, than in aggravating hatred and anger and in making men strangers to each other. In the same Eucharist, and in the same Spirit of the eternal Pentecost, what are our quarrels of a day, and our great din of battle! It is easy to cause disunion, and selfishness has been thus long employed; it is divine to reunite, to pacify in light and justice, and giving to each his due, to ask nothing for oneself, but the joy of service.—*Beati misericordes* (*Matt.* v. 7.) I thank you, O my God, for Your invisible action which brings together again brothers who have long been enemies; I thank you for making me understand how truly we are one, and by what eternal bonds You have bound our destinies together. Thus it is that when the least of the little ones strays away it is almost as if I lose myself, and when You bring them home again to Yourself, it is to the delight and joy of the whole family. *Congregavit*. Be always He who gathers together, for disunion lies in ambush for me and slays me, and that which You do in the whole Church. You have need to do each day in me.

Gather up my thoughts when my memory lets them fall through the loosened meshes of the netting of my mind, and remember in my place all that I forgot and that I ought perhaps to keep a hold on. I have alas, forgotten those who have been good to me; I no longer know at all what I owe my brethren. Gather up all their scattered rights, and take from my works, take above all from Your mercy what will pay off all my debts.

I have, alas, forgotten to repair my negligences and I have offended You, without having thereby troubled my memory! I have treated Your commands thoughtlessly and Your desires like common birds that one does not even look at and which chatter among the leaves without attracting any attention. Gather up all my obligations in relation to Your justice, and all those providential desires which I have so proudly slighted and let me expiate here below these old offences and all the evil I have committed, of which my memory has lost the trace.

I have also forgotten, and that perhaps is well, I have at least in part forgotten, what I have done for You; I have kept no count of the hours of holy watching, of the hard sacrifices, difficult resolutions and whole-hearted prayer.

I no longer know what I offered to You, what I gave to others, nor what they have paid to me. My accounts are in confusion; I hate to keep all this history of my earthly journey in my archives, and of whole long periods of my existence I no longer know anything, or I remember but vaguely that I was in Your presence. *Congregavit*,—I consent most willingly to die bit by bit, since You gather up, in order to change into life eternal, all the fragments that my weakness tears from me, all that my hands can no longer hold. Be to me my interior strength and the cement of my existence, my security and that in which I end. And when the finishing touch has been put to me, when You have gathered all and harvested all, may I receive from You, for ever, my final form.

L

Memor vulnerum tuorum
The remembrance of Your wounds
(Medieval Hymn.)

I SHOULD wish to be able to meditate on Your passion and Your sufferings with the loving discretion of a disciple and the holy reserve of true adorers. Shall I tell You, O my God, that I am at times troubled by the way in which they reproduce Your painful agony, and by all the literature that has been poured out around Your physical distress. I do not much like that they should analyse with too great minuteness, and describe Your ineffable sufferings in the superlative mood. Rather than allow my nerves to shrink at the story of Your anguish, I prefer to kneel in stillness near Your blessed Cross and to let myself be taught by Your great silence.

To move men to pity over the misery of a man is not moreover to render homage to our faith. The pagans saw Christ suffer far more clearly than our imagination can ever help us to see Him; Pilate looked upon Him bleeding, heard His words, and knew all the details of His death. But this spectacle did not draw him near to the Redeemer, his soul was not thereby enlightened.

Christ suffering is far more than a hapless man, whom they are persecuting, and if we need do no more than pity Him, behold so many others too, tortured men whom the Chinese and the Red Indians laboriously hacked to pieces; there are sights of horror scattered plentifully all through human history. . . . But why reopen these dreadful archives, dreadful and yet so ordinary? Is the Passion but a somewhat more pathetic chapter in this collection of cruelties?

Thus it is that sentimental protestants and doubting modernists have looked on it; they have stopped short at the surface of things; they have not wished to see beyond the exterior. In memory of Christ suffering they have devoted a worship of retrospective tenderness and of useless emotion. That death upon the Cross is, they tell us a distressing tragedy. We admire the greatness of soul of Him who, to the end, wills to pardon and to bless. Perhaps through inadvertence something of this error has slipped into the wholly external manner in which at times the Passion is represented to us? For this pity for a suffering man is not the only nor the true fruit of our Holy Week. It is not, indeed a bad fruit, but it is an insufficient one. The question is to reform ourselves, more than to be filled with pity.

The invisible is always the meaning and the cause of the visible to us; Our Faith ought to furnish us with the meaning of things. What then is the invisible in the Passion? The Blood, the blows, the cries, the scourges? No. All these relics are infinitely precious, and we can be indifferent to nothing that concerns Our Christ. But that which is of moment, that which gives unity and a soul to all the rest is the invisible: it is the salvation of the world accomplished through these redeeming sufferings.

Intuens in ipso non tam vulnerum livorem quam mundi salutem (Breviary— Seven Dolours). That was what the pagans could not see and that is what all hearts illumined from on high should discern on Calvary.

I gaze, not upon a man who suffers, but upon my God who saves me, and I end each of my thoughts with the *propter nos;* it is for me, for us, for us all; this suffering is alone of its kind, for it is redeeming.

It seems to me that meditating thus upon Your Passion, I should no longer call upon my nerves, nor overexcite my ever unstable imagination by pictures of horrors. I can think peacefully, in a filial way with You of Your sufferings and understand them as You do in their source so full of life. I am no longer merely an onlooker, I know what others, who have but their own eyes and their own feelings do not know, and I give thanks, I am filled with immense gratitude in thinking of Your so blessed Passion—*tam beatæ Passionis (Canon of Mass).*

This prayer does not force me out of myself, it does not carry me abroad into the tumult; it can be with me everywhere, without distracting me from my work, and I treasure the memory of Your painful redemption, that I may adore You in silence and may bless You—*adoramus te, Christe, et benedicimus tibi. (Lauds: Exaltation of Holy Cross.)*

Your Gospel is so restrained there where it speaks of what men made You suffer. Our curiosity is apocryphal when we wish to know more, and when we refuse to stop ourselves upon the threshold of Your Mystery.—*Et crucifixerunt eum (Mark* xv. 25)—that is all but it is enough. You have been fastened to the wood, so that we may always know where to find You, and that You may draw all to Yourself. Your Holy Church does not suffer us to picture You in forms of horror, and nothing is better than the simplicity of our Catholic Crucifix, which is to accompany us maternally even unto death. Holy Church has wished to soften its aspect, but it still remains pathetic and eloquent, though it does not freeze us into stupor or drive us into paroxysms of fear.

My God how I love this wise and gentle spirit, so true, so human, which You have spread over all the sacred pages which tell us of Your agony! You call us ever to what lies within, to the affirmation of Faith; and the visible manifestation is but a leading us by the hand to the invisible reality. It is always in Your company that we must pray about all things.

Fill me with Your truth, I beg of You, and deliver me from all orators, from all those who treat Your Passion as a theme for declamation, and who imagine that the extravagance of their physiological descriptions and the profusion of their phrases will be able to give anything to souls except a passing shiver of terror. I have no need of the canvas of an artist; I admire them, of course, but a plaster crucifix fastened to my wall, and a little metal cross hung round my neck is enough, is it not, O Lord, to keep me from ever forgetting the immensity of Your redeeming love? *Memor vulnerum tuorum*.

LI

Plorans ploravit in nocte
She wept all her tears in the night
(*Lam. i. 2.*)

MY GOD, steep my heart in pity, to preserve it from rigid pride. I fear not to love men enough. I have heard it said so often that compassion is somewhat feminine; and I know not why, all tenderness is looked on with suspicion. To make away with Christian charity, unbelievers have talked a great deal of altruism, and have called themselves humanitarians; and Your disciples have somewhat timidly come to the point of distrusting this love of humanity, and they willingly speak unfavourably of universal brotherhood. These words have so often been soiled by lies and deceit, that sooner than purify them we neglect them, as with the word love, of which we scarcely dare to speak, as no other expression has been more desperately defiled than this heavenly word—*unde nec reputavimus eum* (*Is.* liii. 3).

I must have an immense pity for all men; I should love greatly all the sufferings of the human race. What can I do, my God, to break down my narrowness, and to come out of my selfishness; to interest myself in my neighbour as in myself?

In the silence of the night what is that wail of desolation, and from whom come those sobs from the depths of the darkness? Jerusalem is sorrowful, but Jerusalem is the world of souls, and when I think of all the griefs of men, my existence seems to me to be too easy, and I long to bear a burden on my shoulders.

All the dead waiting in the night! They are still of our own Church, these suffering ones, and I cannot remain unmoved by their misery. If their voices could but pierce through our repose, and wake us from our slumbers! But we are interested in our own affairs, and we easily resign ourselves to the inevitable when there is question of the long-drawn privations of our neighbour.

I wish to have pity on the ignorant and also on the perverse. Ought not severity to be directed, first of all, towards the powerful, the learned and the strong? In dwarfed or even vicious beings, is it not a whole world of unrecognized grace, and of longing for good that is sobbing thus and calling to us. I shall speak no evil of those who fall; I shall pass no judgment on the guilty people, but only on the sin, for sin is our common fault, and in condemning it I do not think of exalting myself. A little truth would reform so many of our violent judgments, withdraw the bitterness from so many of our spiteful appreciations. Why should we have no pity for those who stray and who stumble on their journey? Is not all misfortune in some sort a holy thing?

Pity disarms me. That is true, very true and so much the better, for it is not against our fellow men that we should use the sword, but against the evil which has conquered them; and in spite of the apparent paradox, it is in order to render him a service, and not to punish him, that we kill the unjust aggressor. If he identifies himself with sin then we cut off both together, but as soon as this union is no longer evident, we must spare even a guilty man and respect in him the possibilities of revival. To take upon myself the action of the law, and to punish delinquents, is to add a crime to their crime and so to make the world less worthy of God. Pity disarms me, but it is inevitable that honest and charitable men should be duped, as long as covetous and selfish people surround them; and is it not good to put once for all into the common fund of virtue, this contribution, and deduct beforehand from our expenditure, the cunning of all those who exploit it? Was not Christ Our Lord Himself most odiously exploited? Is it quite certain that we ourselves never joined the ranks of those profiteers? And did His meekness ever withhold our pardon, because we had taken advantage of the ease with which He granted it to us?

All that dies should kill us just a little; all that weeps should find in us an echoing sympathy. Pity will be clear-sighted and will not scatter at random dangerous affection or doubtful consolations. There is a necessary sternness, and intrepid wills are not fashioned in eiderdown. But this sternness and this severity must not issue from a natural harshness; it is too often the evil that is in us that pretends to correct the evil in another.

Teach me, O my God, to look upon humanity as You yourself behold it. May nothing of my *bourgeois* vanity, of my self-sufficiency as a scholar, yes, even of my pride as a believer, come to hinder a true love and active sympathy towards all my brethren in the flesh. Our race is scattered over all Your earth, my God. For thousands of years humanity has been upon its onward march, since the beginnings, when man, having escaped from Your guardianship, took his physiological place among the primates, quite astonished to know himself to be animal. It has marched onward since those far distant times, so distant that our imagination goes mad with reckoning them, and during all those thousands of years You have been at Your unhurried work upon these sons of the First Father, preparing among them Your eternal Tabernacle, *deliciæ meæ esse cum filiis hominum* (*Prov.* viii. 31).

And to-day again, this great sob that breaks the silence of the night is the sob of humanity which calls to you. On the banks of the

M

Ganges, or in the pagodas of China, round the fires in the woods and in the depths of floating keels, those who sigh and sorrow do not know that it is You who are wanting to them; those who pray with sincerity do not know that You are near to their distress. I wish to love them with You and as You do, because You are their Master and because the Universal Shepherd embraces the whole flock in one glance.

When, burdened by myself and my own interests, I shall be tempted to complain, to murmur, to draw attention to myself and to win compassion from others, make me hear afar the confused groanings of those who seek You and who suffer, and may the *plorans ploravit in nocte* come and banish all those cares which concern myself alone.

I shall no longer despise any one. I shall no longer hate anything but what You hate Yourself, that is to say all that lessens and destroys us. I shall see all men, born in suffering, dying in anguish toiling here below to know and to forget, to build and to destroy, to cancel the past and to prepare a hope. I shall see them, all the sons of Adam, my brethren, and I can then well re-echo after You: *Misereor*.

LII

WHEN He met His disciples His first word was not a command, nor a warning cry, nor a reproach nor a regret, it was a peaceful word of encouragement. *Pax vobis. Nolite timere (Luke* xxiv. 36).

Shall we then allow ourselves to succumb to indolent quietude, as in those too comfortable armchairs, which urge us to nothing but sleep? And shall the fear of God play no more an essential part, in the economy of our interior progress? Must it be thrown aside as too coarse an element, without an effort being made to understand what a strong impulse it can give to love and to confidence?

It often seems hard to us to harmonize in equilibrium absolute confidence in God and fear of Him; it seems to us very difficult to work out our salvation in trembling, while keeping at the same time the filial confidence of those who do not distrust Providence and who confide themselves without anxiety, as children do, to their heavenly Father. Fear and confidence succeed each other in our souls and drive each other out, and we come at last, perhaps, to think that we have to make a choice between these two unfriendly sisters. We are alternatively terrified by the remembrance of threats, and our scruples make us doubt our pardon, then again the story of the prodigal son returns to our minds and we hear the divine word: I have cast all your past sins behind my back.

How is it possible to reconcile these dissimilar ideas? We cannot treat God otherwise than as a Person; and to change our attitude at pleasure, to pass from terror to confidence, to believe God is angry with us and immediately afterwards that He forgives us, is to put something artificial and conventional into our piety and this kills it. We must look our God and our Judge straight in the face as true hearts which have nothing to hide. *Deum videbunt (Matt.* v. 8).

Fear is not terror. To fear God does not mean to dread the caprices of an oriental potentate, whose anger blazes forth for no reason, and whom we offend in spite of ourselves. God is not far off; His grace lays siege to our souls and does not wait to come to us until we are tottering to our fall. To fear God is to dread the divine anger, but this anger has a clearly defined object. It is not loosened for some involuntary infraction of the supernatural protocol, and the Word made Flesh did not show Himself to be very punctilious on questions of etiquette. To fear God is to fear that which causes the anger of God, and sin alone, that is to say guilty desertion,

unfaithfulness that is acquiesced in—sin alone, displeases eternal
Justice. Only the lie of hypocrites refusing to accomplish what they
know to be their duty, only this lie is odious to Substantial Truth.

Since to fear God is to fear voluntary offences, those theorists are
very superficial who, misunderstanding the words of the Apostle,
tell us that fear is good for beginners, and that there are little cross-
country paths leading by love alone without fear, up to the summits
of perfection. Fear should increase daily in the souls of believers,
because they understand more fully each day that sin is the only
evil, and because each day, too, they realize more deeply the powerlessness of their own wills. We shall no longer then speak ill of fear.
That would be to calumniate most foolishly our foremost safeguard.

But if we fear sin, we are carried by the whole impulse of this
aversion towards the remedy, and towards our protecting securities.
The remedy against sin past, present or future is not to be found in
ourselves any more than fresh water can be found by digging in the
sea. Powerless to resist even mortal sin for any length of time, incapable by ouselves of remaining erect for long in the paths of
mere natural goodness upon our crippled feet, we have need phy-
sically, absolutely, of the invisible grace of God that we may not
perish in death.

Thus the more we fear sin the more we draw near to the Father
of orphans, to the powerful and good Master, who alone can cure
our misery. God who punishes evil with one hand, holds in His
other the remedy against evil, and the more we fear, the more we
trust.

Let pagans full of human ideas who ignore the mystery of grace,
let them declare, that fear always drives people away—*Procul a Jove,
procul a fulmine* (Latin proverb), and that those who fear are without
joy. When we feel ourselves growing dizzy on the steep paths along
the precipices, we cling to the face of the mountain and with all the
energy of our weakness we bury our nails in its fissures. Is there any
need to reckon up the dangerous weaknesses which drag us down
towards mediocrity, towards base satisfactions, towards opulent
laziness and little meannesses? Then let us cling to the rock—*petra
autem erat Christus* (1 *Cor.* x. 4)—and may our hold on it be the more
absolute as our weakness will have become the more evident to us.

Fear and confidence will unite themselves in one same prayer,
blending in the one same attitude of soul. We shall no longer have
to pass from hot to cold, we shall no longer run the risk of ruining
our spiritual health by these sudden changes, and clear-sighted
peace, wholly steeped in humility, will begin to make its home within
us.

An interior life in which fear is not an essential element has little

in it but illusion. And the day the bubble bursts it will be seen that
it was but pretentious nothingness. An interior life, which does not
end in confidence is a failure, but an interior life which was not begun
in confidence is erroneous from its very start, and the consequences
of this initial error are harmful.

To see ourselves as we are, and to know what God wishes to be
for us, is to unite complete stripping of self with total surrender into
the divine hands. Our safety does not lie in ourselves, and the keys
of our house are given over to Him who opens and shuts as a
Sovereign, without rendering an account to anyone. *Claudis et nemo
aperit* (*Apoc.* iii. 7).

LIII

Vos me amastis
You at least have loved Me
(*John* xvi. 27.)

AS He said this to His Apostles a few moments before their great desertion, we can perhaps take up His words and, in spite of our misery, apply them to ourselves without presumption.

More is gained from the human heart by trusting in it and by acknowledging its worth than by surrounding it with suspicious contempt, and showing it that it is unworthy and base. Often the only means of making generosity spring up in a soul is to praise it before it really exists. Men become, at times, capable of playing the most heroic parts, simply because they have been trustfully asked to assume them.

You at least have loved Me; In spite of all my weariness and all my gloomy and disappointed boredom, this astonishing word could revive and gladden me, if I had enough faith to believe in it. Is there pride in meditating on it and in thinking it is true? That it is true in those around me, and that it is not false within me, that, in truth, yes, I have loved You, You who have made me and redeemed me?

This meditation is not a fruit of pride as long as we have understood that love in us is the flowering of grace, and obedience to the divine initiative. The love which joins us to Christ is a gift which comes from Him. How then could I be sinful in admiring it and in affirming that it is of good alloy? Only those heretics who think they are themselves the origin and the cause of their own virtue, only the old-time Pelagians and the stoics of our own days withdraw their thoughts from God when they contemplate what they imagine to be their own work, and the result of their sole effort. But we know that nothing of good is found in us except by Grace, and that our virtues are the victories of the Spirit of Our Lord—*quia in nullo fidelium, absque tuo auxilio, proveniunt quarumlibet incrementa virtutum* (*Holy Sat. Prayer of* 12*th Prophecy*).

And so we can humbly admit the truth of His word and tell Him that He is not mistaken when He calls us His friends.

Vos me amastis.—Yes, My God, they have loved You passionately, in spite of mourning and of tears, those men, my baptized brethren, who carry on among us, since the beginnings of Christianity, the tradition of the priesthood. You alone have stored up the immense harvest of active love which has sprung up for centuries around our country presbyteries, and in our great restless towns. What have they not done for You, all those Crusaders of devotedness? What have You not asked of them? They have left family and country as Abraham going forth from Chaldea; they have lived for You alone, and they have died without complaint having desired only You.

I praise You for having been the centre, the soul, the light, the peace of all these lives, and the plenitude of so many and such immense desires, which have been fulfilled eternally through You. Your Church has never been unworthy of You, in spite of the great scandals of which we catch a glimpse in its history, and for not one single day, has the prayer of upright hearts failed You, O Invisible Shepherd of souls.

Vos me amastis.—And I, too, O my God, it is true, I, too, have loved You; I was proud to bear Your Name, and I suffered when I saw that You were slighted. Your people are truly Yours and the grace of love binds the innumerable branches to the stock of the eternal vine. We loved You in days gone by when we were little children, and You came to us on Christmas mornings a little Child Yourself, so full of mystery and so strong in Your tranquil silence.

And we have loved You in our Communions, since the first, and in all those that followed, in which we have told You of our miserable weakness and promised that we would work with You.

And later again we have loved You nailed to the blood-stained wood of Your blessed Cross, and we have not wished to live our lives as strangers to Your sufferings.

The glad Christ of Easter; the Little Jesus of Christmas; The Sacred Heart of *Paray-le-Monial* . . . we have loved You in all Your hidden works, and in all the souls whom You have made holy. Because she is Your Mother, we have honoured and loved her— *Sancta Dei Genetrix;* and because their bodies have borne witness unto You we have kept the bones of Your Martyrs in precious caskets.

And it will always be thus.—*Vos me amastis.*—Suffer not that anything should separate us from You, suffer not that anything should part the Shepherd and His flock, the Master and His disciples, Christ and His Apostles.

We wish to work to the end, as a chosen company, resting on Your word and knowing that You count on us.

Yes, count on us! We shall gather great crowds again around Your Tabernacle, as formerly in the far-off centuries, when they elbowed each other in the Churches at the hours of common prayer, and when the voice of a whole people answered as one man, to the *Sursum Corda* of the liturgy.

We shall make You reign within our family circles, we shall surround the Christian Name with honour, with loyalty and with energy; and in order that when we are no longer here, Your praise may not cease among us, we shall teach the little children that they have a Master meek and humble of heart, and we shall tell them how they should join their hands and bow their heads in the Holy Church, the depository of the true promises.

Vos me amastis.—When I am weary of all and of myself, when my fruitless efforts shall have fallen back upon me, and when my most treasured thoughts shall have perhaps been cruelly made game of; when I walk alone and doubting, asking myself if I have not wasted all my life in scattering it thus in the service of others; when my stars are veiled and the voice of gloom speaks loud within me, to chase away the demons of the twilight and to keep my soul within Your radiance, I shall only need, O Lord, to hear from Your own mouth this heavenly word, and to know from You Yourself that You do not doubt my fidelity. And when I shall have finished with all here below, come to me in my agony and again bear this wintess to me: *Vos me amastis;* and grant that I may be abletto reply: I is most true.

LIV

IT was said of Him, that He had appeared as a new thing, but when examined more profoundly, He revealed Himself as very ancient—*qui novus apparuit et vetus inventus est* (*Epistle to Diognetus, 2nd Century* (?)).—And in truth, if He is to fill my whole mind, if He is to bind me to Himself by all the fibres of my soul, He must be the light and the solid reality of all my past.

Though I have the duty of living in the present, I cannot abolish my memories, and I hear them as they call to me in days of crisis and of sorrow, and I am tempted then to fly off to those shelters, hidden as they are, like some leafy cover in the silent forest; I am tempted to seek refuge in that which no longer is, and to lull myself to sleep with the songs of other days.

This past which I cannot abolish, can be sanctified by Him, as He fills it with His unchanging presence.—*Qui erat*—He *was* before my beginnings, He *was* while the course of my days rolled on; He was calm and all-powerful over all that changed, like the constellations above the moving floods.

And when I look at my past, it is He whom my eyes meet, it is He whom they should meet if my vision is not distorted.

Bound up with every detail of my life since my earliest remembrance, Christ is a familiar thing. He has the calm gentleness of an age-long companion with whom we have shared everything, anguish, joy, danger and success.

He is the only true companion—*se nascens dedit socium* (*Verbum Supernum*)—the only one that I can re-discover in the depths of my secret thoughts of which He was the witness; in the depths of my most intimate desires of which He was in the secret, and which He Himself inspired. Am I too bold in thinking that He has served me— *non veni ministrari sed ministrare* (*Matt.* xx. 28)—that He has helped me and that my memories should be imbued with grateful tenderness for the divine self-sacrifice which He has poured forth upon me night and day. He has been my security and my healing, and no good has ever come to me but through His hands. Therefore what dull and stupid blasphemies have not those lamentations been over my pretended misfortunes? and what selfish ignorance do I not show in pouring forth my grievances as to the harshness of my lot, to everyone I meet! Leave all such ways to those who have never believed in the Redeemer and who do not know that unwearying mercy has never ceased to watch over them.

And I have served Him for so long! My past can be explained in the light of this grace, for any good that I have done I also owe to Him. We become attached to those whom we have served, to those to whom we have given much, because in their hands we find again our being and our life, and because they have become one with us. My God, I have given You my time and all my days. My time, which was not of much value in itself perhaps, but I have no other, and it is upon its web that all my life is woven. When I give it to You, it is rather like the farthings of the widow, for it is my whole fortune that I give. My days! You have taken them each time that prayer, charity, work or illness have hindered my free usage of them. All that is Your part, and if I rejoice as I look upon the years that have gone by, I rejoice because of all that You have withdrawn from death by taking it for Yourself.

We cannot easily do without things with which long usage has made us familiar. They have an aspect, a character which makes them sympathetic to us, and at times the soul goes into mourning when it parts with them. *Mane nobiscum Domine!* (*Luke* xxiv. 29), My Lord, the Companion and the Master of all my Christian ancestors, You who received their childlike confidences on the days of their First Communion, You who sanctified the death of all those who wait for me beyond, You who inspired all heroism and all that was just simply virtuous in Your faithful ones, You who are unseen, because You fill all, as air and light, grant me to attach myself to You by all my powers—*totis medullis cordis Deo adhærere* (*Imitation Bk. I*, 11)—and to sanctify all my memories by Your presence.

A man without memories is almost without a meaning. All nobility is acquired, wounds are only glorious as reminders of old combats. I would not wish to suppress that which was Your work, but neither would I wish to look upon You as a glory that had vanished. Memories filled by You alone, will prevent me from vilifying the present, and the glow of my past days will carry me, I hope, towards more total generosity.

You took an interest in the child which I once was, and Your desires forestalled the awakening of my consciousness—*et visitatio tua custodivit spiritum meum* (*Job* x. 12).

You escorted my strange, fantastic will with jealous care, hindering it from pushing its inherited madness to extremities, and of thus beginning again the everlasting story of the prodigal. You appeared at all the cross-roads of my journey, each time that I hesitated and was uncertain as to which path I should follow; I look in vain for some moment in which You were inattentive to me or absent from me, but all moments have been filled by You as by the waters of a lake which forgets no single crevasse. I give thanks to You who were.—*Qui erat.*

Grant that I may never more see in my own past what pagans discover in their lives; grant that I may not grow bitter in counting over again the harvests which could not ripen, and the injustices and the affronts and the misfortunes which have fallen on me. I know so many who in this way founder in premature and crabbed old age, and who complain of the deficits in their happiness as though it were some criminal injustice. Prevent me from ever becoming rebellious and discontented. May my past, peopled by Your sole love, perpetually give joy to my youth.

I put this past into Your hands, I restore it to You who were, and who therefore know it all; and relieved thus of the weight of anxiety, I salute You immortal King of all the centuries, conqueror of all corruption.

LV

WE pass our life upon earth in holding on to that which is escaping from us, in desiring that which we have not got, and in regretting that which no longer is. We live in the past which has ceased to be, in the future which does not yet exist; we live in the unreal, in the imaginary, and we forget to live in the present and the actual. We seem to be unaware that this present, which our restless home-longing despises and disdains, is alone rich with true wealth, and that to seek elsewhere that which should make us live, is to become the dupes of our mirages and of our voluntary illusions.

The greater number of men live in a perpetual state of postpone-ment, putting off to a hypothetical to-morrow, of which the dawn persists in never appearing, all necessary reforms and decisive actions. And when they do not turn towards this lazy future, they shut themselves up in the past, in order to censure the days in which God has actually placed their lives and to delight themselves with vanished things.

And yet, behind the veil of men who are born and die, behind the moving picture of events which succeed each other, a reality subsists, always one with itself, the reality of the Word made Flesh and never ceasing to dwell amongst us. And it is in this reality that we should live and it is this that we must understand, for this is the unchanging present which judges us. Yesterday and to-morrow do not exist.

Christ is always full of freshness for the present is ever young, and that which fades is that which can no longer free itself from having been. Christ is always full of surprises, as a word which is uttered, as an event which happens, as the birth of morning.

His disciples merely by remaining faithful to Him, share in this unalterable freshness.

We do not love the present enough. It seems to us to be too narrow to enfold the breadth of our ambitions. We do not know that this present is the symbol and the gift of the eternal Christ, and that He will never meet us but under the appearances of the actual *Hodie*—to-day.

Bethlehem is still to-day, and Easter was not yesterday. For Beth-lehem is the Birth of Christ, who through grace is born at every moment in the depths of souls. And the glorious resurrection is again Christ who triumphs over all the dead in the heart of humanity which He delivers.

He always speaks in the present. Protestants have said, that in some far off time He sacrificed Himself and that it was a finished thing; that formerly He forgave sins, but that these pardons were nothing more than memories; that words of healing fell from His lips in a far-off past. And they have reckoned up the centuries to measure the distance which separates our lives from His.

As though He was not at all times Himself, and as if His actions were subject to that corruption which kills our own. It is not yesterday, it is to-day that His pardon lies in wait for us, and it is to-day that His grace speaks to us, to-day that His eyes, the eyes of the Redeemer, are fixed upon ours—*palpebræ ejus interrogant filios hominum* (*Ps.* x. 5). The liturgy teaches this clearly to us when it repeats indefinitely throughout entire octaves: *Hodie Christus natus est* (*Vesp. Christmas*)—To-day Christ is born; *Hodie melliflui facti sunt cæli* (*Mattins, Christmas*); to-day the heavens have dropped down sweetness. I should keep within His sight, I should listen to His word, as to the watchword of this actual day. This is no pious fiction, it is the truth of our Faith, a consoling one without doubt, but above all an enlightening and an invigorating one. For the light which falls strongly upon our souls, leaves no room for anything ambiguous, and very few there are, who have the courage to lay hold with both hands of the present and to refuse to slumber in procrastination.

Christ is urgent and decisive, like the minute which we live, and which is full of chances that nothing will again restore to us. And our love, the answer which His own love has prepared, should be alive and strong, without hesitation and without regret.

We would advance quickly if we only leant upon the present, like skaters skimming over lakes covered with thin ice, for whom to stop short would mean to perish. *Tempus instanter operando redimentes* (*Col., St. Stanislaus*)—minutes, wholly laden with true-hearted acceptation and abandonment, are worth more than long lazy years drowned in dead memories and unreal desires. Not to value the present moment is to turn our back on God. At each moment we have a wonderful work to accomplish. And if the present is hard and piercing like the point of a knife; if it admits of no discussion and desires to be obeyed, it is because Christ is more than a dear memory and a sweet hope, He is an inexorable duty.

Achimilech in his homely sanctuary took care that the loaves of proposition were always hot, fresh from the oven, on the altar of His God. The homage of the present moment is of more worth than complaints and gloomy weariness, and the offerings which are unworthy of God are all decaying leaven and all hardened dough.— *Nova sunt omnia.* (2 *Cor.* v. 17.)

The Christ of the present is a most efficient educator. He drives away dreams, self-occupation, little tricks of selfish policy, and indulgence towards our pet desires. He leaves us a prey to the one Truth and shows us opportunely, our own indigence.

Teach me, O my God, to love the present moment and make me understand the infinite riches which the spirit of faith can find in it. I shall then cease to be a discontented exile, and to carry within me a whole cargo of ridiculous ideas. Perhaps by living in the *hodie*, I shall have a foretaste of the eternal, and perhaps, too, knowing that You are ever the same, I shall be wearied of my perpetual changes and of the contradictions which destroy me.

LVI

Qui venturus est
He who is to come
(Apoc. i. 4.)

IN our finite life the present drives away the past and kills the future in becoming it. Points of view succeed each other without attaining to unification, and we cannot live in one thing and in one moment, without dying everywhere to all the rest.

But Christ is total and overflowing. He is the calm serenity of things that are past, the unique splendour of all present developments, the mysterious promise of the future. All this is re-discovered in Him who is the bond of all the ages, and who re-unites everything in His own person.—*Omnia traham ad me ipsum* (*John* xii. 32).

I have not, perhaps, thought enough of Him as of the One who is to come and as our Hope. I have not allowed that desire of the prophet to penetrate to the depths of my prayer: *Utinam dirumperes cælos et descenderes* (*Isaias* lxiv. 1).—If Thou couldst but rend the veil of Heaven and descend towards us!

He is to come! He is the guest who is announced, whose arrival we await each evening. He is the still unuttered phrase, the dawn that the midday has not yet dried up: He is the Promise, like the flower which has not yet unfolded, and He has many things to say to us which we cannot bear as yet.—*Quæ non potestis portare modo* (*John* xvi. 12).

He is to come again, even to this race of men which He has totally bought back, but in which His work is not yet finished, and which, in the darkness, knows not as yet the name of its Saviour. All Apostles, the obscure as well as the renowned ones work for this spiritual coming, and it was towards the Christ to come that Saint Francis Xavier hastened his footsteps. Where are they whose hearts were on fire with love for those morrows they themselves should never see, but which their laborious waiting had prepared for the One Master? When we look upon ourselves in this perspective of the Kingdom that is to come, is there still place for our petty complaints and our mean grievances; and does not our inertia appear to us to be a guilty thing, like the *sans gêne* of one who would stop his carriage in a narrow and obstructed road, and sleep there to the injury of all who wish to advance? Idle lives retard the coming of the triumph, and the work which we have not done, hinders others from doing theirs. When the mortar has not been prepared, the bricklayers with their trowels in their hands stand idle, and it is a lost day for all.

He is to come, we must love Him because He has not yet told us the whole of His Mystery, and because the morning star will arise in our hearts in the hour of His choice; on the day in which calling us to Himself He will show us what He has prepared for His disciples. Our faith teaches it to us: He is at work, and we do not know His secret—*nec in cor hominis ascendit* (1 *Cor.* ii. 9). He is a beginning, but without losing thereby any portion of perfection; a beginning because His claim is always new, and because we are unable to keep upon our feet through our own strength or that of our acquired habits.

We have not a wide enough conception of the work of the Christ that is to come, and at times the Church appears to us under the *bourgeois* and mean aspect of our own thoughts. We look on her as a sort of benevolent society, which only asks to be let live in peace, without making any disturbance. We imagine her as peopled only by those who resemble ourselves—a dignified assemblage of the right kind of people!

As if a single morsel of the dough could be untouched by the action of the leaven! as if the Church were not wholly outstretched towards the future, towards the promise, towards the life *venturi sæculi:* as if she were anything else than Christ Himself continuing His work, and putting the whole world on the way towards its final meaning.

Qui venturus est.—Simple people have, perhaps, understood this better than the learned and having nothing much to gain from their present life, they have quite naturally concluded that it was preparing something far better than itself. Hope would be a heresy and not a virtue if Christ were not upon the horizon of the things to come. For it is through Him that all our fullness will come to us, and the glorious *consummatam est* will be uttered by Him when all those whom the Father has given Him are gathered together for ever in the home of the family.

My God teach me that I am a link in the chain, make me understand that we are all on the march towards Your day, and that attitudes of final repose are not allowed upon the road. Grant me, above all, not to shut myself up in narrow thoughts and not to cut short Your action to the measure of my feeble powers. In prayer I shall have the most profound respect for Your presence, because You are rich with all the treasure of the future, and because Your secret is not yet unveiled.

I shall try to understand You, to have intuitions of You, and since You are to be found at the beginning of all roads of the past, and at the termination of all paths of the future, I shall feel with joy that I am Your prisoner, incapable of escaping from You, and needing but to think truly in order to meet You.

Be my desire! I cannot but look before me towards that which mounts up there below, on the far horizon; it is indeed my death which now advances. And here nearer to me it is a sorrow that is imminent, a danger that is growing great, it is "trial" in the infinite variety of its aspects; but nothing of all that is the end and crowning of the edifice. That which is to come is not death, nor mourning, nor suffering; that which is to come and which will remain, is You alone. All the rest is but a means or a way. The paths of the Son of Man, which those who follow the Baptist occupy themselves in making straight, and hope to level, these paths lead far beyond the present moment and the dying day—*quo tendimus*—towards all plenitude.

I have at times tried to find a name by which to call You. Your names are multiple, there are some which are appropriate to every predicament of our souls, to every state of our conscience; but it seems to me that this is not the least eloquent, it is a veiled name, but yet without disguise, it is very simple and very deep and I who pass, pray to You "who are to come".

N

LVII

In vineam meam
In my vineyard
(*Matt. xx.* 4.)

TO suffer, to be despised, or even to die—these are not the things which man dreads most of all! He can be reconciled with sorrow, he accepts contempt, he does not refuse death, at times he even seeks it. But what man dreads above all else is to think himself, or to know himself, to be useless.

We ask thousands of soldiers to die in battle, the meaning and the manœuvres of which escape them wholly. And they accept to vanish thus, with eyes bound, in the furnace of war. They require but one guarantee, and that is, that this cruel death may be of some real use. The soldier will die to cover the retreat of his comrades, to extricate his neighbours from difficulties, to hinder the advance of the enemy, to bring in the wounded on the field, and even, for the paradoxical reason of carrying in the dead! But that which they do not forgive, and that which they do not allow, that which will be for ever intolerable to them, as intolerable as a blow on the cheek or a splinter in the flesh, is that the commanders, through carelessness or ignorance, should make them die without reason, or live without work.

That which man dreads above all is the curse that weighs on the unemployed. Thus in the Gospels one of the most utterly brokenhearted words is the answer of the workmen of the eleventh hour to the Master of the vineyard: *Nemo nos conduxit* (*Matt.* xx. 7) no man wanted us.

Whether it is work or love, strong arms or pure eyes, timid avowals or virile promises, all that is offered vainly, becomes changed for us at once into inexpressible bitterness. Man is always down-hearted when he sinks into being of no account, for the end of this fall is nothingness.

I must have work, just as I must have bread; if my days are empty they are nil, and if my existence is fruitless there is no reason why I should cumber the ground.—*Ut quid . . . terram occupat* (*Luke* xiii. 7).

This seems a hard saying, O my God, for looking round about me, I perceive they are innumerable, not only the powerless who help no one, but the infirm whom we must support. Age and sickness, vicious habits and ignorance, have put it out of their power to be useful to their neighbours, and if we compare the world to the trees in the orchard, the pitiless pruning knife should for the good of the whole, cut off all these weakened ones and all these parasites who live miserably on the energy and resources of others.

Teach me how it is that a cancer-stricken patient in the corner of a ward in the hospital for incurables, can still be of use! Show me how a drowsy old man, warming his fingers without uttering a word, in front of an iron stove in a hovel, can still remain of inestimable worth and fulfil a divine function. Tell me what help You have got, and what riches You expect in the case of that little child, which has not as yet opened its eyes and which will never have seen anyone down here below, because at its birth death watched for it, as its prey, and it disappeared before the evening of its first birthday —*de utero translatus ad tumulum* (*Job* x. 19).

Such a heavy belt of fog lies over our earthly life, the haze of ignorance and the clouds of doubt; we feel our way towards You, and our paths wind in and out, and when at last we manage to find You, all these twists and turns upon our journey seem to us to have been of no use, like those long hours of waiting, when the fishermen on the banks of a river lay out their useless bait to tempt the sluggish fish. Are the good tidings of the Gospel in reality so full of light that they can pierce our chill mists? Can we walk joyfully in Your light—*in lumine tuo* (*Ps.* xxxv. 10)—certain that all our hours have a meaning, and that thanks to You, the curse of the unemployed is no longer inevitable or necessary? Of what use can I still be, when I am nothing better than a remnant? And if I should find myself lost upon a rock amidst the waves, having alone escaped from a sinking ship, could I still be of help to those who would not even know that I was occupied in dying? Would not my solitariness separate me from the whole human family?

Solitude is non-existent; and the useless thing is also non-existent in His common, eternal and living work. We are never alone but when we go forth from the Word and exile ourselves in the night— *erat autem nox* (*John* xiii. 30). We only become useless when we separate ourselves from the Vine, in order to belong to ourselves, *ad nihilum valet ultra* (*Matt.* v. 13). But since He came on earth, and even before His coming—all those who join themselves to Him, share in His possessions, and are, like Him and through Him, redeemers of their brethren.

For it is the invisible which everywhere in things of faith, gives a reason and a meaning to what is visible. A man with his fingers so eaten away by leprosy that they can be of no more use, yet supports the fragility of our virtue on those unsightly hands. That which is of moment, that which is true, that which simply *is*, is not that which describes us in our natural relationships with one another; that which *is*, that which is true, that which is of moment is what we are in Humanity, in the only total and subsisting Humanity, in the Word made Flesh who gathers up and reunites all that is found in our being.

When we love Christ, we give a meaning to the universe, we have something to say to the persistence of the stars and the return of the seasons, *omnia propter electos* (2 *Tim*. ii. 10). Half a dozen just men would have saved Sodom and Gomorrah from destruction and the townspeople would never have known it. To them it would have seemed quite natural not to disappear beneath a rain of fire! But it was the contrary that was natural, and the continuance of those guilty cities could have no true explanation except in the mysterious influence of those anonymous just men.

You who are called the useless ones, you who wear yourselves out in inglorious labours, you, children, dying before you have ever smiled, you, old people with the earth already up to your knees, you, the sick, the suffering, the poor, the desolate, in the invisible world which alone counts, you are the most active instruments of the redeeming will, and it is through you, as much and even more than through others, that Christ carries on and finishes His work.

LVIII

Omnia traham ad me ipsum
I *shall draw all things to Myself*
(*John* xii. 32.)

IT is an excellent thing to correct our faults, and for centuries ascetical writers have given us the most apt advice on this matter. They have pushed this study of interior strategy to the uttermost, they have shown in well-compiled treatises, how we can make head against our evil passions, and what special ruse should be employed to exorcise each one of them.

It would be folly to pretend that a vigorous work of clearance is not imposed on every soul that desires to make progress. It would be dangerous to allow people to believe that the toil of the ascetic could, at any moment, be given up without danger. Our brambles, even when burnt or cut down to the ground, grow vigorously again from the root, and as soon as we stop fighting against ourselves we are overcome by our mediocrities and hemmed in by our weakness.

But perhaps it is possible to add a chapter to the manual, and to complete, in accordance with the most authentic traditions, the ordinary teaching of the ascetics. Many souls have sought long for their dominant fault, who have never asked themselves what was their dominant attraction.

And yet the cultivation of our spiritual attractions is as fruitful, and as necessary as the extirpation of our parasitical faults; it can even help in this work of extirpation, by hindering the defects from springing up again too quickly, just as the serried ranks of corn hinder the growth of the grass. Our defects and our virtues can only expand within us, and it is the same place and the same will that they both dispute. In making virtue grow we then cut down our faults.

Cultivate our spiritual attractions! There are evil tendencies within us, but there are also higher propensities; there are roads which go down, but there are also paths which mount, and those heretics who declared that our nature was wholly corrupt, have been cast out by the Church.

God who knows our weak places uses them as ways of reaching us, for we have points in our armour of selfishness which are vulnerable to His grace, and when He comes as a thief, He knows well by what place He can penetrate into our house. Grace and nature are not hostile to each other, and God finds in our being, accomplices who are favourable to His projects. The work of the Creator is in harmony with that of the Redeemer, and my character facilitates the design which the Holy Spirit is carrying out within me.

A supernatural attraction, in which the longing of my soul and the desire of my God meet, may carry me towards prostrate adoration, or towards jubilant gratitude, towards poverty, or towards humble silence. . . . Each soul has its own *nuance*, which must be grasped and which defines it far more truly than its defect.

When we say: I am proud, we have not shed much light upon our interior. For there are so many forms of pride, from ostentatious vanity which refuses to work, to the fever which meddles with everything; from a stand-off scepticism which refuses to mix itself up with men, to the fawning servility which begs for a few words of praise. Pride is a very vague term, and the proud are met with on every path: talkative or dumb, gloomy or enthusiastic, fearing nothing or despairing of everything. . . . Pride is the illness, but to know that we are ill we do not always need to have a doctor, that which is of interest is to know the nature of the illness.

Try then to specify your spiritual attraction. When you have taken some generous resolution, what was it that determined you to do so? There are people who pass their whole lives in perpetual thanks, and who out of gratitude to God are never wearied of giving. There are some who are filled with joy by this one word "give" and to them life has ever appeared to be an unreserved oblation. Others again there are who are only happy when their hands are emptied of all possessions, and who wrap themselves up in the First Beatitude as in a warm embrace. Many, who know that nothing is ever wanting to God, find repose in this plenitude, and in spite of all whirling eddies they remain happy and at peace because God alone is most High—*tu solus altissimus*. There are some who are never set free until everything fails them, and they make the *Magnificat* of humility flourish on the ruins of all earthly hopes. Others again desire to repair, and answer every question by these words: we must love God for those who forget Him, who offend Him or who do not know Him. . . . Supernatural attractions are as numberless and as varied as are the characters of men. Was it not the influence of that special end which we have pursued from the first beginning of our conscious life, which set all our activities in motion? My spiritual attraction gives a unique physiognomy to my behaviour and marks me off from all my neighbours.

And now, O my God, see me here before You, begging of You to enlighten my darkness and to remember all that I have cost You. It seems to me that in moments of difficulty, I turn, as it were spontaneously towards that quarter of the horizon whence I know light comes to me, and that like the thirsting stag, I inhale, in the scorching air, the freshness of the distant springs. I know that such and such a thought would be decisive against my covert rebellions; I know that if I kept myself in the light of a certain truth as wax beneath the rays of the sun, my unyieldingness would soften and I should become pliant in the hands of Your providence. I know that in the name of gratitude they could get everything from me; I know that if I go upon my knees to adore You, I shall find peace, and that all my evasions shall cease and all my grievances vanish. I know that upon such and such a road of truthful thought, I shall meet You, You the Inevitable and Supreme; and when I wickedly desire to persist in my evil ways, I take great care to prohibit these roads and I bar up the interior paths of salvation. But You are all-powerful and You draw my better self towards You. I can never find myself quite at ease with the mediocre, because I exist only through You and my completeness is found in being joined to You.

LIX

Relicto eo
Leaving Him there
Matt. xxvi. 56.)

PRAYER should be perpetual within us, but this constraint is a burden to us, this command irritates us. We seek to excuse ourselves. We create pretexts, and as to create means to make out of nothing, we are never at a loss at any moment, when there is need of finding some pretext in order to excuse ourselves from doing a thing.

We say: I can't always pray, I have too much to do. We add further: I can't pray always, for I have nothing to say. Nothing to say, too much to do, these are, in general, the two excuses to which all the reasons given by the active or the lazy, can be brought back; the reasons alleged by hurrying souls and by sluggish minds! And yet there cannot be valid reasons for dispensing ourselves from a divine command. If prayer is the soul of our life, it is foolish to invoke the necessity of living in order not to pray, just as it would be ridiculous to appeal to the intensity of the work which is required of us to justify a regime of starvation, or to allege the urgency of a decision as a reason for not taking any!

I cannot always pray, I have too much to do. As if prayer was in the first place a search and an effort.

It is first of all an offering and an acceptation. And those who have much to do, have much to offer, they should offer all they are doing. And those who have much to do, have much to accept, for every action brings a repercussion, every movement carries in its train some bruise, and every workman is a sufferer.

The prayer of offering is necessary to us and it is always possible. For to offer my actions or my rest, does not mean to turn away from what I am doing in order to murmur some prayer by stealth, it more truly means to keep the candour of untroubled eyes, the calm of an upright intention, and to act and rest and even amuse ourselves for God alone and because it is right. What is offered is thereby consecrated. I should offer all my instruments of work to God, for they only exist because He has given them to me, that through them I might go to Him. Pictures of the saints, in defiance of all iconoclasts, show them as holding in their hands, in order to give them to God, the implements of their torture or simply of their work; and from the traditional plane of Saint Joseph to the quill-pens of the doctors, all these attributes symbolize what they have done, or endured.

I do not offer You my blood, O Lord, for to-day no man asks it of me, nor even my sweat! I a man of the north more accustomed to winter than to summer; but—*atramenti vectigal* (said of Suarez)—I offer you all this ink spread out in the form of words on all these sheets of paper; I offer You my files as a judge, or my notebooks as a student; the registers of my accounts, or my manuscripts as a philologist; I offer You my needle as an embroiderer or my rifle as a soldier; for all this human work, with its silent joy or its dumb reproach, this work of the electrician, of the professor, of the policeman, of the lawyer, all this immense work can be worthy of You; provided it is honest work You are to be found at its beginnings. My prayer then will be as long as my work, and it will invade all my repose, like a perfume penetrating oakum; and I shall make of my entire life a continual oblation, a homage without a break.— *Oportet semper orare* (*Luke* xviii. 1).

I cannot pray always, I have nothing to say! Pitiful excuse, hidden error! You have nothing to say? But prayer is not first of all a discourse, it is not the phrases which honour God, nor the far-fetched ideas, nor the correct words, nor the cold accuracy of grammarians. Prayer is not ruled by syntax, and dictionaries are quite useless to the illiterate people who contemplate. Prayer is not first of all a discourse, it is a waiting, a welcoming. It is the waiting for Him who comes into the world, the waiting for the redemption which is being accomplished, and for the Kingdom which is approaching. If I have nothing to say, I have much, I have everything to wait for, I who am bereft of the only real good.

Discourses have wearied me with all their high-sounding and somewhat hypocritical words! their strained declamations, their oratorical feats, and their tragic tone. I can bear them no longer, O my God, between You and me. Even to express my sorrow, I prefer the sobriety of our traditional acts of contrition to the exaggerated lyricism of men of letters and of poets. I prefer to repeat to You that I repent with all my heart for having offended You by my sins, and that through love of You I detest my wrong-doing; I prefer this bare, unvarnished formula to pathetic exclamations: *Quis dabit capiti meo aquam et oculis meis fontem lacrymarum* (*Jer.* ix. 1). If prayer were a fine discourse, I should have excellent reasons for neglecting it.

But to wait for You, and to receive You, is to pray like the elect of Sion. I can and I should at each moment wait for actual grace, and welcome within me the progress of Your liberating invasion— *illum oportet crescere* (*John* iii. 30)—I must wait for You as for my cure, and as for my completion; as for my pardon and my glory, for nothing ends and nothing good is being prepared except through You. Those who have refused to receive You have remained in darkness, and those who have not consented to wait for You, have been called bad servants by You!

Perpetual prayer of souls which are always open to receive You. A mirror never wearies of reflecting objects; an echo is never tired of sending back the voice of the waterfall—*abyssus abyssum invocat* (*Ps.* xli. 8). When the mirror has reflected the entire world, it is quite ready to begin again, it is still fresh and active; and after having repeated throughout a thousand years, the clamour of the cataracts, the echo is neither hoarse nor weakened; it is as clear and strong as at the moment when under the pressure of the waters the rocky barrier first gave way. To reflect is the very essence of a mirror; to repeat is the very being of an echo, and *to be* does not weary us. My prayer should become so intimate, so perpetual that it should be nothing more than the conscious union of my will with Yours, O my God; it would then no longer tire me, and I should no longer have to allege my weariness in order to dispense myself from it. For to reflect You and to repeat You; to be Your reflection and to be Your echo, is the law of my nature and the requirement of Your grace. And to pray is to have attained finality.

LX

Tene quod habes
Hold that which you have
(*Apoc. iii.* 11.)

I WISH to arm myself with Your peremptory command against the anarchy which devours me, the scattering of my powers in which I faint away; and against all those contradictory absurdities which tear me to pieces. In order not to lose myself, I shall try to keep hold of myself.

Foolish people have told us that watchfulness is not necessary, and that the research of the practical took away from our prayer its nobility and its great dignity. As if to be of use was a disgrace! as if to be in touch with the real was a blot! Prayer which should be in no way directed towards the practical would be a pastime of the cult of the beautiful, a way of amusing ourselves among the clouds, a valueless frivolity. Our prayer must end in action, and must put to right our natural deviations; it must restore to us or preserve for us the health of our souls, and through it we must become less vulnerable. The streams of prayer should converge in resolutions.

But it is necessary to understand what a resolution is, and what connection it should have with prayer. Many people imagine, no one knows why, that the resolution of a retreat is the real fruit of those laborious days, and that it grows at the end of the branch of prayer of which indeed it was the only goal. And so, it happens, that we do not dare to take those humble, simple resolutions unadorned by sculptures or by graceful curves. We do not dare to say that after eight days of spiritual exercises, after thirty hours of meditation on our knees, after such sublime reading in presence of our Crucifix or before the Tabernacle, we have decided to get up when we are called, or not to talk about the rain or cold, or to smile at that specially tiresome person. We do not dare to state as the two sides of our equation the immense effort made and this puny result; and remembering the old fable of the mouse and the mountain, we think we are ridiculous to exhibit such a commonplace resolution, so straightforward, so easy, so ordinary, and to give it as the result of this general mobilization of all the powers of the soul. What! can it be possible, that in order to make yourself get up in time, to obey your alarm clock, you have, for a whole week, refused to see or speak to anyone, you have gone off to take refuge in a sanctuary of recollection and silence, and there you have been asked to meditate on the salvation of your soul, on the martyrs and the apostles, and to examine the urgency of a complete conversion!

And so not to appear ridiculous, we become so, and we invent sublime, well-built, stirring, rugged resolutions; well-riveted, like faultless armour plate, and terrible as an army in battle array. But time takes swift vengeance, and makes short work of such resolutions; they nearly all die the day they come to birth, because they have been sown upon the rock—*et non habebant humorem*—(*Luke* viii. 6). They die as all dies that is artificial or inadaptable: life passes on and leaves them there. Life does not see how to assimilate them, any more than a man can digest a stony nut which cannot be broken. All these magnificent resolutions are but as fish bones, no one can feed upon them, they are indeed inglorious rubbish. Shall we then despise all resolutions, and forgetting our daily lessons, set out to sea without oars or compass, set out for a pleasure trip and not for a voyage?

A resolution is indispensable, but it is not the fruit on the tree; it is the stopper in the bottle, or the lid of the hermetically sealed jar, or the iron hook in the wall. It is not the result, but the keeper of the result.

We do not blow a glass bottle in order to put a stopper in it. And this stopper is not the end of all the work of the glass-blower. But it is not therefore any less indispensable, if we wish to keep wine safely in our flask. We do not make leather bottles in order to strangle their necks with a narrow strap, but if this leather band did not exist it would be useless to fill the bottle at the fountain, we should find ourselves thirsting in the first stage of our desert journey. If a resolution were the result of prayer it should be in proportion to the effort put forth; but the keeper of that result may be very modest in appearance and yet fulfil its purpose excellently. Who dreams of carving the cork stoppers of our bottles, or of embellishing their wax seals. No one asks them to be beautiful; but to be strong, not to allow themselves to be corrupted, and to let nothing pass them. If the cork is good, the liquor is in safety.

It is extremely difficult to put faith, hope, and charity, or the four cardinal virtues into the form of resolutions, and yet all are very necessary. We can, however, easily keep our charity under control by a humble practical resolution, just as we set a little girl who knits and sings, to keep a whole herd of horned cattle. When we have decided to get up at the right time, we have evidently not upset the equilibrium of the planets, and our modest resolution is but a hook in a wall, but as long as the hook does not give way nor allow itself to be drawn out, it will hold up at its own level and keep stable, all that we wish to hang upon it. And just because we get up in good time a courageous regularity and a kind of beneficent responsiveness will reign throughout our day.

Thus the best resolutions are never found in groups. They do not grow stronger by being added to. He who adds on indefinitely to the hours of his sleep is not more rested; and he who increases his food ration every day is not on the road to health but to death. Numerous and simultaneous resolutions get in each other's way as runners on a narrow track. One resolution is of more worth than two, and two are better than three, while beyond three we may well question if there can be resolutions, just as we can question whether there are many men of over one hundred years of age in any town. Here and there they can be found, but they have only just enough strength not to die.

Teach me here again, my God, to follow Your calm and balanced wisdom; make me adaptable to the life which You have fashioned for me, and drive from my soul those pretensions which I call chivalrous, but which are but childish dreams. My virtue is not in the clouds, my duties are not among the stars; but to be good is to think and to act as You do and with You.

LXI

Redimentes tempus
Exploiting our days to the full
(*Eph. v.* 16.)

MY days advance one by one, in a long file, like the petitions of beggars, like the moans of the sick, like the rhythm of slow breathing, and they give its measure and its punctuation to this poem which my life should be. There are many on which nothing is written. I leave a blank line. What will You say of so many useless days, You who judge an idle word? What will You say of so many comfortable idlers, whose only excuse is precisely that they do nothing?

Dies mali sunt (*Eph. v.* 16). Because of the all-invading evil round us, I should wish not to waste one of my days. I should wish to make use of the least moments, not from any niggardly motive, such as make the petty tradesman hug his possessions and gather up the crumbs, but out of highest respect for Your gifts, and for this time which You have granted to me. I should wish to make use of the least moments, not with frenzied and nervous anxiety; I know too well the blunders that are accumulated from over haste, and that at times I must allow some play to the imagination and always leave room for thought.

But I can make the time which You have allotted to me yield up all that it contains. I can spare myself no trouble and dig deeply in my days. Some moments are vaster than others, not because they last longer, but because they are better filled and because our souls are more completely in them. If I lived thus, giving all my mind to my least undertakings, working hard, devoting myself unstintingly, perhaps I should save the world by my sacrifice and make the best of each of my moments resound to the end of the universe—*in fines orbis terræ*. (*Ps.* xviii. 5.)

For I am answerable with my whole existence to the sphere in which You have placed me, and my particular duties are but applications of the general scheme outlined in my social duty. Bound up thus as I am, with all that suffers, and with all that falls, it is in vain that I seek to secure to myself any false independence. My days are not my own. I need never ask at what rate they are being paid. Rather should I ask, what I myself have paid for this day received; what work I have freely given to balance in the eternal scales, the twenty-four hours which have been advanced to me.

They run one after another, these my mortal days like hounds at the hunt; they fall one by one like great drops of water into a pond where they are lost to sight. My past drags on my present and in the flight of the hours it is my life that is being consumed.

My God, Redeemer of our great family, do not suffer that any ridiculous melancholy should come to hinder me from rejoicing as I see the oil in my lamp grow lower, as I watch, each day, my reserves of life so steadily desert me. Teach me to grow old aright, without murmuring and without laziness, not that I may isolate myself, but that I may augment myself, refusing ever to appeal to work already done as an excuse for not putting my whole effort each day.

My past days have perhaps brought nothing to maturity within me. The seasons have gone over my soul without stirring and without refining it. I am left worn and rough, understanding nothing of all that is being done around me, and firmly fixed in the determination not to move. My days, the price of my purchase, the only means I have of doing good, these days so laboriously reconquered by my God from the evil which imprisoned my life, should all be stamped with the divine effigy as those coins of the tribute with the effigy of Cæsar.

Those who do nothing are murderers, murderers of themselves and of their neighbours, murderers from a great distance perhaps, like those men in our arsenals who neglect to prepare the protective weapons which will be needed in the hour of the combat in the still far future. All those obstruct our roads who think that any slack effort will do and is even creditable, that an intermittent desire saves us from being base and that we can saunter through our lives like a bored or jovial pleasure seeker without ever bruising ourselves against hard realities.

The most busy people are always those among us who are the most prompt to undertake more work. At the early Mass in our Churches it is the working people who are gathered there. Those who have nothing to do are quite content with carrying on that agreeable occupation, and never have time to render a service.

If You came back, my God, how would You judge our lives? If You should appear among us should we not act as schoolboys caught in a fault, who assume a studious attitude when the master raises his eyes? I think You would find words of mercy for all self-sacrificing people, who, saying nothing to anyone, and making no fuss about their martyrdom, live for the service of others and find sleep impossible when they have not laboured to their utmost. Their virtue is not always in the best style! There is dust on their sandals, and they have been so much taken up with their neighbour that they have forgotten to look at themselves in their mirror and to adorn their lives. But they understand how to redeem the time—*redimentes tempus*—and their moments are of more value than the long day of the disdainful, bargaining pharisee. They have never grumbled when they have been asked to serve a stranger. Their self-sacrifice has indeed appeared so natural that all those who benefited by it thought it was quite superfluous to give thanks. We do not thank a tree for giving us its shade, or the engine-drlver for driving his engine! Who will grant us to find a dozen or more of such reapers for the needful harvests? We are above all intent on being leisurely, cold, correct and prudent, we study how to conform ourselves to this century, and time never presses unless we are waiting for some service to be rendered to us, or when we collect the money owing to us, or decide to take our rest. We have kept a clear remembrance of the *Requiescite*, rest yourself, but we have forgotten the essential little adverb that modifies it: *pusillum*, a little moment.

LXII

IT is not enough to keep our lamp alight. We must not only have the means of providing oil for the flame that is burning, but also for the flame that will burn. Instead of lessening the work of the flame and lowering the wick, we must increase its resources, and keep all its brightness. The greater number of people, unfortunately, measure their work by their courage instead of expanding their energies in proportion to the need there is of them. They do not wish to exhaust themselves; but there are two ways of avoiding exhaustion: either by diminishing our output or increasing our gains, and the wise virgins are those who take with them a provision of fresh oil and who without detriment to the present moment, wish not to forget in advance what the next moment is to bring.

Oleum secum.—It is a load to carry, and therefore an annoyance, and many will not accept this increased burden, which is the condition of real growth. They drag themselves along in a small way, without any security and without safeguards; those safeguards which we must ourselves carry, as divine graces. In order to be protected from any chance scarcity we need much prayer, much love, and some virtue to spare.

When the flame of energy burns low and dies, a strong desire is needed to rekindle it, this desire which has not yet shown itself in action, and which dwells in the depths of the soul as a reserve supply. We are at times astonished at the tenacity of people who are in appearance most tractable and easy to handle; on some point or other they will not yield, and they put aside unweariedly all obstacles; they pursue their idea or their mania, and make a way for themselves as a flame does. *Oleum secum.*—They have laid in a supply of energetic will power.

Oleum secum.—In order that a life may glow, it must have work which somewhat overflows it; more to be done than can be done! so that our activity may find something on which to spend itself. The reserve of work ought always to be at hand, and when the flame flickers or crackles for want of fuel, instead of waiting till the dealers in oil come to tell us what we have to do, we must immediately infuse ourselves with new duties and our days must never know the gloomy slothfulness and fœtid smoke of idleness.

In critical moments those who carry oil with them stand out in the crowd of Christians who are all apparently so like each other.

They are those who are not surprised by weariness and who continue to shine placidly, because they are able to renew themselves. Everything wears us out, and if we have made no provision against this wear and tear, we shall fall back into impalpable dust, like the stone of monuments which is silently worn away. Everything uses us up, even doing good; at times weariness in well-doing takes possession of us, and we are depressed at having but one narrow path in which to walk, and at being unable even to turn our heads toward the horizon of joys which seem so easy to obtain. All wears us down, but everything in us can perpetually renew its youth, like the flame which never dies of itself and because it is weary of burning, but only because it is no longer fed and no one gives it anything more from without. Its capacity for being renewed is indefinite. The grace of God can be the oil of our lamp, and if we co-operate, with it, our will although so frail and weak, can shine without ever failing —*fulgebunt sicut stellæ in perpetuas æternitates.* (*Dan.* xii. 3.)

Reserves of peaceful resignation, of silent courage, of persevering prayer, of tried knowledge and of kindly counsel —*Oleum secum.* The utilitarianism which has in view the immediately useful is nonsense, and he who has only what is needed to live for one moment is just a dying man at the last second of his agony.

My God, I have never understood Your wisdom, and I thought that all was useless which did not at once make the flame of my life more brilliant. I disdained all lengthy, abstract, and dry study laborious and exact calculations, methodical and leisurely observation, perpetual asceticism with its repetitions and its insistence. I thought as many of my neighbours do, that we should direct our energies towards the practical—which is true—but I also thought that the practical was opposed to theory and study, which is folly. I thought the best thing was to work as an Apostle, which is true— but that the Apostle had no need of accumulated thought and—even more than others—of perseverance and of calm—which was folly. I wished to live like a dancing flame, forgetting that all within me dies, and that it is You and Your Spirit that I must keep—*lampades nostræ extinguuntur.* (*Matt.* xxv. 8.)

The wise virgins and the foolish ones! It was in vain that I looked at the light of their lamps. I could not distinguish which were the prudent and which the heedless; the flames seemed equally clear in all. But it is later, at the moment of crisis, at the moment when strength is exhausted, that the separation between them will be made, and that the breakdown of the unforesightful ones shall be without remedy.

Save me, O my God, from foolishly frittering myself away. Save me also from husbanding myself like a miser, and from limiting my outlay of virtue. In order that I may always give to the uttermost, without fearing that the prodigality of my efforts should empty me, be my richness and supply all my deficiencies. May Your power and Your inspiration pass subtly into me. I must hold out until the dawn; throughout the livelong night my watchful fires must burn. You do not suffer us to be less generous to-day than yesterday, and less so at the third watch than when twilight fell. Your exigencies remain ever the same; I have no excuse when I decide to love You less, to serve my brethren less, and to bring, in deduction of my actual debt, all that I have already paid to You.

Master, both austere and kind, like the reaper's hook which in cutting down the corn gives it its true value and its final meaning, like the sickle which forms of all those blades a harvest, I love You, because You will not suffer that I should make myself grow less, and because You exact from me that my soul should know no falling off.

LXIII

Gaudium plenum
Complete joy
(*John* xvi. 24.)

HE has himself told us that this was the ultimate end of His revelation, and that we ought to draw joy from all that He has said to us,
from all, even from His commandments, even from the news that
He would leave us—*gauderetis utique* (*John* xiv. 28)—when returning
to the glory of His Father. Joy is a word of Eternity; it is possible
so to fix ourselves in joy that neither death nor suffering can dislodge
us from our place. For the Christian all days are gala days, and he
calls the cause of his joy by a divine name—*Dei Genitrix*. The Gospel,
the good tidings, ends in Saint Luke by that exultant prayer—*cum
gaudio magno* (*Luke* xxiv. 52)—and virtue which does not lead to
luminous plenitude, virtue which has no interior smile, no spring
of joy, has not as yet taken its perfect form. It is constrained and
hard, meritorious doubtless, but unfinished.

It is strange, nevertheless, that as a rule we give so poor a welcome
to holy joy. We see, as it were, some impertinence or danger in it.
It seems to us that gaiety is a kind of conceit. He who says: I am
happy, seems to acknowledge that he wants for nothing, and does
not that imply forgetfulness of his present faults and of all his
weighted past? The ancient Greeks imagined that the gods were
jealous of the laugh of a man, and that their spite pursued on earth,
those mortals who did not weep enough. We have inherited something of these pagan terrors, and we dare not receive joy as a river,
nor peace as a harvest. We keep our joy in secret corners; we hide it,
fearing to lose it, and we only taste it stealthily and in haste, like
greedy children who steal dainties from a storeroom of which the
door has been left ajar. And even from these too short joys, we
retain, as it were, an ill-defined remorse. Our attitude of mind not
having been frank, our soul not seeing very clearly, we keep an
impression of duplicity and weakness; and we persuade ourselves,
with reason alas! that our joys are slaveries, and that in tasting them
we are unfaithful to our God.

Is it thus we should receive the Fruit of the Holy Spirit? Is it by
this unworthy attitude that we imagine we show respect to the
message of Christ? And is there not much pusillanimity in not
daring, nobly and greatly, to declare that all goes well, as nothing
is wanting to us? In reality, he who says he is happy gives up something which men fundamentally desire: he surrenders all claim to be
pitied and to be consoled; he renounces the profitable gestures of all

beggars; he gives up borrowing the energy of others; and he even becomes a debtor to all the weak, a purveyor to all the starving; he becomes the one who gives, because no one gives to him, and because all forget even to thank him. We are always equivocal and hybrid; we wish to keep secret all the advantages of our situation and to remain rich, while at the same time entering a claim for the privileges of the poor and exempting ourselves from common burdens. We wish to preserve our health because we hold to it, and at the same time we desire to be coddled a little as sick people, because it is pleasant. We wish to keep the use of our two feet and yet to be carried in portable chairs. And when we say joy is not for us, we lie, and we blaspheme the word of Christ.

For joy, true Christian joy is deeper than sorrow. There is within us—and we know it—a last stronghold where we can always meet with Grace and solder ourselves to the ultimate. But to reach that point courage is often needed, and to remain there calls for heroism. Joy is not an idle heritage; it is not a pleasant feeling; it springs from a principle of faith, and it has to be conquered as Jerusalem of the Crusaders of old. There is much blood on the road which leads to the glory of the resurrection and to perpetual joy—*æterna perfrui lætitia*. (*Liturgy, Vespers of Our Lady.*)

Those idyllic shepherds who have sung to us of effortless happiness were either pagans or simpletons; they have forgotten what we are, and have forgotten that in order to continue calm and steady in the tempest or the battle, to smile at death, at one's own or that of others, we must go down as pearl-seekers who dive with closed eyes, and recover possession, in the very depths of our being, of our willed and total acquiescence in the designs of Providence. The joy of knowing that God is making use of us, that nothing of all we do is lost, that the eight Beatitudes are eternal, and that Christ and I are not two but one! Where are those who consent to put all their happiness in their duty? And where are those who dare to say that they have no duty? From that it follows that there is always a marvellous and most safe jewel-box in which we can place our joy; for the divine will has assigned a duty to us to the very end, so to the end, too, this duty can protect our holy joy.

We begin with unreasonable demands; then we declare that our happiness consists in seeing all these demands satisfied; then we complain that men and things go all wrong and do not appear to trouble about our desires; then we lay the blame on God, *who has abandoned us*; and finally we declare that happiness is an empty word, and we pursue with sarcasm or with tales of our experiences, those who speak of it and who pretend to have discovered it in the Gospel.

All that is quite logical starting from the one initial absurdity of our unreasonable claims. It is not God who abandons us, it is we who have never beheld in Him the First and the Sovereign, and who have *humbly* and urgently submitted for His approval an already completed plan, like the draft of a law submitted for royal sanction, which cannot be retouched! It is we who have defined happiness as the satisfaction of our own claims, without even troubling ourselves to put order and coherence into our pretentions; it is we who have fallen into the double error, always the same in the spiritual life: of taking a creature for God, and of treating God as a creature. We have not perceived that our happiness lay in being ourselves, and that our nature, that is to say we ourselves needed only to serve God.

LXIV

Omnia in ipso constant

In Him all things hold together
(*Col. i.* 17.)

I LOOK round about me, O my God, on what men call in a
neutral and general way: things. Their immense number disconcerts
me, their inner mystery terrifies me. What am I among all these
undecipherable countenances? What connexion does my being keep
with the trees of the century-old forests and with the geological
fossils? I find it strange, odd, disquieting to pass my life in the midst
of a creation which I can scarcely understand, and which does not
trouble itself about me; into which I seem to myself to have fallen
by chance, and from somewhere else, like an intruder among
strangers! Neither wind nor cold, nor the sea nor gravity seem to
know that I suffer, or that I think, and for long ages this indifference
of nature, so near to us and so remote, has fostered our melancholy
and has been food for the metaphors of poets.

I have been told that "things" were objects of knowledge for the
mind of man, and means of action for his will. This is doubtless true,
but I should like to know what is this knowledge, this science, and
to what this action tends, and how that it can all be concentrated
in one single source or centre of being scattered among
trifles. For everything that I do bring back to the conscious
principle of my life is but the restlessness of one walking in his sleep,
and a foolish distraction. I can bury myself in these dreams and these
distractions but I cannot believe in them; I can occupy myself about
them all, but I cannot bring that pathetic interest to bear upon them,
which stirs me whenever I myself am in play. To understand does
not mean only to classify methodically, but it means to become one
with the object understood. How can I become one with this impenetrable and cold world? At what point shall we try to meet each other,
and by what means—tearing off its veil—shall I be able suddenly to
recognize in it the face that I already know, the familiar features of
my race? For I am certain that at bottom this world and I cannot be
two strangers, and if we do not seem to be in accord from the first,
it is because we are parts of a far greater whole, and we are but
stating the conditions of a higher harmony; we are like two straight
lines which cut each other abruptly, and in so sharp a way that they
form by their very divergence the figure of an angle.

Can it be that my only connexion with the cosmic world is that of
a passing spectator? Is my life but a surface phenomenon, like the
path of a pen on white paper, like the track of a frail insect on the
surface of sleeping waters?

I recall that in the days of Genesis, man then innocent, gave a human name to each thing, and that Creation, wholly directed towards him, had a friendly and a kindly meaning; this meaning was man himself, towards whom all converged spontaneously.

Of this marvellous language which tamed the elements and charmed all creatures, nothing is left since the original break was consummated, and man chose to profane the world and to make things unholy. The human meaning of creation has been altered; for the universe has turned its back, and nature has escaped from the transgressing hand of the sinner, the father of the race. In vain would man have sought for himself in a world which refused to acknowledge him, and in which he would have found nothing but rebellion and resistance, contrariety and punishment. His spirit even would have wept in darkness.

But that which the first Adam destroyed, the Second has rebuilt, and humanity comes to its completeness in the perfection of the Son of Man. The name which the father of the race has given to things is forgotten, but the Incarnate Word who upholds all through His power, has inherited all that is—*quem constituit heredem universorum* (*Heb*. i. 2)—and it is His Name which now sums up the world and gives a meaning to creation. We can no longer be "perfect" that is to say be ourselves, except through Him, and when we choose to escape from Him we fall back into the second death. Outside of Him nothing holds together, and nothing is in equilibrium—*propter quem et per quem omnia. (Heb.* ii. 10.)

Thus the mystery of "things" now only tells the story of the Redemption; and the work of Christ has not been cut short at the frontiers of the moral order, as later day protestants have thought, separating the Word and Jesus. The role of Christ is not only to teach us the rules of good behaviour, and to open a school of virtue; His Divine function is not only to distribute advice, to broadcast His assent and to encourage us to live well, but it is to penetrate all things in order to give to each thing His being and His worth, and to bring all back to that luminous Principle from which all came forth—*et per eum redire omnia in integrum a quo sumpsere exordium (Holy Sat. Prayer, Second Prophecy).*

It is always the last word which gives the final meaning to all the others, as it is only the last act of our earthly life by which it should be judged, and the last battle that makes a war victorious or a failure. An achievement, being an end, gives a meaning to all that has gone before it.

Knowledge is then a holy thing, as is also the struggle of industry and the grouping of men in social frameworks. Christ extended to the infinite measure of His mission, the Redeemer who saves our body and our soul, is in truth *Salvator mundi*, the Saviour of the entire world torn by Him from the senselessness of sin.

It would be well to re-read some day or other, in order to understand them and not merely to pronounce them, the words of the Holy Spirit speaking through Saint Paul; it would be indeed well that our Christian pride and our intelligence should rise to the height of these absolute points of view. That which is being done in us, is the buying back of a universe, and the meshes of the netting are only upheld by the vast whole; when we repair one we are working for the whole.

Give me, O my God, this true view of things: so much so, that I shall no longer be obliged to turn away from the marvellous rapture of Your cosmic work, in order to seek You in a little sanctuary, where occupying Yourself with me alone, You will abandon the fast world to its fate Give me true sight which will embrace Your redeeming work in all its immensity, both its past and its future; and grant that, like the prophets of old and the great patriarchs, I may be able to contemplate Your far-off glory, and to adore You on the heights.

LXV

Omnibus omnia
All things to all men
(1 *Cor. ix.* 22.)

THERE are two ways of understanding renunciation. It can be made into a form of annihilation and tend towards extinction. It can also be made into a form of growth, and instead of directing it towards increasing our insignificance, it can be given, as its end, union with God. How can we possibly grow greater by renouncing ourselves? The Gospel is, throughout, the answer to this question; and for those who cannot read the Gospels, the practice of the Church is an all-sufficient teaching. So sufficient that it explains the meaning of the texts themselves and hinders us from folly.

To renounce oneself is to disappear, so they say! It is to be unconcerned about everything, to react to nothing and to become a cipher. Thus it was the Quietists thought, and the Church condemned them without mercy in spite of the example of their exalted virtue. To renounce ourselves in order to become less would be a singular way of understanding the fullness of the message of Christ. That was most certainly not what the angels announced to men in the night of the Nativity. To lessen themselves, to pillage and plunder themselves, to ruin themselves in the nothingness of folly and vice, men had truly no need of new teaching. Since the sin at the beginning of things, they had inherited this art from their first father. They knew instinctively by which actions they could destroy themselves. Unconcern pushed to its final extreme is crime become a custom, which only stops short because it finds nothing more to trample on. I cannot be impartial as to whether I am in truth or falsehood, in justice or violence; I cannot hand over to others, as a cast-off garment, my sincerity and my virtue; I cannot be indifferent to my own interior purity, nor allow whoever wills to come and wipe their dirty feet upon my threshold. I cannot yield up my body to the pleasure of chance encounters; I must guard myself as a thing of infinite price, and the apathy and unconcern of guardians is always treasonable.

I cannot even be unconcerned for others; I should suffer what they suffer, and find fault with what they do ill. There is no people so remote that it has not the right to obtrude itself into my pre-occupations; and hunger and thirst after justice should hinder me from sleeping. He who renounces himself in order to suffer less, and who, like the snail draws in his jelly-like horns lest they encounter something hard, that man is far from the practice of self-renunciation and has reached the point of seeking nothing but himself; and what he, perhaps, calls his affection, is only some animal weakness. Let us leave to pagans the care of hating the common herd and of driving them from their path.—*Odi profanum vulgus et arceo* (Horace *Odes* iii. 1).—That fashion of withdrawing from men is the vilest of hypocrisies; for to think of nothing but ourselves, or our rest or our pleasure, or even to think only of our own virtue is to be a stranger to all catholic interests. The schoolboy who renounces knowledge and cares nothing for the results of his study is an idler who is punished; the soldier who withdraws from fighting and cares nothing for the results of the campaign is a criminal who is shot; the father who abandons his wife and cares nothing for his home carries within him the soul of an adulterer and absolution is refused to him.

But we can and we should renounce ourselves by blowing up all barriers of our narrow interests in order to blend our lives in the whole work of Christ. He who renounces his own judgment under religious obedience, does not give up judging, and he still has an opinion. He is even asked to be of the opinion of the one who commands, and to approve the order that is given to him, which he could never do if he had made a clean sweep of the faculty of judging. He keeps an opinion and the right to have one; but the renunciation of obedience consists in putting himself, in the appreciation of things, at the universal point of view, which is by definition, that of authority. The Superior acts for the good of the whole, and it is in this whole that I should work. If I make my own all the motives for the order given, my obedience will be blind, not because it sees nothing any more but because like justice which has bandaged eyes, it sees only one thing: the supreme end, the one goal to which everything, including the one who obeys, must remain subordinated. Obedience does not give us the soul of a slave Quite the contrary, it is the only way of giving those who serve the souls of leaders.

The religious who through his vow of chastity has forbidden himself to love a woman as his own, and to concentrate his affection and his interest on any one person, this religious does not seek, as has been said in jest, to escape the burden of a family. It is not that he may be less a man, that he wills to be more chaste. But, not having pledged his love to any one person, he can with a free heart put himself at the service of the whole world; he can love without coveting, for he has forbidden himself ever to be a captive; he can bear in his own soul the secrets and the anguishes of others, and each one can call him Father, because all will call him father in the same very high and universal acceptation of the word. His vow enlarges him, just as it would be with a flame, which instead of remaining imprisoned in a small dark lantern and lighting one corner of a village street, should be set up in the firmament among the stars to illuminate with its modest ray the million eyes turned towards it.

Teach me, O my God, Your great, Your very great wisdom, that higher knowledge of which Your disciple Paul spoke, which would cancel so much darkness in me. I always think that I can guard myself best within narrow bounds, and I live like the gold fish in a small jar scarcely bigger than themselves. I have not yet experienced what we become through You, when we abandon ourselves to Your plenitude, nor have I realized why, from the very beginning and even to our own days, Your faithful ones, those who have understood You, have by instinct compared You to the ocean and to the abyss.

The soldier does not diminish himself in renouncing himself, because the renunciation is a service to a cause far greater than the interest of any passing individual. Could I possibly fear to grow less by putting into Your hands, for Your work, as we give an alms which is changed into love, my life and my affections, my time and my tears, and all in me that could, had I so willed, have served for myself alone, and have vanished with my mortal life.

LXVI

Ego sum veritas
I am the Truth
(*John xiv.* 6.)

THAT which should make us love the true, says the old author of
the *Paradisus animæ*, is that Christ is the Truth. We would most
probably have corrected this sentence had he submitted it to us;
under pretext of improving it we should have written this empty
banality: We must love Christ because He is the Truth. We are so
convinced that the abstract precedes the concrete; that logic is
anterior to reality, and that law, necessity and justice are the primeval
things. We do not know that primeval justice was The Just One,
and that necessity only exists under the personal form of the necessary Being. Truth is not first of all an abstract equation, and it has
never been real under that aspect. Truth is for itself all that it is, and
Truth is first of all a Person, it is God. Christ being God personally,
could say without metaphor and without exaggeration: *Ego sum
Veritas.* Truth is I myself.

The consequences of this fundamental principle cannot be exhausted in one day. Rightly understood, it would restore its youth to my
whole life, and unify activities which appear to be most completely
disunited. For if Christ is Truth, as He is personally and substantially
Justice, then the search for knowledge and the social equilibrium of
the world instead of being concerned only with the domain of
abstract ideas, take a Christian meaning and become the *building up
upon earth of the Body of Christ.*

I have asked myself, O my God, how my studies, my researches,
my reading and my notes could be directed towards You. First of all
I said to myself that this study did not necessarily distract me and
therefore it was not in itself inimical to my devotion, that it could
adapt itself to my piety, just as two neighbouring people who do
not know each other and think each of their own affairs. But that is a
most insufficient and injurious solution. It gives no intrinsic value
to my scientific efforts; It does not explain to me why I can, and why
I should push these efforts to the uttermost, nor how I am Yours,
not in spite of what I know, but by reason of the light which the
truth known, has been able to put within me. When I study the
history of vanished civilizations, when I strive to reconstruct
Ninive or Byblos; when I identify old texts or grammatical forms,
how can all this interest You?

I have tried to answer this question, which cannot be evaded with
impunity, by saying to myself that I could unite myself to You by

means of the intention underlying my work. I wished to study for Your greater glory, I directed my studies to the good of souls, I persuaded myself that knowledge had a moral value from the secret idea which urged a man to study, and an apologetic value from the lustre which it gave to Your Church in the face of unbelievers. My work would be yours because You would approve of my intention, and because without this work there would be nothing but reprehensible idleness. I remember one of your faithful servants who made a scientific collection of butterflies, and who said to me in excuse: Well, after all I must do something!—I was never able to believe that this commonplace formula explained his entomological passion, nor the joy that took possession of him when he found some unknown lepidoptera.

If our knowledge only touched You through the intention of the *savant*, then, as this intention could also be found among the ignorant and the mediocre, You could not care whether we knew more or less than they. And it would be true to say that the content of my knowledge was a matter of indifference to You. It would then be with human knowledge as with bouquets of flowers which we should only choose by weight; chrysanthemum or lilies, tulips or columbine, no matter, we only think of ounces and pounds. The special flower-element would have been abstracted.

But if Truth is not an abstraction: if it is a Person and my Redeemer, then quite independently from the intention, knowledge is in itself good, even for a mortal man, and to know is to build up Truth and therefore to build up Christ among men. Science then becomes a divine business, which can without doubt be profaned, as the Bread of the Eucharist is profaned, but of which the most intrinsic law is identical with the very knowing of the Saviour of all men. Science must lead to this knowledge which is life eternal, and the complete revelation of what we are. All that turns science from this end, is sacrilegious, as he would be sacrilegious who would treat the Wine of the Sacrifice as merely an intoxicating drink.

Thus it is that those who do not find their path obstructed by other more urgent and more immediate duties, those who have leisure to learn, cannot let their minds lie fallow under the pretext that virtue alone is sufficient. We have need of something more than a mere excuse, we need a reason of greater urgency to dispense us from labouring to know; and if God treats ignorant people with more mercy, it is only because His providential arrangements have deprived them of so excellent a good.

Wherever truth is spoken we stammer something of the Person of the Word who is the Truth; and I can love my studies and my books as we love the stones of our house and the air of our native land. It is impossible that the last word of all human effort towards knowledge, should not be by right the one Christ. But man has the terrible power of making use of things against their end, and of soiling them by thus misusing them. To misuse science is not to pursue it too much, but to pursue it badly, that is to say to make it evil or not to take heed of concomitant duties. We are spirit and body, one and many, of to-day and to-morrow, and our obligations ought to be so arranged as not to be mutually destructive, they should be on good terms and not quarrel with each other. We can sin because we refuse to resign ourselves to our necessary ignorances, which are the conditions of greater knowledge.

What is true of science is true also of all human effort. Christ is Justice and He is the Life, as God is Being. From the blow of a blacksmith's hammer to a treatise on civil law, all that tends to order, peace and justice, all that mounts upwards and improves, all rises and tends towards God Our Saviour, the Truth made man.

THIRD
SERIES

DUC NOS QUO
TENDIMUS

PROLOGUE

TO THE THIRD SERIES

Ubi sum ego

There where I am

(*John xvii.* 24.)

IN a far deeper sense than we imagine, this present life is the prepa,
ration, the noviceship for our future life. It is the preparation for it-
not only because our good or evil actions will merit for us reward
or punishment on the other side of the grave, but because, even here
below, we are beginning to do what we shall do throughout eternity.
We are acquiring habits, approving principles, cultivating desires
which, long before the hour of death, already give to our soul its
special physiognomy, and fashion for us the face of one saved or
that of one lost.

The only thing then that is of consequence to us is to learn our
avocation of eternal happiness, to make trial of the function of the
elect. Grace in us is the beginning of glory; faith is already the
foundation of the beatific vision; charity regulates in us the perfect
union of our will with the divine, that union which will know no
break at death. The whole spiritual life is thus but the art of finding
God. It is excellent to trace out a programme of action; it is useful to
mark out our roads across the future, but above all it is necessary to
arrive. It is by its results and not by its ambitions that we judge of
the value of a method.

To find God! *Christum consequi!* In the fourth addition of the
Spiritual Exercises, Saint Ignatius tells us, so clearly as to admit of
no misunderstanding, that prayer is good when it leads to this end,
and that all effort to lead it elsewhere, or to make it leave this blessed
sanctuary, is labour lost, a superfluous and unrighteous solicitude,
sine anxietate progrediendi ulterius. For God is the ultimate goal, and
when we are conjoined with the Infinite we have only to rest in
giving ourselves, just as a ripe fruit which allows itself to be gathered
from the end of the branch.

To find God is no ordinary science, and yet the roads which lead
to Him are numberless, and the feet of little children, far in front of
us perhaps, have trodden them in all simplicity. Our difficulty is to
become simple once again and to look at things with unclouded
eyes. Our difficulty is to accept, to keep quiet when we have been
placed upon a stretcher, and not to call Our God, a God who frowns
upon us and is far away. We waver between revolt and despondency,
between weakness and pride, when, if we would but throw ourselves

on our knees before the one Redeemer, we could, perhaps, with light, regain our equilibrium. If we would but strip ourselves of all resistance we could meet with the Eternal.

To reach God! This third volume of thirty-three meditations tries to show that the thing is possible and that the conditions for success are fixed beforehand. There are sacrifices to be made, or rather there is one total, absolute sacrifice by which alone we shall be able to join ourselves to God. It is quite useless to wish to escape from this sacrifice of spiritual surrender, of poverty and of abnegation. The exigencies of the God-joined life are peremptory. The half-hearted learn it to their cost.

How we can go towards God; how He Himself comes towards us: such were the subjects of the first two volumes of this series. To-day we would wish to explain where it is He leads us, and towards what final end, His grace, capturing our will, intends to conduct us. There is no other goal but God; all ends by coming to the Saviour, and when our tendencies are in harmony with His, this ultimate meeting is Life eternal; and when our guilty will is antagonistic to His, this meeting ends in hell. Our whole existence is staked on this alternative. In order to prepare for unchangeable states it is necessary to reflect in silence; and in order to consent to indispensable sacrifices it is well to examine that to which they correspond.

If in these pages some expressions are found which appear to be rather harsh, it is hoped that no one will read into them anything of contempt. To-day we are certainly no better than our fathers, but we accept more willingly perhaps, to be brought, without circumlocution, face to face with the real. A religion which should offer itself with advantageous reductions as goods at a clearance sale, would certainly be foreign to the spirit of Christ, and could only meet with contemptuous acquiescence. Why should we not quite tranquilly admit that the truly Christian life is boundless in its exigencies, and that, in order to serve God according to the measure of our grace, we must suppress all the selfishness of our special points of view, and rejoice to be used for the one great work of the Redemption.

Otherwise nothing has been changed in the form of these little meditations, and those will be mistaken who hope to find in them either lyricism or controversy. Uninterrupted lyricism becomes speedily ridiculous; our prayer should be uninterrupted, it cannot therefore be developed, without serious harm, on the poetic mode. When, from the depths of our soul we shall have submitted ourselves to our whole duty, when dismal surroundings, lustreless spheres of life, dreary work are no longer obstacles to our prayer, then we can begin to pray always, and we shall find God unceasingly. In the desert we find all or nothing according to the desire we have brought with us. He who desires laughter and feasts dies there; he who seeks for solitude and peace returns and finds his refuge there. From the day that divine Grace implanted in us this need of reaching God, from the moment that we became the sheep of the fold and the sons of the house and the branches of the vine and the witnesses of the Word and the Apostles of the Gospel, it has become impossible for us to perfect ourselves unless we attain to the living and eternal goal, the Redeemer, the Son of Man.

In these volumes we have as it were put only dry crusts of bread. But because of the virtue of so many unknown Christians, the blessing of Christ will perhaps consent to transform these tiny fragments, as formerly in His own Galilee. May He be thanked beforehand. *In quo crescentes quotidie, ipsum tandem adipiscamur omnes. (Ignatius of Antioch.)*

PIERRE CHARLES, S.J.

Louvain. Feast of Saint Francis Xavier, 1923.

LXVII

Usque ad summum

Up to the brim

(*John ii.* 7.)

TO stimulate my laziness ten thousand pedagogues offer their good services. I am surrounded with heroic models; books swarm which set glorious examples before me. Why does all this disturbance leave me so cold? In my monotonous life, with the short breath of my desires, O my God, is it a mistake not to run the risk of climbing up the mountain peaks, but to seek instead, in my own zone, without music and without exploits, the measure of my perfection? You have nowhere said: Blessed are those who dream. I shall look then in Your Gospels, not for the foremost roles, but for the hidden immolations. It seems to me that they are of my variety, and that without pretentiousness, I can slip into their ranks.

When, at Cana, in order to strengthen the faith of Your disciples, You showed Your power and changed water into wine, near to the great amphora ranged against the wall, were standing the silent waiters. My God, I think these faithful, unobtrusive men can teach my duty to me. They said nothing, but in passing, almost as it were by stealth, Your Blessed Mother, who knew You, whispered to them: Whatsoever He shall say to you, do ye. The hint was understood. And when Your command rang out: Fill those water pots with water—without a word, by one swift act they filled them to the brim—*usque ad summum*. That was all and it was quite enough. No one could possibly ask them for another drop. Up to the brim! That is again a formula of perfection.

Do You desire that I make it mine, make it ours, O my God? They only poured insipid water, they had no other; and their poverty, by its contrast, was about to make Your power flash forth. I too have nothing but my will, my desire, my days and my years, and all that, poured into the eternal amphora, is very tasteless and colourless, without aroma and without vitality. I am at times dismayed, when I see that throughout whole periods of my life my memory yields up nothing but what is trifling and spiritless. My days have glided by like worthless water in the fountain basins of stone. My desires have poured themselves out upon my inglorious labours, and my fidelity itself has been in no way striking.

Usque ad summum.—But I can at least fulfil my duty to the uttermost, and not hold myself quit, until I can do no more. There is a way of pouring common water with a royal gesture, and of accomplishing a simple duty with perfection. I look round. My amphora

is not full. Through negligence or avarice I have not given You all
I could have given; I have kept back the disposal of my life, instead
of handing it over to You. I wished to save some outlet for my
liberty, and to keep the power of leaving You, as soon as Your
infinite perfection wearied me. I said: Let us take care not to give
too much; not to run to excess in self-sacrifice, or to lose any legitimate chance of enjoyment. After all, You did not tell those waiters
to fill the vessels to the brim. You left it to them to understand the
meaning of Your precept. What is it to fulfil our duty? And why
should we only stop short at the limits of the possible? Am I obliged
always to do the better thing? . . . Shall I spoil the divine work
because I adroitly hold back from the Supreme Master that which
He moreover has not demanded? Thus does false prudence argue
and harangue within my soul when I have to determine what part
shall be Yours, my God. This wisdom argues and I listen, and I try
to be cunning and to find out comfortable little solutions; to save
appearances and yet not to sacrifice more than I must. . . . And
these hateful bargainings, these miserable waverings, hinder me
from being free and from pouring into my life the maximum of
fidelity.

Usque ad summum.—Up to the brim, like little children who love
with their whole hearts, and sleep with clenched fists, and who run
at the top of their speed, laugh without restraint and weep their
very hearts out. It is because I am whole-hearted in nothing that I
have no meaning for myself and that my life appears to me like a
great note of interrogation, like a timorous stammering, a perpetual
holding back, a never-ending false start. Blessed are those who one
day said to God: Behold all the years that I shall have to live; see
them in their number ranged along the walls of time . . . Lord—
usque ad summum—up to the brim, without any reserve, by perpetual
vows I fill them with fidelity. You shall have them all, and it is You
who will fill my life.

Duty, dull and ordinary, self sacrifice and work . . . *ad summum.*
To fill my mind with light, as much as it can contain; to fill my will
with a mighty love, to fill my memory with healthful thoughts and
undying recollections, to give my whole energy to my task and all
my life to my neighbour, would that not be for me, O my God, the
sole salvation, and for You the only triumph? You need these hearts
full to overflowing; for all that was poured into the water-pots of
Cana was changed by You into miraculous wine, and it was therefore
this wine they would have wasted. Help me to understand this Gospel, to understand that I lose everything that I keep back from You.
I ought to deliver up all my treasures to You; and then I should know
that You are the Master, that all good comes down from You, and

that Your blessing upon my insipid virtues will give them the power of bringing joy to Your chosen ones.

Is there anything more ridiculous than to treasure up pure water when the springs are never-failing? Is there anything more senseless than to keep for ourselves ever-multiplying mediocrities, instead of making over all to God by one great, calm act without recall. I see those whom You watched at Cana while they carried out Your orders; I see them; their steady hands, without a tremor, poured on until the water-pots were full, and I say to myself that, through You, I may perhaps be able to understand the infinite meaning of this humble symbol.

LXVIII

THE most magnificent treatise on Architecture provides no one with a roof; for a shelter from the rain the rusty corrugated iron of an outhouse is of more value than the pages of Vitruvius. It is not enough for us to know and to think and to imagine and to infer, we must put our hand to the trowel; our trade is that of a builder. The works produced by us will judge us.

To build we must toil. I admire those people, without however understanding them, who speak to us of the service of God as of some soul-stirring poetry and an unfailing ecstasy. The hands of builders are grazed by the roughness of the bricks, and, from long use of the trowel, their palms have become hardened and their nails are all misshapen. Stone is resisting and heavy. We must strike upon it to make it obey us. It is rugged, full of sharp corners and cutting edges; it revenges itself on a man for the blows which he gives it, nor does it of itself take up its permanent place in its little bed of mortar.

I ask myself if I have really understood this harsh lesson. Hare-brained as I am, I have perhaps imagined that we could build with words, and like the heroes of old pagan fables, raise walls by blowing on our reed-pipes. Hard work dismays me. Is it really necessary to hammer the nails in order to drive them into the walls? Could we not try a method of persuasion, or at least work by pressure and not by blows? Could we not gently wear down the irregularities of the stone, instead of demolishing by one blow of the chisel, all that projects? Could we not build without hammer and without noise, without violence and without blows, by a simple decree, or a simple desire?

All those who are afraid of the real have thus wasted their time in foolish day-dreams. My God, help me to love hard labour. The stone of the building is myself, with all my fantastic forms, with so many outstanding defects, eccentric desires and lawless pretensions. The stone is myself with all that holds and clings to my soul, and which must be left there upon the ground before I can become, in Your hands, the docile block of granite, for ever steadfast. Your Providence has been obliged to hammer long on my resistance, to tear from me all that I would not willingly forego. These retrench-ments seem cruel; your chisel and its rough blows have at times caused revolt to surge within me. For so long now You have been hammering and I have said to myself, to prove You in the wrong, that You were implacable to my misery, that You were jealous of all that I desired and that Your sole thought was to thwart me. I have held such opinions, Lord, they are absurd it is true, but appearances were against You, and a stone would need to be very intelligent indeed not to harbour any bitterness against the workman that cuts it into shape. This intelligence has failed me. My lamentations have been but the measure of my stupidity. I always believe that the savage state is my normal one, and that those who mould and train me are dangerous enemies. I shall try with Your grace to resist no longer; I shall hold no more to my angularities, nor glory in escaping from Your mallet.

Aedificantes.—You are the builder, but I too should be one. It is not enough that I offer no resistance. You ask me to work efficaciously and to build. The weary work! The same action repeated one hundred thousand times; all those nameless stones, marked, as they are to be dressed, in accordance with an identical formula; and the wall which rises up, always the same at every level! You do not ask for projects of sublime virtue, but for efforts of real virtue. I wish to leave lasting work and to wound myself in working. My God, let us together bring forth solid virtue. I have never quite understood the meaning of that old word, a truly ecclesiastical one, *to edify.* I believed it meant something guarded, close, silent and attenuated. . . . I had not heard the noise of the building yard ring in its syllables, and I had not noticed that You asked me to be a builder, and to line up my good works methodically along the course of my days. But see, in my soul there is nothing that is firm, and in my actions there is nothing well advanced. Could You build with my weakness? Must I not renounce the hope of making my heavy indolence and my unstable clay rise up in the air? No! Palaces and churches and whole towns, to last for ever, are built of kneaded clay. It is sufficient that it allows itself to be well beaten and baked, then its native softness does not hinder it from enduring even as the granite of the mountains. My weakness will not be an obstacle if I accept to be kneaded by Your hands and to be passed through the kiln, keeping, even in the hour in which my fidelity is on trial, the form which You will have given me.

And if I am heavy, heavier than I think and certainly heavier than people have believed; if it seems that I can never raise myself, nor, above all, remain in heights of serene adoration, my God, I shall remember that stones, heavy slabs of stone, intersect each other in the vaults of Your Churches, and in the soaring mullions of stained-glass windows, and I shall say to myself, that upheld by the whole, they play their part most suitably, raised thus over our heads. Then perhaps, thanks to all those who in Your Church are in their places; thanks to the prophets and Apostles—*super fundamentum apostolorum et prophetarum*—thanks to all my neighbours, and to all the unknown people who have prayed for me; thanks above all to the Corner-stone, to the Chief Key-stone—*ipso summo angulari lapide*—which the Father has given to us in Your Person as Redeemer; thanks to Your plan of salvation and to Your mercy, I shall perhaps be able to keep my place not too unworthily, I, too, in Your heavenly Jerusalem and become of some use in Your eternal work. I do not refuse to hold firm, but I am incapable of putting myself in place. I have no meaning unless I stay in Your hands. You alone know what is to be done with me and to what idea my being answers in the concert of Your Glory. *Electi lapides.*

LXIX

I MUST confess, O Lord, this seems to me a hard saying. I have feared it at times, and I dared not look it in the face. It appeared to me unreal and as disquieting as a ghost. When death comes to take away her children, surely I cannot say that the weeping mother is happy; when I see those little ones resting their pale faces on their white pillows, and lying there so weak and suffering, I dare not say they are about to be a cause of joy to their sobbing parents. My God, I have so often had to comfort those in sorrow, tell me then, can we, without cruelty, scatter Your message over all those griefs, and offer our congratulations when the time comes for condolence? I know indeed that this *Beati* would rouse revolt and ring like derision in striking thus upon real suffering. For in truth, my God, we suffer, and suffer much upon our earth, and if the race of man has never ceased from weeping, it is because death under every form has never ceased from its hard blows. I wish that You would enter with me into that room where brothers and sisters, father and mother are all in tears; I wish You would visit that house with me—I know it well —from whence the children one after another have gone forth in coffins, each just a little longer than the last. An abode of happiness! Why should we take from these unfortunate ones the thing to which they cling in their distress, the right to bewail their sorrow? Why say to them—it seems so tactless—why say to them we envy them their lot, and that they do not understand their good fortune?

Tell me, You who formerly taught Your Apostles—*domi*, in secret—the hidden meaning of the parables, teach me the meaning of Your strange expressions, and remove the scandal of these alarming paradoxes. I fancy that up to this I have understood nothing of this beatitude of tears, and I am always inclined, when I do not understand a thing, to believe that there is nothing to be understood.

Beati qui lugent.—We can then weep without incurring blame or being mediocre. Tears disqualify no one. I believe indeed that, at the time when You spoke upon the mountain, in the world of those days, this would not have been admitted. Tears were considered a weakness, in calling them a blessing You at least cleared them from this opprobrium, and You have thus allowed us to be true. Your teaching does not say that it is wrong to weep. You put aside that stoic harshness which saw unreasonableness in sorrow, and you will not reproach mothers who weep for the death of a mortal son. It was not with logic nor with sophisms that You wished to heal our wounds; and in order to beatify our tears You first of all allowed them to flow in torrents. We are already so accustomed to this gentle wisdom that we no longer thank You for having taught it to us, or for having taken from our sufferings all semblance of cowardice and all the harshness of remorse.

But that is not all. You have never said that suffering does not hurt. You have only declared that those who mourn have, in Your eyes, a special right to consolation. You have promised that towards them Your justice will be biased and Your severity without a sting. To have been unhappy is already a little like to be deserving. And from eyes that have wept much, Your judgments will not readily cause fresh tears to flow.

I thank You for having hidden these good tidings in our miseries, and for having taught us, not that suffering was a pleasure, but that it concealed a hope, and offered a protection. Under our sorrows we are sheltered from Your severity, and that which the hermit's long practice of virtue produced, true tears can also bring to flower.

Your wisdom is so harmonious and so balanced, but we are slow to believe, and Your Beatitudes, to be rightly understood, have need of an inward grace to interpret them to us, and of that healing peacefulness which, unknown to us, You pour into docile hearts. The chief of Your consolations is that which enables us to stand firm under the storm and not to scatter ourselves abroad in useless lamentations. Teach me to suffer well, to suffer as I should.

I cannot say to the sick and to orphans that they are happy, and that all the world is envying them, and yet I can truly say that a divine vocation has marked them for its own. To please You, they need wipe away no trace of tears. You are not one of those easily offended masters, so convinced that their mere presence is the height of happiness to others, that they are annoyed, as if it were a failure in politeness, when any look sad in their company. You have not asked that children should grow up in order to draw near to You. Like all our little ones, who are restless, and ill-mannered, shocking to our refinement and fastidiousness, those Galilean rustics had gross defects and were wanting in good breeding. You took them as they were and closed Your Redeemer's arms around them. You always take men as they are. You do not ask that we should have ceased from suffering and from weeping in order to come and claim our places in the Kingdom and appropriate our share in Your mercy. The only evil tears are guilty ones of anger, jealousy and hypocritical weakness.

And now I ask myself if I have filled up the measure of my tears. I fear that to the paucity of my merits will be added the penury of my sorrows. I fear on Your side a too kind Providence! When I see others weeping round me over some grief in which I have no part, I have a vague, uneasy impression that I have deserted my post or that I am not taking my share of the burden.

I shall pray to You for those who mourn. In former days this was done with love throughout Christendom. I who up to this, have not had experience of long and merciless illness, and have only seen in others continuous and devouring sorrow, I beg of You to put well in front of me, in Your Grace and in Your Paradise, all those poor people whose eyes are wet with tears, the desolate, the abandoned, all to whom life is hard and whose hearts are bleeding, all the sick and all the destitute. Fill them, console them according to Your promise and do not trouble about me till after that.

LXX

I HAD been told that kings were becoming rare. I went down into the streets and I found them by the hundreds! The little children of the poor! I watched them for long that I might discover what God wished to say to me through them, and find out what alms their care-free ways would offer me in the shape of timely lessons. These little ones behave as kings; alone of all people they are everywhere at home. I have seen them going into our museums, flocking together in crowds before the great glass cases where the mummies of the Pharaohs sleep; setting out to hunt for birds' nests, and greeting with clapping of their hands the great international express as it dashed along the lines. Each day their wonder is renewed; it is for them bands play, for them the wedding coaches draw up in lines before the churches, for them the great shops are lighted up. It is for them the rain pours and the sun shines. We, the disagreeable, busy people, scowl when it rains, we have to save our hats and boots, but they! they laugh in the downpour, one would think they had ordered it expressly for their own enjoyment. They play for hours under a cracked gutter, and they organize naval expeditions and cruising squadrons of floating sticks in puddles of water. They find a treasure in an empty sweetbox, and they beat rousing marches and all-conquering airs on a broken kettle. In this one word *play* they have hidden more good fortune than Cæsar had in his expedition into Gaul; and Alexander was less happy on the evening of Arbela, when he had defeated Darius, than they are when they have gathered up the chestnuts from under the yellow leaves of autumn, or when they have caught a cockchafer in the beech-woods.

My God, You would certainly love these little kings were You to return amongst us; You would gather them together as in former days, You would tell them stories, and You would repeat again to all disdainful people, that unless they became like these children they would never find their way into Your home. You would love them, but no, You do love them. It is impossible that You could have commanded us to model ourselves on the Galilean children whom we never met. Your models are contemporary, as Your commands are eternal, and it is round about us we should look to learn how to fashion for ourselves royal souls, and to understand how to become masters of the Kingdom of Heaven—*ipsorum est regnum cælorum.*

Dissatisfaction consumes me. I no longer enjoy anything beautiful, for covetousness has denaturalized me. Men are strange beings. They imagine that in order to possess a thing they must be able to exclude their neighbours from all share in it, and that padlocks, grills, gratings and safes are the conditions of all real wealth. If, O my God, You had not placed the stars out of reach of their hands there is little doubt they would have already extinguished those lights, they would have surveyed the firmament, under pretext of not leaving it unemployed. They do not know that at the fountain-head of all real virtue there must be a royal and magnificent reckless ness. They do not know that the faithful soul is delivered from all anguish and all fear, and feels herself at home everywhere, because she wishes herself to be everywhere in Your home.

I wish that I could walk through this beautiful dwelling-place which is Your work, with the serene tranquillity of the children of the poor playing on the grass. It is not necessary to become childish once again, but it is necessary to understand that all voluntary thralldom is childishness, and that liberty of spirit is Your gift.

Jealous, vindictive, spiteful, pleased with nothing unless it be in some way connected with ourselves, and foreseeing by shrewd examinations what our sacrifices will bring us in return, our calculations burden us and joy passes us by. This Beatitude! We leave it piously, like a faded flower between the leaves of the Gospel: it is no longer anything more than a touching theory. We have disco- vered convenient commentaries which allow us to be avaricious and covetous. Who amongst us would agree to take at one sweep all the baggage which he carries round with him, and to make a great pile of it by the wayside, leave it there without an inventory or a back- ward glance, then go off down the road singing softly to himself the Magnificat of freed souls, and the hymn of the Beatitudes?

And yet, my God, it would mean deliverance, and in this poverty of spirit, desiring only You, I should rejoice at all that happened to me, and still more at all that did not happen. Day and night would abound with messages for me, and I should at last realize that the whole sky, peopled as it is with stars, was shining for me. Each time that we examine ourselves to find out why we have done wrong, we discover, at the starting point of our calamity, a desertion. We have not believed in the beneficent power of poverty. So it is, that to describe the heroism of her Confessors, to explain the deserts of millions of the unknown faithful, the Church takes up the words of Scripture and is content to say quite simply that these friends of God have not put their hope in wealth and in possessions. *Qui non speravit in pecunia et thesauris.* (*Eccles.* xxxi. 8.)

Wealth, my God! Is it of money only that they speak to us? No, but of all riches to which we cling and of which money is the symbol. The children of the poor, with a candle in a paper lantern at the end of a stick, and with a gold paper star as a diadem, each year at the time of the Epiphany, in our small provincial towns, begin once more the journey of the Magi. Had I the same faith and the same simplicity could I ever think of despising Your gifts; could I pass, disdainful and sceptical, through the midst of the piled up wonders which make the world of souls and the world of things? Should I not be as these little ones each evening, exhilarated by the summer sun or enchanted by the winter snow, falling to sleep trustfully as they do, without a care, in obedience to the prayer of Compline: *in pace, in idipsum dormiam et requiescam?* And heaven! What is it but the Beatitude of the poor of whom You alone have become the riches.

Q

LXXI

WHO? The rich of course? Not at all; the poor shall enjoy this plenitude.—*Edent pauperes*. I wish, O my God, to come back once more this evening on this eternal lesson of poverty. We need it. We are dying from not being truly poor; we are going astray because this light-house, which is unequalled in power, does not shine before our blinded eyes and because we have forgotten by what roads of deprivation we reach at length eternal opulence. Poverty! We despise it, and the poor man too, in spite of our beautiful phrases. Tattered and miserable poverty, who among us will consent to kiss its feet? Who above all believes that it would be an honour to him to do this? Who dreams of saying thank you, not to the one who gives the alms, but to the poor man who accepts it?

Poverty would overthrow our false ideas. It alone is splendid. It is true. . . . Our middle-class way of life understands nothing about it. Our luxury is wholly in error, and we alas! believe that virtue is a kind of luxury. Our sole accomplishment is that of producing pagan and futile ornaments and we have not yet learnt to look at the beautiful countenance of simple things. All declamation is a sin against genuine poverty. And I declaim without truce throughout the course of my life. I vociferate, I gesticulate and apostrophize; I set myself in relief and inflate myself that I may occupy more room. There is nothing less poor than all this eloquence. Sometimes even when I speak to You, my God, this luxury of bad taste finds its way into my discourses. I come into Your presence bedizened with accessories, I utter stilted compliments and like a *parvenu* I make my gilding glitter.

Who is there who has ever fed himself on rhetoric? Whose hunger has ever been assuaged with the pulp of phrases? Who has ever grown stronger by absorbing long words? Truth, poor and honest, such as it came from Your hands, my God, that alone can strengthen us. All that we add to it is harmful—a deceitful wealth, which my soul, through Your grace, begins to loathe. The forest is not tampered with by gardeners so that it may appear greater or less savage; in the stables the cattle bellow unrestrainedly; and the fruits of the orchard have not retained their bloom when we gather them on the damp grass after the storms of autumn, but they are without sham and they give themselves for what they are worth.

I have need of this sincerity. I see people who, in order to influence their neighbours pretend to be well up in matters of which they are wholly ignorant, or to know things their laziness has never allowed them to learn; I see some who put all their hope in a policy of bluff, and who conceal their emptiness under borrowed formulæ, under conventional axioms and premeditated silences. These are the false rich, all their tinsel is an injury to the simplicity of Your Grace.

This does not mean that we should be bearish and do away with politeness. Only savages hold that truth requires us to be rough and off hand. All restraint that we impose upon ourselves in order to be useful to others, to ease their burden and make their labour lighter, all trouble that we set down to our own account is a pretension that we abdicate, and a forward step on the royal road of all-sufficing poverty. But that which is odious is to hide ourselves behind lying appearances and to deceive others as to our own qualities or to the worth of that which we do. I will not describe my virtue of deal as heart of oak; I will not dye my evasions in the colour of prudence, nor dress up my inertia in submissiveness. I will not call my incapacity for thinking, good sense, nor twist my customs into venerable traditions. I will not let people think that I have known a thing for long which a chance communication has just taught me, nor that I have pondered deeply upon problems over which my mind has merely skimmed. My entire life, established upon truth, would be a life that was poor, beautiful and holy. Rust and moth could not consume that which no longer had within it any falsehood.

But I am afraid to be nothing more than just myself; and, having no weapons to defend myself, I seek at least for a mask behind which I can hide. Much courage is needed to be voluntarily poor and not to add apocryphal accessories to the essentials which alone should suffice for us. We despise all that is not noisy and gaudy; we construct complicated façades, we fasten pendants and scroll-patterns to the ceilings of our houses and we overload with ornament our furniture, our discourses and our way of life. When will You come, O my God, to restore our lost sincerity to us, and to put upon our eyes the remedy which gave back his sight to Tobias? Make us see the splendour of that which is unadulterated; in the path of that ray of light we could understand the wealth of poverty.

The joy of a frugal life and of geniune feelings! Joy of simple love, of straightforward trust, which blooms in clumps like the potentilla, on the poorest soil; joy of possessing nothing but that which is eternal, and of having dissolved our miseries in the whole-hearted sincerity of their avowal; oy of being poised in equilibrium and of being able to keep, in our grown-up souls, the freshness of childhood! After all God has no accessories and His riches is His being. There is no need to twist and turn my virtues, nor to take affected attitudes and give myself great majestic airs, but only to establish myself for ever in the true as in my home.

Purify me, O my God, from being a flatterer or from desiring adulation; hinder me from delighting in what is false; give me an over-mastering love of the real. Sweep from me by one final act all craftiness, all mean ways and petty subterfuges, and all that childish strategy which we think so very clever. I desire to be honest, honest in the same way as things are honest, in the manner of the lilies of the field and the sparrows of the streets; You yourself proposed them to us as our models. What a relief, my God, to be no longer obliged to occupy ourselves in constructing falsehoods.

LXXII

Discipulus ille non moritu
That disciple will not die
(*John xxi. 23.*)

WHEN on the day of the Ascension, You were lost to sight in the far-off mists upon the mountain planted with the olive-trees, Your disciples, not knowing what to make of it, remained for long with their eyes fixed upon Your wake, believing that You would reappear and continue Your discourses with them. But You did not reappear upon the mountain and their eyes sought You vainly in the evening when in the Cenacle, the doors being closed.

And yet You needed to have witnesses of Yourself here below. When You were gone it was these Your Apostles, who would continue Your life. In looking upon them we should find, in their words and in their actions, the relics of Your teaching and of Your commands. When speaking to them You had said: He that heareth you heareth Me; and he that despiseth you despiseth Me. They were Your living signs. The Christians gathered round them in order to keep near to You, and listened for the echo of Your words in their voices.

But death did not forget the sons of men. One by one Your Apostles passed away and John alone was left, John of Ephesus, who had leant upon Your breast on the evening of the First Eucharistic feast. And a saying went abroad among the faithful: *Discipulus ille non moritur*, that disciple will not die. He will remain, a persistent watcher on the ramparts of the Holy City, until the day when, coming from afar in the dust of the roads or on the summit of the clouds, You would reappear to judge Your servants. Was it not indeed necessary that one of those who had known You should remain among us to recognize You on the great day and to say to us: It is He indeed! Was it not necessary that one human soul should be able to bridge the space between Your two comings with his own experience, and in the face of all the illusions and deceits of Antichrist, to guarantee the identity of the Son of Man?

Discipulus ille non moritur.—Why then did he also disappear when the number of his days had been accomplished? Why did he go off to sleep in his tomb like the prophets of old? Who now is to carry on this holy office and reveal Him who is to come?

The disciple who does not die, O my God, has been long since placed in our midst by You, and the day on which You said of the poor that all that was done to them was done to You Yourself, that day they began their holy mission among us, and the *mihi fecistis* has consecrated it. That disciple does not die. *Semper pauperes habetis vobiscum.* (*Matt.* xxvi.11.) If we had more faith, we would look on them with more respect and with more tender feelings.

But we have forgotten this, and our faith is slumbering. We have not met the gaze of Christ in the eyes of the poor, of Christ Himself who watches us.

When he took bread into His Venerable Hands, He gave it to His Apostles saying: This is My Body delivered for you. And from that day, because of this word which consecrates them, the faith of Christian souls prostrates itself before the Hosts in our Tabernacles, for under these mean and humble appearances faith sees Christ present, whose power never dies.

When He wished to carry on His work here below, He passed on His power to His disciples, not permitting that our obedience should ever attempt to distinguish between them and Himself: *Qui vos audit me audit* (*Luke* x. 16)—and from that day, because of this word which consecrates them, the faith of Christian souls bows down before the priests, for under appearances which are very weak and often very rough, faith sees Christ present, whose power never dies.

When He wished to teach the world the secret of universal love and to sow amongst us the seed of supernatural mercy, He said, thinking of the poor, of those who suffer and who have nothing: All that you will do to them you do to Me, I do not wish that between them and Me your love should ever attempt to make a distinction. . . . And since that day, because of this word which transfigures and consecrates them, the faith of Christian souls should go on its knees before the poor, and see, beneath those disconcerting and miserable exteriors, Christ present, whose power never dies.

The witness of Bethlehem and of the days of distress, the witness of the Son of Man who had not where to lay His head; the witness of the Man of Sorrows crushed by a whole people; the witness of the Redemption and the symbol of crippled humanity—*discipulus non moritur*—this witness, this disciple does not die, since the poor are with us.

Why ask by what name they are called? Let no one question them —*scientes quia Dominus est* (*John* xxi. 12)—all those who suffer, apart from sin, are in some way "the Lord."

When I wish to renew the strength of my faith and make myself familiar with the features of my final Judge; when I wish to prepare for the Second Coming, in order to make no mistake on the day of the great summons, but to recognize instantly Him, the mere sight of Whom will be eternal bliss; when I wish to rid myself of all my miseries, I shall draw near to the poor and shall try to touch the hem of their garments. My God, the poor hold a sacred office in our midst. We ought not to forget it. There is a Christian way of looking on them and of drawing near to them. Forgive me for not having understood it sooner, and for having kept untrue thoughts in my hard heart. I was unwilling to see in these needy ones anything more than importunate beggars; I thought that my obligations were satisfied if I threw an alms to them, adding a forced smile and some stiff phrases on great occasions. I did not dare to allow Your light to enter freely into my soul. My prejudices have created darkness within me. . . . I have found Your poor tolerably troublesome. It seemed to me that their chief business was to thank me, and that they acquitted themselves very badly of this obligation. I have even calumniated them in declaring them to be incapable of truly noble virtue, and in attributing the monopoly of worth to people of my caste. And yet this poor abject man, empty of valour and of grandeur, clothed in rags and misery—my act of contrition cries out to me that it is I myself, and all the disdain that I have had for others, like heavy stones thrown upwards to the stars, falls back upon my own head. Give me this humble heart, which will make me love Your poor sincerely, and reconcile me with that which I am myself.

LXXIII

Infideli deterior
Worse than an infidel
(1 Tim. v. 8.)

I HAVE always thought those people were endowed with a good judgement who acknowledged my intelligence, and that those who believed in my worth showed discernment; but as soon as there is any appearance of questioning my excellence, I ask for explanations, I require proofs and sometimes I demand apologies. I have fed my pride on what was from first to last pure grace; I have sought within myself for the cause of my vocation to supernatural faith and for the well-spring of my worth. Deign, O my God, this evening, by blows of harsh truth to break down this false attitude for ever. I know indeed that I can never become Your Apostle unless humility not only possesses me but enchants me; but I do not see clearly how I can present myself before the unbelievers without servile lowliness and without imperious arrogance, without disdain and without timidity. Since I am to evangelize them, it is necessary that they listen to me and that I command respect; but since You are the one Master, it is necessary that I efface myself and decrease. Could You not, O Eternal Wisdom, enlighten my darkness and remove the obstacles? Show me what I am and in pursuance of what divine plan, the gift of God has been passed on to me.

Your ways are always identical. You are recognized by the same signs. By reflecting on Your visible advent I have every chance of understanding Your secret thoughts, and salutary lessons will follow for me.

You were first of all announced to the people of Israel; it was in a body taken from that race that You clothed Yourself, and it was at Bethlehem that, silent and hidden, You asked that room should be made for You. And for You no room was made, and among those whom You came to save, not one troubled or disturbed himself. You chose this people and this village of Judea. In no other place would You have been received so badly. The Jerusalem of Your choice killed the prophets and stoned Your envoys. She understood nothing of Your pursuing Providence, which spread out protecting wings over all this weakness, as if to shelter chickens. This people, Your own people, You called the people "who hated without cause," and for centuries You had known that they were stiff-necked and hard of heart. Why did You begin Your work of Redemption at the point of most resistance? Why let Your first words of mercy fall upon ears so dull of hearing, and why do signs before veiled eyes?

Tyre and Sidon would have taken haircloth and the garb of penance
if You had but allowed them to see You, and Niniveh, cruel Niniveh
would have been saved by those discourses for which they insulted
You with the name of Beelzebub. Why did You sow Your seed on
rocky ground? Why did You first speak to the most rebellious
ones? . . .

When we wish to remove a heap of sand it is of no use to begin
our work at the top. We can only carry off what is above the spade
and all the rest remains on the ground. We must attack the heap at
its lowest part, and it is quite close to the ground that we must push
in our tool. You came to save the whole human race. Did You
perhaps wish to begin at the very bottom? And may not the people
first called have been the most unworthy? Such tactics are quite
according to Your customs. You did not will to become an Angel,
but to be born of the race of Abraham and to begin the work of our
regeneration at the lowest level of our weakness. It was needful to
gather up mankind from the depths of his misery, and to busy
Yourself first with the most grievously sick, as a doctor who
neglects his convalescents for a dangerous case, and who saves those
who are dying. Your disciple, Saint Augustine, had at first thought
the contrary, he believed that You had spoken to those whom Your
foreknowledge showed You would be docile; but the evidence of
Your Gospel convinced him of his error and he himself refuted it in
his Retractations. No, the first called are not the most worthy and
the marriage feast has not received them. They are not the most
worthy, perhaps they are the least prepared to receive You well.

Ah! if You had been born on the banks of the Ganges, or on the
slopes of Mount Vindhya; on the plains of China or under the sky of
Japan; even if You had appeared among the Redskins whom our
cruel inhumanity has massacred, or among the Negroes whom our
pride is crushing; if You had not chosen to begin Your work with
us, the pretentious, the cavillers and the covetous. . . . My God,
You would perhaps have met with a better reception; they would
have welcomed You gladly, and those peoples, seated in a ring
around the Incarnate Master, would have consoled Your Church far
better than we have done. You chose us because we were hard,
because we were swift to stone our prophets, because the first shock
of Your Redemptive power should fall upon Your most terrible
enemies; because Your first pardon should go to the greatest sinners
and because You always take upon Yourself the hardest tasks.

Thus the Apostle, the missionary should be so humble as to be
almost apologetic for his people. He brings to the Hindus, the
Chinese or the Negroes, not a personal treasure, but the treasure of
God. He takes it to them saying: To you, O people, this treasure

should first have been confided, and my apostleship in your midst is as it were a restitution. Yes, it is more a restitution than a gift. If God had chosen to begin His Redemption among you, you would have taken up the hymn of Christmas with less discordant voices and hearts far more united than are ours. It is time you should receive your part of this treasure, which of course you do not merit, but of which you were less unworthy than we were; and just as the Greeks surpassed the Jews who were called before them, so will you, it is our one hope, surpass us in fervour, in self-sacrifice, in total submissiveness, and in adoration in presence of the sole Redeemer and the true Father.

My God, I beseech You implant these thoughts within me and I shall guard Your gift with humility, and even in Your gifts and in Your favours I shall find a means of beating down my pride. For if ever I should become so infatuated with myself as to believe that You chose me because I was the most lovable, I should become at once worse than the unbeliever—*infideli deterior*.

LXXIV

YOUR Holy Spirit is mysterious, Lord. We hear Him so little, and yet His voice, we are told in the Liturgy for Pentecost, resounds to the ends of the earth; and You Yourself announced Him as the one who would teach us all things and recall to our minds, at the needful moment, all Your doctrine. Ought we not to know Him better? And is it not a scandal that so many of the baptized could answer as those poor men of Ephesus: We have not so much as heard whether there be a Holy Spirit.

The Sanctifier works in hidden ways, unceasingly. Perhaps it is because He is everywhere that we do not see Him; perhaps because He is as the very air we breathe, no special aroma betrays His presence. It is not possible that He has been, as it were, relegated to some out-of-the-way corner; it is not true that a good work however humble can be unconnected with His influence or withdrawn from His initiative. He is the source of all holy inspirations, and it is in His silence that our supernatural being takes its root. Without uttering a word He took possession of us at Baptism, and since that day He has said nothing. Those who work answer, not by words but by deeds, and I should be, in face of all who deny and all who doubt, the living answer of the Holy Spirit.

We always imagine that only the unusual is of importance. The Holy Spirit has moulded the world and souls of men for centuries, and we, blind ones, have not as yet seen anything.

If I wish to judge of the action of gravity, would it be enough for me to handle heavy objects? Would it be sufficient to look at all that falls and breaks itself? The pointed arches under which I pray, and the ceiling under which I work, are only held in place by an effect of gravitation; and it is because it has weight that the slender spire of the church can become a dweller of the air.

Tears flow down the face of a child and the earth turns on its axis, but in both cases it is by the same law. Gravitation enters through the windows of a hospital ward under the form of a soft breeze passing over the damp brows of the patients and making the white curtains quiver; the same law which hurls down the avalanche makes the pink-veined petals fall quite quietly beneath the apple trees; gravitation which causes the air balloon to rise forces the parachute to descend; and the path of a downy feather which is carried by the wind over the meadows and caught by the bearded grasses, the quivering of the flags, the advance of the needle in the hands of the embroiderer, the stability of the continents and the security of fleets, all that stirs and all that stays quite still, all is directed, governed by this invisible power which supports our heads upon the pillow when we sleep and keeps us in our coffins when they bury us.

Your Spirit, my God, is at the starting point of all supernatural movements; it is He who has prepared them before we had any knowledge of them. He it is who regulates the course of the world, and the history of souls, and who must gradually transform all into Your image. When Cæsar advanced into Gaul, he did not know that the Spirit went before him to prepare the way of the Gospel. When Augustus ordered the enrolment of his whole empire, he did not know that he was but the instrument of the Spirit for the fulfilling of the Scriptures. Alexander never knew why he led his Macedonians beyond the kingdom of Porus, and Carthage was unaware that she had a divine mission to accomplish. Your Spirit is not seen, but I know well that in battles which are managed as they should be the Commander-in-Chief is never seen. He is felt everywhere, but is seen nowhere. It is only in disastrous, unpremeditated combats and in days of defeat that the staff, instead of co-ordinating the common action, mingle with it. The work of Your Spirit surrounds us on all sides. He is the decisive cause that is not seen but is everywhere felt, and if we had a more living faith we should fall upon our knees at the mere recital of a page of history, of that history which we, in our great folly, call profane.

In the secret places of our hearts too, the Spirit carries on this same work. We should never end were we to try to tell of all His marvels. He who directs the whole Church and the world, inspires a baby boy in an infant's class to deprive himself of a sugar plum, and He encourages a little girl not to cry although she has a toothache. Since He is at the starting point of all meritorious actions, we have the right to say that, through our mothers, He watched beside our cradles; we have the right to say that through our Apostles He has taken possession of distant continents, and has carried the Good Tidings to the unbelievers; we have the right to say that His love prepared all reconciliations and urged on all self-sacrifice, and that the virtues springing up around us, like trees in a virgin forest, have been born from seeds which He has sown and have grown, thanks to His care.

Lumen Cordium.—What a strange light, and one which divinely illuminates my life and those of others! It is forbidden to see things otherwise than in their relations willed by God; it is false to pretend that the action of the Holy Spirit is limited to a little sphere in the great work of Creation, as if the Three Divine Persons, after the fashion of the gods of fables, had been obliged to share among themselves portions of the Universe, and as if the sanctification of the world did not imply a change, a regeneration of the whole. No, nothing is outside the province of the Holy Spirit. It was He who prepared in a crevice in the rock the hollow in which Rosalie of Palermo lived, and the sacred cavern of Subiaco, and the Franciscan refuge of Alverno. He made ready the Appian way that Paul might enter Rome, and the olive-trees of Gethsemane to shelter the Agony of the Word. He has organized my whole existence, and it is from the depths of the Holy Trinity that this impulse of helpful energy, or of compassion, or of prayer, has come to me. One sole pulsation gives its measured movement to the supernatural life of the whole Church, as one sole force of gravitation causes all the stones of our earth to fall, and as one sole star illuminates all our days and pours its light from the eyes of Abraham even to our own.

My God, Your Spirit is hidden because He is strong. He is silent because He is eternal and He does not hasten because nothing, except that which wills to be lost, withstands His gentleness.

LXXV

THE best method by which to make us realize the value of a thing is, at times, to suppose it gone, and then to examine the extent of the vacancy that its disappearance would cause in our lives. We only know the worth of bread in days of famine; this proverb, old as the world, is still rich with new lessons for us.

I woke up this morning. Before I had time to make the sign of the Cross, at the very moment that I was raising my hand to my forehead, the forehead of one who had been baptized, a phantom voice cried out: Grace is no more! Grace has gone, and with it all its following. Seek it no more throughout this world, where henceforth you will find yourself alone.

Grace has gone. God has withdrawn it. It has been engulfed like the vessel over which the last rings of the rippled waters close. Then the Sign of the Cross has no longer any meaning. I shall have to begin my day without this primordial consecration. From over my prie-dieu, the Crucifix on which I was wont to look has gone. The invisible messenger has withdrawn it. Since Grace was abolished its signs have no reason to exist. I shall never again see the image of the Redeemer. Never again will any sing the *Pie Jesu.* I wished to go to the church. It too had disappeared. In its place was a great empty space: building lands, on which within six months they will have raised up shops and banks. No more altars and no more priests, no confessional and no absolution. In the cemeteries our dead no longer await a blessed resurrection; there is no society of Saints to whom we can direct our prayers. My guardian Angel? Vanished! I am alone. My rosary, my missal, the holy water font, formerly so welcoming, open to all like the kindness of Christ, with no ill-feeling and without any anger; faithful and motionless, and its great Cherubim with outspread wings who held out to us the marble shell! This old font too has disappeared. Our Blessed Lady is no more. Our sister and our mothers will no longer be called Mary. I have no patron saint. Our bells will now be silent. The little convents of the town have been extinguished in the night like lights blown out. There is no Catechism taught in school, no evening prayer, no Vespers and no parish priest. We are quite alone. Rome is no more than the town of Cæsar, Lourdes is but a grotto flooded by the inundations of the Gave, Paray-le-Monial is again but a cluster of wild hazels, and nowhere will our hill-tops now be crowned with great basilicas. Your marriage-tie will not be blessed; your sins will not be forgiven; no one will kneel to pray by you in your agony and your dead hands will not be clasped. You are alone. There is no more grace and Jesus Christ is nothing but a name!

But with the vanishing of the visible Church the welfare of souls is in jeopardy. We are too solitary to be able to fight successfully against the evil desires which dwell within us. The long-drawn patience and the gentle allurements of Grace, the desire for self-immolation, the need of sacrifice, love without reserves, kindness without any discount, behold all this is finished with; and like a flower which we cease to cultivate and which returning to its savage state becomes once more small, without brilliance and without perfume; like a fruit which is by nature sour, and only sweetened by the gardener's care, I feel myself again becoming what I was by nature: vindictive and hopeless, spiteful and violent, desirous of enriching myself at the expense of others, and eager to fleece the weaker ones among us. And round me I see the same hard faces, the same selfish designs, the same evil suspicions and all the bitterness which rises again to the surface like polluted foam and grey-blue seaweed floating on the angry billows. We are too solitary, and this solitude has nothing pacifying in it. It is like the solitude of the damned who suffer from being harassed by each other. Without grace we are for ourselves full of snares and our security has disappeared.

Beyond these visible effects of grace there lies all the immense expanse of the invisible: with life eternal and happiness that knows no twilight; with unsuspected vocations which will flower at the hour of the Spirit; with all that silent Providence which, unknown to us, unceasingly protects us. All that has vanished. . . . There is no more grace. My God, were Grace to diasppear my whole being would be shattered; I should become blind, like animals that live in light-less caverns; I should discern nothing but the rumblings of my powerless rage, or the gloomy sorrows of my cureless ruin. But You are the Saviour, and through You we have the right to look to the Father and to receive the Spirit; through You, our Mother Church abides and watches over us, and there is balm for every wound and useful tasks for all our powers.

Thank You for this immense work! I am so accustomed to Your mercy that I easily fail to appreciate its wholly gratuitous character. I install myself in it, just as we seat ourselves on the top of a cliff without asking permission of the ocean or of the rocks. Thank You for having created me, and still more for having given Yourself—Your Grace!

I understand now how Saint Ignatius declared that it was all sufficient for him, and that with Grace in his life he could want for nothing. Thank You for having allowed me to kneel down before You, for having heard me when I called to You, for not having shut up Your heaven after the great fault at the beginning, and for having had mercy on us! I have no wish to be dispensed from saying my Kyrie eleison. It is not a morbid taste for spoilt things, it is the need of truth that makes me find joy, unutterable joy, in Your pardon. Thank You for Your compassionate Mother and for all our holy patrons; for the unknown martyrs and all the crowd of humble virtues which form a hedgerow by the path of my brief journey! The Angelus has soared above my life, and it is in Your Grace that I wish to die and that I hope to rise again. You are so great and Your mercies are above all Your works.

People have said to me at times: Beware of human respect and do not blush to believe in Grace. My God, how remote and how irrelevant is such a speech! Do we recommend to a fiancé not to be ashamed of the one he loves? Can human respect exist in the company of that in which we glory. *Gratia Dei sum id quod sum.* (1 *Cor.* xv. 10) Your Grace has made me. *Deo Gratias!*

LXXVI

Respiciens retro
Looking back
(*Luke ix. 62.*)

YOU have forbidden us this action. You have said that to turn our heads towards the horizon of the past was to become unworthy of You. My God, I do not quite understand this forcible expression. Does it mean that we should live in perpetual forgetfulness? Should we, as children do, begin each day in our lives with candid freshness, unsullied by a breath of memory? Through Your Church, You recommend us to examine our conscience and to bring to the Sacrament of Your pardon a list of our faults. How shall we succeed in making a good confession if we never look back? How shall we grow in wisdom if we abolish the experience of yesterdays? How avoid future accidents if we never reflect on our old-time mistakes?

And yet Your assertion is absolute, and I already have a presentiment that it must be true. In spite of my darkness I see filtering through Your words a ray of living light, as in the night, underneath a door, we see a luminous pencil sweep the gloom of the threshold. I imagine that if I push open that door I shall enter into Your splendour; I know beforehand that there is a way of abolishing the past which will make me joyful and strong, more true, more pure, more sure of You and less frightened in the face of death. All holy enterprises should be lighted from within like lanterns. Show me, Lord, what it is You wish to teach us . . . *Edissere nobis parabolam.*

To look back is to judge the existing work of God by what it was formerly, and to condemn or mutilate the present because it does not resemble the past. All heretics have done this. They have wished to obey the Apostles, but not the Pope; they have accepted the ancient Gospel but have rejected the infallible teacher; they have told us that beginnings alone were pure, and that to-day has no right to exist except on the condition of being identical with yesterday. Something of this folly has at times penetrated into my mind, and I have caught myself making a minute comparison between my present state and the perfections of my childhood and my virtues as a novice. In life, which never pauses, I dreamt of always beginning the same thing over again, and I have not known how to adapt my rigidity, whole-heartedly, to ever actual duties. I wished to resuscitate abolished forms and to pass once more by the road which in bygone days enchanted my youth. I think that to be young is to refuse to grow old: an impossible thing. When a man and woman found a new family, it is not in order that they may themselves become children as before; and the toys that will enter that house, and the cradles which are rocked in it are not for them. They are, of course, beginning once again a cycle already known to them, but they are now the parents not the children, and the game they are playing is a tragic adventure in which they risk their very lives.

I look at what I was. The sweet virtues of childhood! I search for them in vain in myself! Formerly I believed that with uprightness and self-sacrifice we could be sure never to make an enemy; I already thought of all those whom I should meet upon my roads as of disinterested fellow-workers, toiling in the service of the same God. He who carries no weapons is never attacked, I said to myself. Love of men seemed easy to me, I had not suffered from them. In those days I believed in my own strength of soul, and thought that with method and within a given time, I should be able to suppress defects which were as yet not fully grown. Not having any very fixed ideas, not having studied anything out of the common, wholly encircled with ignorance, and therefore brimful of respect for the learning of others, I did not find it very troublesome to obey, and conflicts of opinion seemed absurd to me. Why, I thought to myself, why not rally to the best opinion, and if two opinions are good why not blend them with a wise eclecticism? Formerly I had no need to give advice, nor had I to take decisions; I had not yet come out of my trench. . . . But to-day responsibilities harass me, and as in great battles, all my powers must work at their highest pressure, and even the time for reflection is measured. Ah! those formidable alignments of the battle! irregular and fluctuating, with gaps which must be filled here and massed groups to be dispersed there, when these are compared with the marching past in great reviews and manœuvres in the barrack yards, how defective they appear! And yet they alone are truly efficacious, and the instructions followed in parades have never saved a single province!

To-day, indeed, I feel that if I paused to look back, the yearning for a form of virtue now impossible to me, would ruin even the possibility of that virtue which is necessary for me. I cannot love men as I loved them formerly; I must love them far more and wholly otherwise, with a keener realism, with a more effective vigour, without deceiving myself as to their worth, without believing that, with words and smiles, we can open out the way of Justice across the thorny ground.

I can no longer obey as in olden days, that is to say without having to confront thought, then non-existent, with the orders made known to me. I must obey far more strongly and far more magnificently. No one will make me yield with petty motives of appeal to feelings, nor yet by angry looks and threatening gestures. I have no right to despise myself to that extent. But the very noble motive of my absolute obedience is, that the whole, of which I am a part, is worth more than I am, and that divine strategy is ever sinuous; it is that nothing exists and has any worth but by being joined with the will of Christ. To-day I need to be far stronger.

Respiciens retro.—If I go back to the days of my childhood, to all that naïve piety, those simple and so straight desires, the poison of the past will fill my present soul with bitterness, and I shall let fall the handle of the plough to weep like a fool. My God, Your Grace, like our years, has its seasons, and our duty is to discern their meaning and to love them with all our hearts. I shall hold the plough and, in spite of the heat or of the winter, I shall drive it straight before me across the stony ground or the too soft clay. To look back, does not mean to think of the past. You have never forbidden that. It means to desire to return to that which no longer exists and hence to deny Your presence.

LXXVII

Nescio, Deus scit

I know not, God knows

(2 *Cor. xii.* 2.)

I HAVE no wish, O my God, to establish my innermost equilibrium on feelings, still less on illusions, nor even on the opinions of my neighbours. I desire to be able to rest upon the eternal, but in excavating the soil of my own soul, I cannot unearth this immovable rock. I can discover nothing in myself but the changeful and the fleeting. Help me to find unending peace.

Scarcely ever do we dwell upon the divine attributes. We look on them only as far-off beautiful abstractions; we speak of them in learned books; but we do not know how to introduce them into the very foundations of our existence, and unless we reflect upon them we make nothing of them.

And yet it is upon them that the Universe is upborne. Sometimes on the top of lofty towers I have leant against the iron balustrade and looked down calmly from the height of this platform overhanging the void, into the vast, dizzy abyss. Ah! that good railing, on the safety of which we can count! If it were not there we could not venture upon those slippery sheets of steel in the wild, blustering squalls; we should not dare to make all those gestures nor to speak to those who were with us, pointing out to them at leisure, the specks that stood for towns on the far-off horizon. But thanks to the railing, that which would have meant the risk of death has become a radiant vision. And of this climb, we keep only the remembrance of a wonderful view, no fear having crossed our path.

I wish, O my God, to lean upon Your eternal attributes. I know that Your knowledge is limitless. Why has this idea never issued from out those deserts of abstractions where I have confined it? Why has it not become the very groundwork of my life?

You know all, and so we meet each other, for I cannot, without lying, affirm that I know nothing. I know You, You—and You know me—me—and on this mutual acquaintanceship we can establish a holy intimacy. All that I know contains You, since if I examine each thing fully I shall see that it is an expression of Your knowledge. If I study it carefully I shall discover, as experts do who examine old china or old pictures, that it corresponds to such a type and comes from such a studio: Your knowledge has contained it from all eternity. When we journey by sequestered mountain paths, what emotion we experience when we discover the ashes of a fire under some rocky shelter, and see on the snow the footprints of explorers. Thus, too, I meet Your knowledge in my own, and I am overjoyed to realize that the same things are known to us. I need not explain to You who my friends are, nor describe minutely the character of my nieghbour. You know it as well as I do. When I study history, I can say to myself that You knew every detail of that tragedy of Cæsar's death, and all the warlike episodes depicted on the Roman tablets. It is through Your domain of knowledge that I wander when I examine the constitution of matter or of life. You have possessed Yourself of all that is true, and the roads by which my mind must travel, in passing from one thing to another, have been traced by You. *Deus scit.*

You know all, and thus outrun me, for my ignorance is vast as an abyss, and left to myself I hesitate and grope my way. You know all. I can then lean upon this eternal, infinite and ever-stable knowledge and leave to You the care to judge me. It is not necessary that I should know exactly how many fathoms deep my virtue goes, nor over how many acres the fleece of my sacrifices can be outspread. It is enough that You should know me and know my little worth, and all that Your love has made good in the deficit of my misery. I cannot tell what goes on in the souls of those who are most dear to me. God knows. But You have undertaken to watch over their salvation, and nothing that could help them will be overlooked by You. I do not know what death discovered of worth in the lives of my vanished ancestors. Rather than lose myself in vain conjectures, and alarm myself without cause or lull myself into security without praying for them, I prefer to rest my De Profundis on Your knowledge, and to recommend all my dead to You, according to Your great mercy.

The joy of knowing is great, but the comfort of not knowing is ineffable, once this ignorance, like a happy islet on a peaceful sea, is surrounded by Your infinite wisdom. By all that I know I am united to You; by all that I am ignorant of I am subject to You. My knowledge is a bond of intimacy, and I respect my mind because it makes me see that which You too see, and because it is filled by Your light. My ignorance, while putting me in my place, makes me understand how far You surpass me and I love to feel my littleness in presence of Your greatness. If You did not know all, my ignorance would indeed be full of anguish, but how can I do otherwise than break forth into gladness when I think that Truth is You, and that far deeper than I can ever go myself, You have penetrated into me. The hidden thing does not exist, the riddles of antiquity are but an evil myth. No dragon will slay him who takes refuge in Your omniscience, and who adores Your infinite light.

When we lift up a slab of stone lying on the wet ground we

discover legions of little woodlice sheltering in the darkness and the damp. The movement and the light terrify them, and all these creeping things decamp at a run, as if they dreaded to be seen. Ah! If Your light, O my God, could fall unhindered on all the grotesque and nondescript fauna that swarm in the depths of my soul! If my anxieties, my regrets, my scruples and my remorse could feel themselves struck by your silent ray as the greyish backs of the woodlice! It seems to me that if I kept myself for long under the splendour of this truth: God knows; if I allowed my night to be traversed by these tidings, my soul would be delivered from many parasites. I should cease to be breathless, struggling and disheartened in the dark.

Tu qui cuncta scis et vales (*Lauda Sion*). O You who know all and whose unchangeable wisdom contains the whole meaning of my existence, grant me to rest in You beyond all that can be desired, to rejoice In Your infinite knowledge and in my own limited knowledge and unfathomable ignorance; grant too that the blessed joy of truth may flow from all sides into me.

LXXVIII

Orta tribulatione

When we begin to shake them

(*Mark iv.* 17.)

PIETY is a very weak word to express a very strong thing. The type of the pious youth or of the devout contemplative has been so distorted by stupidity, worn so threadbare by language, that we can now see nothing more in it than what is shapeless and vague; even virtue itself, that hardy word, has taken somewhat languishing airs.

Souls formed by You, Lord, are strong souls, why do we find so few around us? Why am I not myself more fearless in the face of difficulties, more steadfast under trial, more firm before invading weariness or unforeseen danger. Why, when they are shaken, do Your servants allow themselves to be uprooted? Why do the long years of their training too often only succeed in keeping them good while they last, and leave them so unarmed in the hour of stern duties?

Confused thinkers have answered me by speaking of the negative method and the positive method, extolling sometimes one and sometimes the other, but they have never been able to define clearly what ideas they had hidden under these words, and I fear very much that there may be many an error in these divisions.

Others, taking the cure for the remedy, have said that we should give people a sense of responsibility and leave them some initiative, and they have prepared magnificent schemes of education, in which they perpetually assume the problem already solved.

Why do we not keep to Your revealed Wisdom when we seek for answers? Is there need, on these essential questions, to consult any other masters but You?

You have said that we should take root in deep earth. Roots are not watchwords, nor commands, even if numerous and precise; they are real, intimate convictions which have grown slowly and from within. There is nothing easier than to give orders; there is nothing more laborious and at times nothing more despairing than, from without, to help convictions to form themselves. To say what must be done in such and such a case is ordinarily quite simple; to indicate how it should be done, and to supply the method, is already a more complicated affair; to state precisely why it must be done, and to give convincing motives is an exceptionally arduous task and one which tempts nobody. Those who command have evidently the right not to make their reasons known on all occasions, but they have not the right to have none. They cannot dispense themselves from thinking under the pretext that others will carry out the orders. The duty of being loyal is an absolute one. It is not because a thing is difficult that it ceases to be necessary, and it is most necessary to have principles for ourselves and to give them to others.

People imagine that with feelings and affection they could become strong and make great progress. Sin ruins this illusion every day. Some fancy they could tame the horses of the steppes between a pair of shafts, but their wild nature, restrained for an instant, recovers itself and escapes the moment they are out of harness. To train disciples there is need of a faith, allurements are not enough, there must be a doctrine. No one can deliver us from our responsibilities, for if I obey I still shall have to render an account of that very obedience, and if it is meritorious to keep my vows and to submit myself to authority, it is just because such an act never ceases to be free, the author of it remains always responsible.

When those who believe are roughly shaken, far too often they become unsettled. Their faith is a routine faith, and their virtue is perhaps merely the absence of occasion for doing ill. My God, give us vigorous recruits such as Your Church calls up in days of crisis. Rain down strong virtues on us; grant us to be totally sincere, and to love You, knowing well the reason why. It is pagan love that is blind. The beloved of the Canticle is so clear-sighted that she recognizes the spouse from afar, merely by the colour of his hair: black like the plumage of rows; *nigra quasi corvus*. To understand the "why" of our duties is a blessed labour. Your Church has condemned all who despise reason or who would do away with profane philosophy. With our principles in harmony, in agreement with the real and in accordance with the true, we could more easily resist and stand firm when contradictions shake us.

Long experience has proved to me that resolutions, even the most determined ones, are easily overthrown, as warlike statues are made to rock upon their pedestals by the simple movement of a lever. To Fell a fir a greater effort is needed, for the tree is closely united to the soil which feeds it. My God, convictions which are more tenacious than decisions, vigorous faith which logically precedes Christian practice, the impulse of the mind towards Your truth—of all this You alone can plant the seeds within me—*incrementa virtutum*.

A strong conviction has sometimes unfortunately a rough appearance, and those who will energetically are apt to jostle their neighbour. The swimmer can only advance by cleaving the waves, and the forest road makes short work of all the trees upon its track I do not see how I can be very strong for myself without being a little hard on others, and I wish to do no hurt to those around me.

It is from You that I shall get this supernatural tact. I want none of that soft weakness which imagines suffering is an evil, and that a gentle soul never causes any. Without the suffering that has fashioned me, I should be nothing. The aim of life is not to rock my neighbours and to sing soothing lullabies in the ears of all the world, but to bring forth its uttermost perfection from the Divine work, and to make the creature worthy of Christ. If in order to attain to this it is necessary that our neighbour should suffer and should weep, it would be criminal on my part to spare him from these effects and to deprive him of these merits. But we must not wound without utility; we must neither exasperate nor discourage the weak; and we must not crush the already broken reed. Your Grace has never granted a diminution of Your exigencies; it is implacable and yet so gentle. Make me to its image, O my God, and may my action be like Yours.

LXXIX

Superseminavit zizania
He oversowed it with cockle
(*Matt. xiii.* 25.)

WHEN the servants of the parable perceived that the harvest was being spoiled, they asked their master how this disaster had come about. He did not blame the soil which he had chosen, nor the seed which he had sown. He contented himself with reminding them that he had an enemy, and that other seeds had been sown by stealth among the original grain.

Our religion should germinate and ripen in marvellous ears of corn. You, O my God, are the source of all beauty and of all grandeur. The Christian soul, while simply docile to Your Grace, shares in all Your perfections. The soil is good, the seed is excellent. Why then do we see so many unsightly objects growing in our furrows?

I am not speaking of sin. That is, of course, an enemy, but we know that it is evil. God has to guard His work in us against our vices, which is in no way astonishing. But that He should have to protect it, even against what we style our virtues, is stranger and perhaps more serious. People imagine that to be pious it is necessary to assume unpleasing attitudes, to isolate oneself from all that moves or hopes or works. They think that piety is the enemy of good taste, that all elegance is a frivolity and that the intention alone being meritorious, the technique of performance is negligible. They think that to be militant one must be aggressive, they see nothing in the Crusades of olden days but the fighting, and forget the deliverance of the Holy places and the purification of Jerusalem. They appeal to the certainties of faith in order to dispense themselves from making their own minds work. They flatter themselves on being obedient. They are glad to have superiors, not that they may thus enlarge the horizon of their activities and serve eternal causes, but merely in order to rid themselves of responsibility and care, and tranquilly to enjoy the role of the driving-belt for transmission of motion in a machine.

We say: I wish to avoid pride and we fall into immovable sloth; I wish to fly from ambition and we take refuse in paltriness; I wish to obey and we become incapable of self-command; I wish to save my soul and we neglect those of our neighbours; I am satisfied with being pious and we refuse to make ourselves of use.

I have seen earnest apologists try (as they themselves expressed it) to make unbelievers "swallow the faith" by showing them that one mystery more or less should not alarm any one, and that in reality we knew absolutely nothing that was quite certain. They began by enumerating triumphantly all the mistakes of science; they inculcated contempt of knowledge, disparaging the claims of the light which is within us. All is soot and smoke, they said, why be scandalized if our dogmas are but little satisfying? Poor human reason is not worthy of so much consideration. In the midst of so many theories all more or less deformed, and of certitudes all more or less ambiguous, you will be able to make a little place for the Credo.

Thus did these sowers of cockle speak, full of the best intentions, and their perfidious seed choked the plant of uprightness and sincerity in the minds of their hearers, the corn of light and daring which was rising fearlessly to the truth. Faith is not a mutilation; it is not a holocaust of our thought, but a sacrifice of oblation, a homage of deference, like that of the disciple offering himself to the master, like that of the thirsty man who puts his lips to the cool spring, like that of the seed which offers itself to the furrow that it may bear fruit. The first lesson of faith is one of dignity not of abjection; it is a divine respect for our power of knowing, that astonishing power which enable us to attain to God. When I think of it, O my Master, when I think that I know, that my mind rests on eternal foundations; when I think that that which is for my mind a contradiction is in itself impossible, and that what I can prove logically can be falsified by nothing whatsoever; when I think that it is the laws of being itself which I calmly analyse, I say to myself that the glory of being a man should make my weak heart break with joy, and that all those blaspheme, unknowingly, who, in order to make me accept the faith, begin by depreciating our intellect. Why do they clothe Your supernatural truth in these cast-off garments of a discouraged scepticism? Was it not that old man, Ignatius of Antioch, who wrote to Polycarp: *Postula intellectum ampilorem quam habes:* Ask of God that you may have an even greater intelligence.

And the nervous people who think that Your grace is weak or absent-minded, and who never trust in the future; those who sow their pusillanimous seed in Your field; those who pass on sighing and moaning, full of ridiculous lamentations and of pessimistic predictions, why do they give this funereal and lachrymose picture of the Christian character? Can it be that You no longer have for us words of eternal life? Youth they tell us is in full decadence. All is going to the bad, and everything will yet be worse. Let us close our doors on the little flock of the Faithful; let us at least keep what is left to us; raise the draw-bridge of the city, lower the portcullis, keep within doors and wait till Providence undertakes to change everything. . . . Feebleness and shame! Since You, O my God, have found hardy virtue each time Your powerful Grace has sown it, why should these people cry-down beforehand Your harvest of to-morrow? Youth is in no way under condemnation to do worse than we have done; it is not even condemned to do as badly, and if, determined to forward it to the utmost, we were to throw into this work all our devotedness and our valour, our time and our life, You would succeed in making of those who will follow us a generation of Christian men and women incomparably better than we are. Is not that the watch-word to pass down from the elder to the younger in Your Church, as men pass orders from one to another all down the lines of combatants? Our joy should be to know that after us others will do better than we have done, and that they will serve You, my God, with more intelligent energy than we have been able to give. We are the sons of a promise, and our prayer can hasten the hour when the bearer of the Keys in the Church will be Japanese, when black Africa will have its priesthood, its hierarchy and its crowds of faithful; the hour when the Pentecostal miracle will be as it were repeated, because every idiom on the earth, the voices of all the continents, will be united in one same acclamation, and will express for all but one sole meaning. . . . May no cockle spoil your work!

LXXX

Pro mundi vita

For the life of a world

(John vi. 52.)

MY God, I fear that the unceasing flow of our meanness will wear down the sharp corners, the trenchant edges of those absolute commands, which You have thrown into our existence. I am afraid that we may not be exacting enough with ourselves and that, without knowing it, we shall put, in the place of Your thoughts, our hesitating little cogitations, and in the place of Your peremptory commands our pitiful wiles and our imbecile contrivances. Our task is a formidable one. When I think of it I shudder. With You I have to give myself for the saving of a universe. How shall I set about it and who will tell me what means to take? When I examine what Your Grace demands of a true missionary, I, who have not gone out into distant lands to bring back the unbelievers to You, I seem to see that all my prayer must be directed towards obtaining adequate powers from You for these Apostles.—*Pro mundi vita.*— They have to give life to a world, and they must render an account for the success or failure of the enterprise, since You have put it into their hands.

In order to convert others, people sometimes imagine that it is enough to love. I have heard this manner of discourse: Love, they said, be zealous, sacrifice yourself and don't worry about anything else. Lord, I can but think that this wisdom is very short-sighted, and that You demand quite other depths of immolation from those whom You associate in Your work of redemption.

No, whatever they may think, to love is never the first duty, any more than to love is the highest happiness. The first duty is to know, the highest happiness is the possession of Truth. So much the worse for those who refuse to accept this austere lesson; all that they build will fall back into nothingness. To land in China proclaiming that we love the Chinese with all our hearts is neither naturally nor supernaturally the best tactics. Were a man to enter my room and fall upon my neck declaring he would never again leave me, I should at the least judge him to be tiresome, touching perhaps, but extremely stupid, and I should make arrangements to get rid of him. Before setting ourselves to love we must learn to respect as is fitting, we must study and acquire information; we must even give up that secret pride which hides itself under an appearance of compassion. When anyone pities me for long they end by irritating me; they seem to think I am incapable of bearing my trials decently, and in their effusions of tender sympathy I do not find enough respect for my own person. To respect a child whom we educate, to respect the mind we have the mission to enlighten, to respect the will without breaking or deadening or enfeebling it; not to impose ourselves with our prejudices as if they were the measure of all things; with our habits as if laziness had no part in them; with our personal tastes as if we were the lords of the world; this spoliation of ourselves is terrible, it rakes our selfishness to its depths, and many perhaps have died in foreign lands without having understood that because they ignored these grave duties, their apostolate, like the withered fig-tree, was blighted from its beginnings.

To despoil ourselves to the depths *pro mundi vita!* When You made of Abraham the father of a great nation, the heir of the promises, You told him to quit his country and his kindred—*exi de domo tua et de cognatione tua*. He was obliged to consent to this total transplantation and no longer to consider himself as a citizen of Ur in Chaldea. My God, I sometimes think that those whom You have predestined to become fathers, according to the spirit, of Japan or of India, those who are to give a Christian soul to these old worlds will not be able to do so, but on condition that they themselves are Japanese or Hindu. The respect for these peoples must have become so great, the sympathy must be so complete, that these apostles will appear in the eyes of their future neophytes as the living incarnation, as the stupendous realization of all that Your Grace had whispered to them through the centuries. The day on which the Japanese will say in presence of a missionary: That is what all my ancestors and I myself have desired to become; there is the full flowering of all those hidden virtues which were germinating in us; to be a Christian it is not necessary to curse Japan; nothing of good need be disowned but all completed, all consummated in Him who is not come to destroy but to make perfect; to be a Christian all I need is to be Japanese in a holy way; just as to grasp the meaning of a difficult text no word should be suppressed, but all should be arranged in accordance with the thought of the writer; the day on which all Asia and all Africa will thus prejudge the tidings of salvation, the propagation of the faith will be possible and the elect will rejoice in heaven.

After all we do not kill a child to regenerate it, we baptize it. Nothing that Your Grace has produced need be destroyed. And all that trends, even from afar, towards Christ, by the roads of kindness, of courage of loyalty and of forgiveness, has You for its guide and, without knowing it, obeys You.

Between the colonial agent and the missionary the exterior difference is not very great, and the martyrology of the former is more blood-stained than that of the latter. From the deck of the liner both make the same signs of farewell to their families, and the casual onlooker might say that an explorer and a pioneer of religion followed analogous careers, the one in the service of science, the other in the service of the Faith. And yet the difference should be absolute. The missionary should leave everything on the quay, the colonist takes his country in his baggage; he goes off to live among the Chinese, the missionary goes to become Chinese, and henceforth his father and mother and sisters will be that China which he must beget in Christ. He must love all, not with a love that is merely kind in act, which pours out upon others the surplus of its own wealth, but with a love that is watchful, that understands, that sees intuitively and adapts itself, one that makes use of all that it discovers to complete that formation of Christ which has been rough-cast by the Holy Spirit in those around it.

And I, O my Lord, I too must be received into the service of the Universe; I have no right to narrow down my field of action. I have the duty of guarding the whole world for You or of bringing it back to You, and until my last breath even in my uttermost weakness it is in dying each day to myself that I can hope to make You live in all Your redeemed ones.

LXXXI

Cum esses sub ficu
When you were under the fig-tree
(*John i.* 48.)

GOD is admirable in all that He consummates; He is not less soul-stirring in that which He prepares, and since we are on the road towards the end, and our consummation is not as yet the reality of to-day, we can usefully meditate on the divine action in its quiet progress.

The Ascension is a glorious ending and our litanies call it admirable; the Resurrection breaks forth with the Alleluias of Easter, it is another ending and a consummation; all Your manifestations are solemn and splendid, and I do not wish to be sparing of my gratitude for these helpful feasts. I treasure the memory of the kneeling crowds and of the Blessed Sacrament carried in triumph in the midst of light and song. Yes, all that is very good, and we can never praise Him enough who is seated upon the Cherubim and looks down upon the abyss.—*Qui intueris abyssos.* (*Dan.* iii 55.)

But the Redeemer is so many-sided in His aspects that our devotion never finishes the round. And I wish this evening to reflect on that silent Providence, which, slowly and with love, prepares all that is to come.

When You looked on Nathaniel, seated under his fig-tree, he was not conscious of this glance, nevertheless this divine scrutiny was already full of predilection, and, unknown to him. You caught that dreamer in the nets of Your Grace. I love this silent action and this deliberate look none saw. To-day, most certainly You turn Your eyes thus upon some little boy, playing at marbles or chasing dragon-flies, and the child has no idea that You have predestined him to be, in another fifty years, Your vicar here below; he does not know in the least that You will entrust Your Church to him. None amongst us know it, but Your watchfulness precedes our feeble judgments, and You prepare unweariedly all those who later on will continue Your work.

You know how to take men; You know how to make Yourself desired. When in the Eastern skies You lit up a mysterious star, of which our astronomers could make nothing, You were gently seeking to captivate the attention of the Magi, and, as yet unborn, You were already organizing the eternal pilgrimage of Faith towards the unchangeable Bethlehem. And I know that throughout the length of my life Your Providence has made stars arise in my firmament. My pagan head believes that the books of my library, and the remarks of my friends, and the thoughts that cross my mind have been regulated by some trivial chance without aim and without knowledge; but when I am willing to listen to the Faith of my Baptism, I know that You have prepared everything, so that, whether by the roads of the deserts or those of the towns, by advice received or books re-read, I may at last come to where You are, whom I adore in truth—*procidentes adoraverunt*. When the warmth of summer evenings seemed weighted with tenderness, it was You who were trying to reach me and who wished to soften my harshness, and I remember how throughout a whole night in an unfrequented spot, You spoke to me through the voices of the screech owls who dwelt in the ruins of an old convent. You drew the Magi by a star; why should it be forbidden to You to touch me and to enlighten me by the scent of the forests or the noise of the waterfalls, by mountains or by twilight? I have seen so many things by the light of night—*in lumine noctis*. (*Jeremiah* xxxi. 35.)

When you prayed that the faith of Peter might not fail, no one knew anything about it. You announced it saying that it had been done—*Rogavi pro te*—I love this secret prayer for Your disciple. He was unaware that at that moment his eternal life was in the balance, and that You saved him by recommending him most specially to the Father. I can believe that for me too, as for Your Apostle, Your worldless prayer has been redemptive; I do not doubt that on the mountain or in the desert, knowing my dangers. You prepared my final liberation by Your all-powerful prayer. And it is this secret story of my life, hidden in the plan of Your love, which enchants and moves me. How could I be vain or believe in my own excellence when I thus see all the beginnings of my virtues lost in You?

When in the midst of the starving multitude in the desert, You had placed a little boy with some barley loaves and two fishes, no one had any idea that You were preparing a triumph and that You were announcing the Eucharist. This child had left his home, carrying with him his poor little provisions, without knowing that Your Spirit guided his actions, and that something tremendous, unique and eternal was about to be accomplished, thanks to his poorly-filled sack. For us the same thing happens. Your Providence provides, noiselessly, for the needs of faith in souls; it prepares relays of energy; it organizes stages of virtue, and at the appointed hour distributes the truest helps.

In the forests You prepared the wood of Your Cross, that solitary tree—*arbor una nobilis*—Your Providence made it grow for this use; You prepared the miraculous fish which was to furnish Peter with a golden stater; You prepared all Your faithful to listen to You like Lydia, the seller of purple, of whom the *Acts* tell us that You had

opened her heart to attend to those things that were said by Saint
Paul.

Deus absconditus (*Isaiah* xlv. 15).—Hidden God, You understand
how to construct, and how to put pieces together, how to join and
how to combine. Was not that Your trade among us—*Fabri filius?*
Nothing else was done at Nazareth. You know how to bring forth
Your eternal work out of all our brokenness. But alas! over all this
Providence we pass heedlessly, just as we cross our bridges without
once looking at the river. You never for a single day cease to be
busy over us, but we never think of this and our wretched pre-
occupations wear us out.

Could we but consent to reflect, or better still, could we but
determine to cease from being blind, we should see that in order
that we might to-day be at Your feet, You have for centuries been
combining world forces, and each good deed we do is an answer
that Your eternal love has never wearied in preparing.

LXXXII

THE words which in our language tell us of Your ineffable perfections have depths of meaning which make us wonder. When I was very small all my duties were summed up for me in one precept only, and they used to tell me to be *"bien sage."* That is of course the childish formula: why, O my Lord, now that my days cast longer shadows on my road, why are the experience and the virtue with which my life should be filled still called by this same name of wisdom? The Greek sages were not children, and in all languages of the world, the old, far more than the children, are the wise.

I need not then emerge from one disposition of mind in order to enter into another. In tending towards You I should not jump from branch to branch like squirrels devoid of reason. I should not change my virtues as we change our clothes. These virtues should grow within us like the tissues of our epidermis, and to reach You we need no more issue forth from the wisdom of our childhood than we need go out of our skin in order to get better. Your commandment remains always the same. There is no twilight or no waning in Your desires. My nature will not belie itself; I am and I shall remain to the end the child of the human race, and that which sanctifies my youth is not out-of-date in ripe age.

To be very wise! I know what little children, to whom we should become like, understand by this simple statement. It means to be quiet and not to disturb the rest of others. Lessons which are always opportune. I turn my gaze upon the minds of our grown-ups, and I find them so ravaged by disquietude, so violently shaken by cloudy emotions, so encumbered with jostling desires, so little placid in Your hands. And when they came to lay open to me their plans and their losses, when they talk loudly and gesticulate in their restlessness, I feel the word of days gone by rising to my lips: Be "wise," calm yourselves, you are not alone.

To be wise in those days meant not to cheat at play, to finish our exercise before we thought of amusing ourselves; it was to learn lessons which had but little that was attractive in them, and to listen for long hours to dull explanations. My God nothing has changed in this but the appearance of the actors. The roles are always the same. Not to cheat in dealings with our neighbour; not to strut about adorned with the mind of another as if it were our own; not to blush at our ignorance; not to rest content with what we learnt in other days but to acquaint ourselves with all that can help us to be of use; never to consent to those little interior disloyalties which jealousy or malice would urge us to . . .! Be wise, and accomplish, at whatever cost, our professional obligations, obey without fruitless complaints, superiors who have but little intelligence, or are unpleasant people; add up columns of figures or count tons of coal; feel the pulse of the sick or drill soldiers; nurse children or listen to beggars without being carried away by impatience and without changing countenance . . . little virtues? No, consummated wisdom. The child has not died that the grown-up should live, it is the child who continues the first effort which he had begun well.

To be wise meant also to break nothing, not to knock things down, not to shout aloud when the sick or older people needed to sleep, not to slam the doors, not to hang out of the windows in a dangerous way, not to play with fire and not to tell untruths. . . . My God, these same perils still to-day waylay me, and the same follies torment me. To break nothing in myself or in others by contemptuous remarks or by disdainful scepticism; not to throw down the timid efforts of beginners by saying they are worthless; not to judge hastily the first good desire which emerges from my failures and offers itself to repair the evil done; not to shout unseasonably, ferocious truths into sensitive ears, and to know how to wait to speak till the audience is prepared to listen; not to blurt out roughly unkind remarks, like leaden bullets; to avoid useless commotions and dramatic attitudes; to make no fuss about our own insignificance, and to accept it modestly. . . . That is the same examination of conscience of the *recta sapere*. How could it be otherwise, since it is Your Spirit which ever remains as the measure of all things? I look at those round about me. They no longer hang out of windows to look at birds; they no longer risk themselves on slippery banks to gather buttercups; but the fascination of evil things has not diminished in these hearts, and when they fall headlong, when they tumble and when they get drowned they have not even the excuse of ignorance, they knew quite well, alas! that an evil and even deadly desire was exciting them.

Grown-ups, who are so like children and who naïvely believe they surpass them by their whole height! Their height! Between this child and this old man there is just the difference of an arm's length. Is that really enough on which to build such proud pretensions?

I shall strive, my God, to be "wise." *Recta sapere*. To see all in the perspective of Your wisdom; I shall not picture to myself that this is an easy business, I shall not believe that I have only to grow bigger to accomplish it.

Wisdom is eternal, as is goodness. They told me to be "wise," they told me also to be good. These two words are holy since they belong to You. I shall never exhaust their meaning, for Your elect, themselves, are just simply "the good" separated from the "bad," and the wise virgins separated from the foolish ones. Wisdom and goodness would preserve me here below from all culpable aberrations, and would give me provisions for the endless duration of my Paradise.

The wisdom which delighted the old Greeks, and which they sought for in the discourses of Your Apostle and in Your redeeming Message, the Holy Wisdom, *Sancta Sophia*, which You brought into the world and which hinders us from dying, fill my soul and my life so completely with it, O my God, that it will never again desert me— *ut mecum sit et mecum laboret* (*Wisdom* ix. 10)—and that it may conduct me, in the hour known to You, to the right hand of the Father in the Kingdom of goodness.

LXXXIII

Cum rediero . . .

When I shall return . . .
(*Luke* x. 35.)

MUCH has been said about the good Samaritan. He has become dear to us, and we long to be like him, since the day when You set him before us as a model, or rather since we caught a glimpse of Your kindness through his. That is as it should be, my God, and no one thinks of grumbling about it, but I confess to You that I am sometimes embarrassed when I want to apply Your parable to so many obscure, meritorious, Christian lives. We cannot all lift up wounded people on the road to Jericho. Your Providence does not always allow us to play these chief parts in the saving of souls. When we are obliged to teach the village children for fifty years, we cannot neglect this duty in order to beat the woods and lanes in search of great sinners. When, in the family circle, we are perhaps the good aunt or the kindly grandmother, we cannot dare to say that we pour wine and oil into deep wounds nor that we save our neighbours from dying under the blows of brigands. There would be something rhetorical in such speeches. Truthful souls will have none of this, and so at times they do not see how to take the lesson of the good Samaritan in a practical way. It seems to them that their lives, devoid as they are of brilliance, are somewhat *manqué* since they have never brought back to an inn, lying across their saddle, the badly wounded man of whom the Gospel speaks. Could it be that Your parable is empty of all message for these upright souls?

In the dazzling ray of the light-house, fire-flies cannot be distinguished; in the splendour of the Good Samaritan it seems that the solid and faithful virtue of his colleague, the innkeeper, disappears! This poor "*stabularius*" has been badly treated by tradition. Scarcely anyone has thought of questioning him. And yet this silent servant is so much to our own image, and divine wisdom has put him in this story for our teaching. When we think of it, we see it is almost on him that the greater part of the work fell, and it was he who showed the most perfect trustworthiness. The cavalier deposited his wounded man, all wrapped in bandages, with the innkeeper: "Here, my good fellow, take care of him!" *Curam illius habe*. Then he took out of his purse twopence, obviously an insufficient sum, and one that he knows will not cover the expenses—*si quid amplius supererogaveris*. And then the last touch which nonplusses all our mercantile prudence: When I return—*cum rediero*—I shall pay up the arrears. There you have a debt on very poor security! It is quite certain travellers run risks in those regions; and this vague indication—*cum rediero*—could only reassure a simpleton. The Samaritan began his rescue work magnificently, but he has just as magnificently passed it on to the innkeeper, and if this man refuses to enter into the partnership, or if he neglects his sick man, the initial fine deed will be without a morrow. The excellent Samaritan has gone off on his horse. *Cum rediero*—God knows when he will be seen again. The innkeeper, in the interval, must turn hospital attendant. He has not even been asked what he thought of it, nor has he had time to give an answer. Dumbfounded or delighted! We do not know.

There, O Lord, is my true model. I have no steed, and I do not frequent the highroads. I have never had the chance of gathering up wounded people in my arms. I am perhaps a nun, shut up in my cloister, or I am myself ill, chained to my bed on my back for twenty years, or I am what the world calls rather cruelly an old maid, and it seems to me You have treated me as the Samaritan his innkeeper. It is not mine to begin a work, but I have to carry on Your work, in secret in silence with all my heart and unto the very end.

Cum rediero.—When You return You will settle all my extra expenses. You have brought me weighty duties, and You have added to them the care of all sorts of unexpected affairs. You have asked me to have the long patience needed for works of healing and of education, You have thrown in my way many inconvenient jobs, troublesome as an embarrassing and pitiably wounded man, which have tormented me day and night. *Curam illus habe.*—Take care of him! My God how often, without having been able to protest, have I not heard these words from Your lips. How often has my neighbour come to me saying, without preamble: See to this! And objections crowd upon me, with at times not a little impatience. *Curam habe* . . . I have no time, and then really this is too free and easy, they cheat me out of my days, they cut off my rest; they confiscate my little joys, and I have not even the resource of showing bad temper! They imagine that my only business in life is to render service! Thus do I grumble knowing well that all these mutterings are stupid and that You are not alarmed by them.

You have forced me to give You credit. I have done more than my duty, I have given a surplus—*supererogavi*. See my life. There are cuttings in my forests, cuttings down to the roots, of which I have never handled the price. See my life! If by chance You never again returned, should I not have been wholly taken in by Your manœuvre?—*Cum rediero*. Ah! we must live by faith, I realize that every day, and it is as useful as it is invigorating. To finish all that Your Providence has begun, to instruct the children that Your baptism has regenerated, to heal the men whom Your Passion has bought back, to speak every day to those whom Your Spirit has called, to console those to whom Your beatitude is promised, to collaborate with You without rest and without speeches, my God, grant me to love this work and to consent humbly to be the innkeeper of the parable playing his useful part, a necessary and inglorious part under a name that is almost one to laugh at.

When we are not the beginners of an enterprise there is every likelihood that it will displease us, because we seek, not good, but renown, and because we choose to appear rather than to be. Sweep away all my foolishness. Grant that I may accept to live where You have put me, to receive, without having looked at them, the wounded whom Your Providence directs to my abode; grant that I may de contented with the lowest wages and that, with all my heart, I may trust in Your return, not so much that I may be paid, but that I may at last meet You face to face.

LXXXIV

I HAVE said many foolish things in my life, my God, to You, to men and to myself. I noticed some in their transit, others too late, but the greater number have vanished without attracting attention in any special way, and I have neither been able to correct nor to regret them.

I wish to thank You this evening, not for the reasonable prayers which I have poured forth to You and which You have answered, but for the ridiculous prayers which I have multiplied and which Your goodness has refused to notice. Your Providence is no less merciful when it resists us. In order to lead people aright we must hinder deviations, and if all my desires had been heard I should very quickly have vanished in the nothingness of my inconsistencies.

I have often prayed without knowing what I was saying, and not realizing by what spirit I was animated, and because You did not grant my petitions I was angry, I scolded, I took up Your Gospels to discover Your promise and to confront them with my disappointments. Did You not say that all that we should ask in Your Name would be given to us? My selfishness equipped with this little method, I flattered myself that I should obtain my ends by holding Your Almighty power in my hands. Knowing quite well what it means to ask, and better still what it is to obtain, I persuaded myself that nothing was easier than to ask in Your Name. So, provided with this infallible receipt, I imagined I should be able to make everything succeed, and my ambitious dreams would come down from the clouds and become reality in my life; my feelings would be sheltered, and death would only enter with my permission; my little prayer in Your Name would suffice to strike with its veto all threatening dangers, and I should live behind this impregnable wall like those fabulous heroes whom no arrows could pierce.

My God, I thank You for never having sanctioned his wild fancy; I thank You for not having spared me, and for having shod me with the heavy shoes of a traveller; for having obliged me to accomplish long stages of the journey with my knapsack on my back in the snow, and for having caused the imperative demands of Your Grace to cry aloud in my soul, waking me with a start from my delusive slumbers. I thank You for not having listened to me, when I demanded for myself privileged treatment, and when I wished to draw You into pleasant paths chosen by my laziness. I entreated

You; and You, full of mercy, refused to hear me. Your severity, perhaps, will succeed in making me love what is strong. I thank You for not having allowed this *prayer in Your Name* to become on my lips a magic formulary at the service of my whims. To pray in Your Name we need a soul so upright and so pure; I am only beginning to understand this. In Your Name, and therefore taking Your place, playing Your part, praying as You would have prayed, asking what You would have asked, and paying the price which You have paid. You redeemed the world, but it was after the *consummatum est;* You have infallibly obtained our forgiveness, but You never refused anything to Your Heavenly Father, and I, always quibbling and so rarely loyal with God, I who refuse to pay my debts, and who bargain for reductions on obligatory sacrifices, shall I dare to fall on my knees, put on a pious expression and say: In the Name of Christ, like Him, I supplicate and I await. . . . What price have I paid down so that I may be heard? Where is my hard-won resignation, where the retinue of my endurance? When have I ceased to live for myself? And that which I ask of God, is it not perhaps another privilege at the expense of my neighbour? . . .

Had You granted all these prayers, my God, my soul would have become sordid. I should have slighted Your Majesty as we despise the waters of great rivers, throwing into them all the refuse of our towns. . . . Thank You for having been deaf to my lamentations and for having pardoned my complaints. I understand better now, at what height You desire to find me. Having vainly tried to meet You on the level of my own life, I have been obliged to mount upwards towards You, and in refusing to be satisfied, You have given full scope to that power of ascension which Your grace has placed within me.

Nesciens quid diceret. . . . Thus it was Your Apostle asked to be allowed to make three tabernacles on the mountain of the Transfiguration. He was less selfish than I am, since he did not wish himself to dwell within these three abodes, and only thought of sheltering You with the law and with the prophets. You did not grant his prayer. You thought of all of us, and You knew that You had to climb another mountain to redeem the sons of Adam. Lord, how often have my good desires been as the blind, but the bustling, dangerous blind people, who gesticulate and excite themselves! You have not ratified them, I thank You on my knees. These good desires would have slain me, they would have lessened me, they would have crushed me in their jarring confusion. You waited wisely until the rough lessons of realities brought light into my mind. A good desire can have a kernel full of folly, I have known many of that type. It is only by breaking them, they can be judged.

You withstood Your Apostles and the crowd that intended to make You King; Your Kingship was to be far greater and higher and infinitely more appealing than all that those good people dreamt of. Thank You for having thought of us and for having fled again into the mountain by Yourself alone—*fugit in montem ipse solus* (*John* vi. 15)—and for not having granted this good desire of Your Galileans. You withstood James and John when they desired to call down fire upon the Samaritans: Your methods of action were quite other. Your Grace can penetrate into closed-up towns and sealed-up souls without anyone being aware of it and You prefer to win rather than to destroy. Thank You for having thus spared, even beforehand, our rebelliousness and for not having terrorised our weakness by granting the disastrous petition of Your "sons of Thunder." You withstood Simon Peter energetically when he took You aside and asked You to think no more of Your coming Passion and to abandon that suffering Redemption. He thought he was saying and doing what was right, but his good desire ran counter to the eternal plan of redemption, and because You did not hear him we can hope, some day, to see You. Yes, Lord, I thank You for all the petitions You have heard, and again I thank You for all those of which Your merciful Wisdom has understood the rash folly, and which it has not seemed to hear.

LXXXV

Minuta duo

Two little pieces of money
(*Luke* xxi. 2.)

TOGETHER they were worth a farthing, but it was with these slender resources that a widow one day forced admiration from the heart of God. It might be said, speaking in the language of trade, that this result was obtained at small cost. But when we examine the eternal values of human acts, we conclude rather that the sacrifice was heroic. One thing remains certain, and the imprescriptible Gospels are a proof of it, with a farthing's worth, provided we have two pieces of money in our hand, we can win for ourselves the measureless love of Christ. Yes, provided we have the two pieces. The whole lesson lies in this detail. For want of noticing it we risk understanding but little.

The poor widow came, then, where the box for alms stood facing her. Everyone throws in something. It is certain that she too will make an offering. There is nothing astonishing in that. To yield up a portion of our possessions to God and to our neighbour; to pay the tithings proportioned to our income; to deduct even such and such a part of our capital, all these are meritorious works certainly, but very human, based on calculations and on cunning, and they in no way savour of the absolute. If the poor widow, in spite of her penury, had thrown one offering into the box, it would have been extremely good, but Christ would not have exclaimed to His Apostles that He marvelled at her. For, after all, the generous poor are not rare. They are even the greater number. Man, in his own distress, does not refuse to share with others We should not be too much elated because we have made two portions of life and of our goods, because we have thought of God and have not kept everything for ourselves. To pass by the box and put nothing into it is impious; to pass through the treasury in the Temple and let fall there a part of our goods is very right and proper, it is the good action of a self-respecting tradesman.

But Christ had seen in the hand of the widow, two little pieces of money. She had taken them out of a miserable sack, where they could scarcely be seen; she held them in the hollow of her hands. Her whole fortune in two halves. And because in front of that alms-box she did not hesitate, because, after having thrown in the first piece, she also threw the second, her two empty hands delighted the Redeemer, and filled Him with emotion. It is the magnificent excess of this little second piece which gives all its value to the oblation.

There are things that we can only give as a whole; even a martyr has no choice between generosity and duty. By dying he does exactly what he is obliged to do, and if he gives in, even at the last moment, if he asks for concessions, he will be called a renegade. But there are also things which we can give in part; there are the counsels over and above the commandments, and it is possible to draw frontier lines in our lives, which shelter us from all reproach and yet leave us masters in our own house. To have two pieces of money in our hand, and having let go the first, to send the second to rejoin it is an absolute and total experience, and in a sense it is a perfect achievement. I can never experience the absolute in wealth, for I can always possess more and better things; I shall never experience the absolute in power, for I could always rule over more men, and exert more influence in the world . . . but poverty and abnegation can be strictly absolute. When my two hands are empty I defy anyone to empty them still more; when I have given up my independence, when I have made myself over to the Divine Will, who will be able to trouble me? He who drinks will never have drunk everything; he who hears will never have finished hearing; he who looks will always find new sights to see; but when I close my eyes I know the meaning of a complete absence of objects, when I shut my ears I know the meaning of a total silence, and when I drink nothing at all, there can be no question of more or less in that act.

The widow with the two little pieces of money had reached a limit. Because her action was without reserve, it was all-powerful. Before her, there had been the public sinner who broke her vase of perfume, that perfume of great price, the very scent of which recalled the dallying with sin. Here it is a poor woman very humble and good, who takes up again that same attitude and gives all, even that which she could so easily have kept.

The sinner was forgiven, and God praised her—*narrabitur quod haec fecit* (*Mark* xiv. 9)—the poor woman is exalted. Whether it be the perfume of luxury worth three hundred pence, or two little pieces of money of a derisory value, it is always by the total gift, by the spontaneous committal of our being to God, that we gain entrance into the fullness of His Grace.

My God, give timid souls the strength not to hesitate. I know some who are only separated from total generosity by the thickness of a sheet of paper, but they have never had the tranquil audacity to tear up this frail obstacle. They dare not place their security in You alone, and we, alas, are reduced to pleading the cause of absolute devotedness among Christian peoples; we have to explain and justify and promise, and while we talk, the crowd of pagans wait for those who will baptize them, and the crowd of wandering ones call vainly in the night.

Minuta duo.—Yes, if you wish it, make two parts in your life, in your days, in your possessions, that is understood. This to the right and that to the left. Arrange the proportions as you please, set going coefficients and divisors. And then, when all these fine operations are terminated, take the two portions of your wealth, place yourself in the long line of the faithful who are advancing towards the treasury of eternal offerings, throw in the first part to God, and then throw in the second also, and keep nothing in your heart but the liberty to serve Christ and the joy of possessing nothing outside of Him.

The poor have been evangelized, said Jesus Christ. They have been, so completely, that it is they who now evangelize us, but our ears are dull of hearing, and our hearts are well defended against surprise attacks of that grace which would make us generous.

LXXXVI

Elevatis oculis
Having lifted up His eyes
(*John xi.* 41.)

IF I could but read in His eyes, I should understand what I am and I
should know what I ought to do, and never again would anything
be capable of unsettling me. He looked at His disciples—*in discipulos*
—He looked at the heavens—*in coelum*—with that were those looks
laden? I want to try to understand.

Why should we not be sincere? Why not relieve our hidden
wounds? When in former days people spoke to me of the Sacred
Heart, the doleful discourses in which they unfolded this devotion
left me cold. Was it simply indifference, or was it bad will? But I can
recall how all my energies responded, offering themselves for the
service of the Church and the saving of souls. I remember too how
sacrifices were won from me, without expense of eloquence, merely
by asking me if I could have the dismal courage to refuse anything
to God. So I cannot help thinking that there was more misunderstanding than perversity in the feeling of muffled irritation which
rose up within me at the story of a God who was, it appeared, disappointed and woeful, and demanded that we should console Him a
little by shutting ourselves off from the crowds. This God who had
not succeeded! who seemed to have planned His affairs badly and to
lay the blame on others for His defeat! This tearful God who wished
to isolate Himself in some little sanctuaries and to surround Himself
with pious souls! I could not bring myself to identify Him with the
Christ of Easter, with the Saviour who loved the multitudes, and
whose immense work is to bring back all men to God. This attitude
of hidden discretion; the little promise added to the great Beatitudes; all this vague and somewhat feminine compassion, which
lost sight of the rugged labours of the Apostolate, how could it all
be reconciled with the sovereign action of the Word, commanding
the sea and the winds; with the glory of the Redeemer who received
all nations as His heritage, with the eternal splendour of the First-
born, of whom we sing in the Credo that Of His Kingdom there
will be no end?

My God I have already caught the shadows of this objection in
hearts which are nevertheless very faithful to You; I have seen the
mists gather over this devotion, in other ways so popular and so
catholic. It was found to be pessimistic and disheartening, all taken
up with gloomy lamentations and manœuvres of retreat. The Great
Redemption being as it were a lost battle, people would fall back, it

was said, on a more restrained devotion, and they would try to save something from the general disaster. Instead of speaking grandly to the whole world, they would speak to "the privileged," to chosen souls, to the fervent, in other words they renounced the idea of conquest and resigned themselves to failure. . . . An unfortunate God could not gain the heart of youth. Youth prefers words of command, even harsh ones to words of commiseration. It is quite prepared to hear peremptory truths; youth believes that the Kingdom of Heaven will be at least as exacting in its demands as the kingdoms of the earth. The young despise those who do not command their respect.

My God, however plausible it may appear, this objection is in reality of no account. It is full of gloomy folly. Those who refuse to enter fully into the Devotion to the Sacred Heart have never understood it. They believe that it is nothing more than a vast charity-sermon preached for the profit of the hapless Christ! They do not know that all the pride of our manhood can receive a tremendous impulse from it. They see in it only the weakness and the comfort of the feeble; they do not know that its demands are absolute and that it prepares a conquest.

Yes, Lord, You could have saved the world by Your sole grace, and You would have obtained far more quickly a definitive result; but in that result we should have had no part. It would have been handed over to us as a strange and beautiful present, like one of those manuscripts covered with an unknown text, which we look at without in the least understanding. The world saved by Your sole Grace could not be mingled with any of our own experiences, no more than the fabulous victory of Theseus over the Minotaur. We should have talked of it perhaps, we should have enjoyed it, but we should not have done it, and we are only wholeheartedly interested in that which we do. Happiness manufactured like sugar would not seem very human to us.

And so instead of doing it all alone. You have put Your work of salvation into our hands. You are the one source of all grace, but without our will You have decided not to succeed. You have wished that the salvation of the world should be our business also, and in order to recall this to our minds You stirred up the faith of Christians in the days of Paray-le-Monial.

Is it really a question of some little devotion? Oh! the conceit of those false wiseacres! It is God who looks into your eyes—*elevatis oculis*—and who says to you: Will you accept to be the saviour of the world? I associate you with my Redemption. Here are the reaping hooks, and there is the harvest; I do not wish to reap it myself, let us share the labour. Your generosity will be the measure of the size of your sheaves. To work then!

And in order to show us clearly that the work is tragic, He has cried out for help! Each moment that passes is weighted with death for men. Unceasingly the heavy axe falls down. Help! Help! When we hear this cry in the night, does it really seem, in its brevity, to be wanting in eloquence, and do we not, with all our power, fly towards the peril?

That God should cry to me for help! If I understood that aright, the rhythm of my life would change, all my pettiness would fade away.

I should feel an immense capacity for self-devotion rise within me, and the glory of self-sacrifice would fill me to overflowing. I can be of use to God, even I, since in His work, if my hand slacked, there would be a blank.

No, there is no question of isolating Himself from us. Christ is always the Christ of the crowds. It is just because the multitudes press and throng that He calls me to His help. Never has He turned away from men, for whom to-day He would again be ready to be led before Pilate; never has He asked that those devoted to Him should cease to be Apostles in order to sing melodies to Him; for the melody of His choice is that of the unison of all souls in love—*in concentu vestro Christus canitur* (*Ignatius of Antioch*)—it is that of creation refinding the voice of its innocence and, delivered from all powers of death, repeating the chorus of Bethlehem: *Carmen Christo tanquam Deo.* (*Pliny's letter to Trajan.*) Who then will dare to tell us that all this is out of fashion? Who then will dare to speak here of pettiness and trivialities. *Fortis ut mors dilectio.* (*Cant.* 8. 6.)

T

LXXXVII

Relictis retibus
Leaving there their nets
(*Matt. iv.* 20.

LORD, You are the plenitude of all things. Explain to me, how it is that, in order to attain to You, we must despoil ourselves. You are overflowing wealth, is it then very logical to make ourselves poor in order to unite ourselves to You? I have heard learned people, apparently extremely wise ones, who, on all this matter, held the most ridiculous opinions. They affirmed that complete renunciation was not necessary for Your Apostles, or at least it was not so neces-iary; they found there was exaggeration in speaking of total abnega-lion, and their dream was of a very comfortable kind of perfection, anwhich Your love adding a beatitude to all legitimate satisfactions, n d the joy of our soul being conjoined with the pleasures of the body, the Christian, Your disciple, would glide along in cloudless days, sheltered from all excess. With the help of a little casuistry to segalize what we are going to do, and a little absolution to forget what we have done, Your claims become extremely acceptable, and the Gospel is shorn of all sternness.

Alas! my God, I dare not say that these subtle poisons have not filtered even into my soul, and if I were to pretend that my principles had never faltered, that I have always got the most out of myself, I should lie in the face of the sun, and the very stones would rise up to protest against my hypocritical vanity.

No, Your claims are absolute. Those who desire perfection may not first discuss Your conditions, but they must accept them all without bargaining. You enter into our lives like a swordblade and we bleed from Your visits. I have seen You thus take people, wrest-ing them from everything in order to fling them into the cloisters of prayer or the wards of the cancer-stricken; I have seen You speaking to humble young girls in terms so peremptory that my cowardice quailed. You did not say: Give something; but by a gesture You showed that You must have all. You did not say: Later on, when men shall have been served, I shall doubtless receive some fragments of your love; but with an all-compelling look, You placed Yourself right across the road and demanded that You should be given the whole future as a gift; that all hopes should be put back into Your hands.

You are hard indeed, You, the Humble of heart; You are so astonishing in these manœuvres of Your Providence, and my weakness has at times shuddered, thinking that You were about to impose the austerity of complete renunciation on such and such a soul, so fresh and still so young.

You are, as always, right. To know it we have but to look at those whom we call Your victims and who call themselves Your chosen ones. With their whole hearts they cling to their sacrifice, not only because it frees them, but because it has filled them; not only for the future glories of Paradise, but for the present rejoicings of love and of grace.

Relictis retibus. Without again thinking of their nets! You exact all, You demand complete deprivation, because You wish to fill all with a new wine, because You wish to transform all into eternal life. You require that we should empty our hearts just as we thoroughly clean a bottle that was filled with some sour liquid, before we pour into it the cordial that refreshes—*Recedant vetera, nova sint omnia. (Sacris solemniis.)* That which You bring to us has no common measure with that which we possess, it is like the temple of wood that must be turned into a temple of marble. This transformation is impossible unless all the pieces of the original and corruptible building are replaced. It is useless to put gold casings over decayed teeth, all that has been injured, or that is about to be injured must first be removed; nothing must be kept of the inaccuracies of a slipshod calculation; only fools imagine that they can see the sun better by lighting candles. So then, because You are unique, incomparable, above and outside of all that exists, You come to blow out our candles to the very last, and in our night it is Your dawn, Yours alone that begins to enlighten us. I remember how in underground caverns, when we drew near to the passage of exit we put out all artificial lights to see, down there, in the bluish vapour the growing brightness of the day.

Your exigencies are so beneficent! I thank You for Your severity as Redeemer, I thank You for never having allowed us to mingle the odour of death with Your perfume of eternity; or to combine in our foolish mixtures the grains of earthly love and the unique incense of Your Grace. Your Apostles were obliged to leave their nets, not in order that they might be the poorer, but because You were on the point of making them fishers of men, and men could not be taken in meshes of string. When we wish to travel by train we must get out of our cart. He who would combine these two modes of locomotion would be ridiculous. The extent of the preliminary deprivation is in proportion to the subsequent benefits. To possess God we must possess nothing but God. Heaven is nought else.

Give me, O Lord, the grace to understand, and the strength to will. I attach myself so gladly to all that passes. I am foolish, blind and mad, and at times I grumble like the wicked servant, finding

You hard and inconvenient. Why do You want to have everything, and immediately, and given gladly? Thus do my foolish grumblings go, and I seek for means of evasion and I apply for delays.

And yet, those who have made the experience proclaim that nothing has ever been wanting to them from the day on which they consented to make You their sole riches. Do not allow, O Lord, that my cowardice should appear to give the lie to their strong testimony: *Te martyrum candidatus laudat exercitus.* Above all, do not allow that under pretext of sweetening it Your Gospel should be made insipid; do not tolerate that maudlin talk should lull those souls to sleep which You redeemed. The day on which we shall believe that an intermittent fidelity and a lax devotion are on the whole very creditable, and that wholesale generosity, vocations to complete self-sacrifice are the exception, open to the intemperate zeal of fanatics, that day we shall be worse than Sodom and Gomorrha and we shall have blasphemed Your Calvary.

LXXXVIII

THEY had persevered during three days—*triduo*—and that fidelity touched Your heart. During three days they had clung to You, and You repaid their faith by a miracle. This crowd! You fed it in the desert. My God, is it pride in me to think that the Galilean multitude must have counted in its numbers mediocrities of my sort, a few at least? It is scarcely probable that all those people were heroes, that all those souls had continually shown themselves to be perfect. In the lot I should most certainly have found a half-dozen of my colour and of my type, the type of a virtue without any brilliancy, and the colour of a desire that is somewhat faded. This thought encourages me. Because of the whole crowd these too were instructed, fed, saved, forgiven. It is always into this compact mass of the faithful that I like to withdraw, just as a wounded soldier retires from the front line of battle to reach some section in the rear. My only hope is that I too may be saved with the mass, carried to right and to left, raised up and borne along by the vigorous virtues of all my neighbours, as we are lifted up in spite of ourselves in a great crowd, and as the fish are dragged along by the meshes of the immense nets, which at one stroke depopulate a whole fishweir.

They did not leave You . . . during three days! My God, I am going to continue my discourse. Listen to me: It seems to me that I have done better than that. Perhaps it is very impertinent of me to say so. But if I did not say it I should hide something from You, and if I said the contrary I should lie to the truth. Three days! Nothing to boast of! With the risk of being hungry and the fatigue of having to go home again! But see, Lord, for far longer time than that my life has been attached to Yours; far longer has my fidelity kept me by You, and to stay with You I have known hunger, yes, of soul and also of body, and physical distress and the weariness of nerves and will. *Triduo sustinent me.* Towards me You have been more exacting and yet I was no stronger nor more capable of endurance than Your Galileans. I have waited for You during many years, I have tasted of Your trials. Yes, You have been hard through kindness; You did not wish to fashion for me a little, comfortable, sleepy life. I thank You for that. I have known long stages in the desert, and nights without sleep, when the heart beats madly like the old-time tocsin sounding the alarm. When people wishing to attract souls say that those who serve You are, by that very fact, steeped in consolation;

293

when Your service is pictured as a perpetual and delicious ecstasy, and Your claims over us are represented as tender invitations and overpowering allurements, my God, my God, I think, in truth they have not said the whole, and that indeed they have kept silence on essentials. There is the clash of sabres in Your words, and terrible exactions in Your calls. *Non pacem . . . sed gladium.* And the grace that is within us is first and foremost a grace of strength, so that our shoulders may not bend, and our knees may not be loosened under the immense weights which You impose upon us. By dint of saying that nothing is sweeter than to serve You, we finish by making people believe that You command nothing that is disagreeable, and that we can calmly excuse ourselves for the omission of any duty on the single ground that it is not free from bitterness.

The delight, the rapture of which You make a gift to Your disciple is the rapture of rough labour, it is the joy of toiling mightily, of never sparing ourselves, of hitting hard upon all obstacles, and of demanding no consideration for ourselves. *Sustinent me.* Such people know how You must be borne with, and what long patience must precede Your miraculous gifts. They understand what it costs our weakness to put our trust in You. They have known what it is to hunger, they have known too that anguish of the weak who feel their last strength ebbing away, and the startling dizziness of faintness in their bewildered heads. My God! You are an austere Master: but that is quite right, I do not complain of it. In our life all that is really beautiful is also strong, from the love of a mother, so rich in sacrifice, to the intrepidity of the soldier who accepts to die, standing, alone, at his post.

Triduo.—I rejoice to realize that my years, passed in the desert place have been long. You will have pity on me, because of the fidelity I have shown in waiting for You, and because I have clung to Him whom the Father has given us as our Saviour. You will have pity on me, that is certain. You only came on earth to save people of my sort. But in looking more closely into the matter, my God I, think that You have already begun for me Your miracle of feeding. I need not wait till my life of faith is ended in glory to know with what marvellous food You sustain the strength of Your disciples, for You have not waited for that consummation to make Your Grace and the power of Your Spirit pass into me. In the days of trial you were my strength, and perhaps I did not know it. I thought that it was from my own provisions I was being fed; I thought my strength came from myself, and yet without You I should have died long since of thirst and hunger.

Sustinent me.—I do not abandon You, but that is first of all because You undertake not to let me go. It is You who hold me up, without saying a word, and who since the far-off days of my childhood, have been so careful not to let me perish from misery. Continue, O Lord, to give this divine alms to me, the mysterious bread, the invisible succour which comes through Your hands towards my distress, for I cannot live except on Your gifts, without them—*deficiam in via*.

Grant that I may love more and more this life of faith, wholly irradiated by hope; grant that I may love this desert-place where You have put my soul, this immense plain with You in its centre, where I stand before You, not alone, but lost in the crowd of my brethren and depending, with them, on Your sole mercy. I am quite determined not to leave You, and if I do not leave You, I shall fear neither the enemy, nor death, and I shall live for ever on Your mercy.

Ego sum via

I am the Way
(*John* xiv. 6.)

THERE is a great sacrament, a deep mystery of love which makes the roads on which we walk divine. I speak of the paths, of the real paths, of those on which we go at the pace of our weariness or of our hopes, of those paths traced by man on that earth which he inherits on the day of his birth, and into which his coffin is, at the last, lowered. Has not theology, in order to describe the race of those who toil, called the sons of Adam *viatores*, the wayfarers?

My God, help me to understand the dumb signs hidden in things, and tell me what is this Gospel of the road. I recall to mind that the Romans already spoke of the sacred way, but they did not understand, they could scarcely even conjecture the truth. Since You await your chosen ones at all the cross-roads, marvellous things have happened on our highways; our whole salvation is at stake perhaps, as we go by some familiar path, as with Saul travelling towards Damascus. . . . To follow a track is to be docile and confiding. When we can no longer find the road we simply say that we are lost, just like those who have not discovered, or have abandoned, the sure straight way that leads to Your light—*per tuas semitas.*

We put our trust in a road. If a river bars the passage, we know quite well that the road has foreseen this obstacle, and that a bridge will be there to get us out of the difficulty; if we have to go through a forest, we know that wood-cutters have gone before us, and that in the midst of the high forest trees, as for a king, our way is opened; the road climbs over mountains or descends them; it skirts the edges of the abyss; it is a little like You, O Lord, in that at the price of immense labour it unites souls and things, gently and without saying a word, *facit utraque unum* (*Eph.* ii. 14)—and also because it draws strangers together.

I do not wonder that the Church has blessed our roads, and that we find in our breviaries, the *Itinerarium clericorum.* To go by the road towards a far-off, invisible end is to begin again the act of Abraham quitting Chaldea, and that of the Magi setting out for Bethlehem; was not it You Yourself who undertook to tell them that another road would be better for the return journey to their own country—*per aliam viam reversi sunt?*

The old highways of Christendom! Those which lead to ancient sanctuaries, and along which pilgrims in their thousands have passed!

No, I cannot consider as profane actions all those steps which I, as it were, lay out in line along the ways of earth. You Yourself came and walked upon our roads; You discussed with Your disciples as to the best routes to follow; You avoided Judea or Samaria; it was on a road that Peter acknowledged You to be the Son of God and became himself the key-bearer; and it is, O my God, on the way of the Cross that You redeemed the world, and that You pardoned me. When I, weak as I am, hasten, quickening my steps on the roads, I do as You did; when to walk wearies me, and the length of the roads exhausts me, I am like You. And it has nearly always been upon our paths that Your all-powerful Grace has willed to overtake us. It was thus with the blind man, Bartimeus, and that Ethiopian whom Philip converted, and the Samaritan woman, and all those whom in the course of ages Your sanctuaries have drawn from afar.

Ego sum via.—Nothing is more unassuming, nothing more imperious, than a road. To right or to left we lose our way. To remain upon it is to be secure. I desire Your Providence to be my path. What can ever be wanting to me if I do not leave You; and if You are my road, to what could You lead me but to Yourself and to the splendour of the Father?

But it is tiresome to keep faithfully to the high road. When it makes windings it does not tell us why. It is dumb as You are, calm as You are. The short-sighted wisdom that reigns within me, invents short-cuts when Your will leads the long way round. I am always tempted to rectify Your trail, and I feel my faith perpetually assailed by imperative "Whys?" Why do You ask such a sacrifice? Why do You land me with these tiresome people? Why do You lead me to total abnegation, to a religious vocation, to trial and to sickness? Why, above all, do You delay so long before allowing me to meet the happiness which I anticipate and the freedom of which I have caught a glimpse? Your road is a winding one, and yet You told us by the prophet and by Your Precursor that Your paths were always in the straight line: *recta facite semitas ejus.* You said that all the crooked ways should be made straight: *erunt prava in directa.* It seems to me that there is a contradiction between Your words and Your actions, and that Your Providence does not like straight roads. . . . Unless, indeed, it is that I am myself again mistaken? I always have the mania of believing that everything that is in accordance with my desire is straight, and that what I think is correct. When my plan and Yours are out of harmony, I pretend that it is You who have left the line. The right moment is always that of my impatience, and I find all clocks are slow as soon as my cupidity does not get what it expects. I foolishly look on the senseless zigzags of my caprices as perfectly straight lines. No, it is You who continue to press straight on towards the term, not allowing Yourself to be disturbed by my actions or my clamour. My short-cuts are actually circuitous roads. And when I look back towards the horizons of my vanished days, towards the stages of the journey already passed, I see clearly that Your Will towards me was one which knew no hesitation and no retrogression. It is this rectitude of Your thought which frightens me. I know that You are leading me by Your Passion and Your Death to the glory of Your Resurrection, and I entreat You to protect me against myself, not to allow me to go astray nor to permit that weariness of being faithful to You should overcome me. Grant that I may be a *viator* until the end, and be Yourself the goal of my pilgrimage.

XC

Judicium est mundi
The world is judged
(*John xii.* 31.)

LORD, that which delights and that which terrifies me in You is that You are inevitable, more than inevitable, final. When You shall have completed Your passage through the ranks of men it will be settled for all eternity that some will have found themselves on Your right hand and the others will have remained on Your left. And then there will be no further question of anything. Each one will be fixed for ever. No one will be able to continue Your work, there will no longer be a Redeemer to save those who have disowned You.

You are inevitable. Light has come into the darkness. The night which has consented to receive this light has itself become sun-lit, and all its original blackness has vanished; but the night which has refused to let itself be penetrated by this ray, that night has not remained merely what it was. It is now a night by choice, it is a night that has despised the light, and its natural darkness is now a guilty darkness. He who will not have God becomes worse than a man, he is a lost man.

And this judgment of the world has already begun. Whether men wish it or not, You are in their midst. They can indeed behave as if they were unconscious of Your presence, but when we feign not to see the corner-stone there is no pretence whatever about the way in which we are crushed against it. You are installed in our Universe, and You judge us all. We remain eternally fixed in the attitude which we shall have taken up towards You. When I meditate upon these things a slight shudder of terror runs through my soul. I cannot bear that which is irrevocable. I am a little like those authors who become almost crazy when their manuscripts are taken from them, and always wanting to make new corrections and amendments, they suffer anguish at the thought of an irrevocable text. For centuries, O Lord, the race of men has accustomed itself to scheming and correcting and beginning again, and the full-stop always frightens us. You are a full-stop, and the last letter of the alphabet; You are that mysterious omega after which there is nothing more to hope for. It is then with You that we must come to terms; it is on You that we must count as on our last hope.

To recognize You when You pass, to know who You are, and to confess it without dissimulation, thus to receive Your truth into our lives is the only way to escape from death. You are present, and yet those who do not wish to see You, do not see You; You speak unceasingly and yet the would-be-deaf hear, in reality, none of Your words, and take us for fools when we listen to Your voice filling the immensity of Your work. The one thing that matters is to lay hold of You as You pass, and I know some who have spent their whole lives seated in the ditches, by the edges of the roads along which You were walking, and who have assured me that they have never met You. You are in the midst of us; Your eyes question us; Your truth judges us, and many come and go, laugh and weep, sleep and think, without ever having been embarrassed in their movements by Your presence, and without having knocked up against You in their work.

And yet all these people have already been judged by You. All those who wish to ignore You, and who shape the course of their lives afar from You, will be able to realize their desire, and will, for ever, be delivered from Your Presence. You are terrible and good, terrible like all that stands firm and does not yield, terrible like the Truth which nothing can persuade and like Justice which nothing can corrupt. From all wilful blindness may Your Grace preserve me!

The culpably blind do not lie when they say that their wide-open eyes reveal no sign of Your presence to them. Their sin is more subtle and their infidelity far deeper. They have put it out of their power to see You, like those Jews whom hate had blinded to such an extent that they judged they did well at the moment when they crucified the Son of God. Long continued laziness, or conceited moroseness, whining cowardice or sarcastic pride, the desire of money or hardness of heart, all these things consented to are the power of darkness within us—*Videte ne vos tenebrae comprehendant*. (*John* xii. 35.) And when I say that I do not see You, it is not always, it is indeed, never, a valid excuse.

If, however, I will to obey You! If only I could promise to shift my course no more, to put myself back without reserve under Your sole rule and to receive my whole life from You! The Fathers of the Greek Church have told us that, in Your Incarnation, You had cured all that You had assumed, and that, desiring to cure the whole of human nature, You had been obliged to take it completely upon You and to become man, body and soul, mind and will. It seems to me that the same thing should take place within me. All that I keep is lost, condemned, judged worthless, given up to death. All that You assume, all that I give into Your hands, all *that* is cured divinized, becomes immortal and enters into the House of the Father. My days are of no value if they are not Yours, and my long drawn efforts only beat the air if Your Grace is not their starting point.

O, my Judge, take all. I do not wish that this title of Judge should chill my confidence. It is, in reality, because You are definitive that I love You. If Your judgment could be repealed, You would be weak, and what help would my feebleness find in resting on Your impotence? But what You will have said of me, no one can ever refute; No one will come to write in pencil above what You shall have written; and the day that, looking me straight in the eyes, You will have proclaimed that I am "one of Yours" and that my trial has ended, on that unending day, I shall bless You without measure for being the One who does not change. You have imposed the obligation on me of hoping for this ineffable happiness and of expecting from You, my Judge, eternal life.

XCI

Et erant valde bona
And they were very good
(*Gen. i.* 31.)

THEY were so very good, those works of Yours, my God, when they left Your hands, that in spite of all our profanations, they have kept the marks of their noble origin. When extremists among theorizers have proceeded to tell the faithful that nature was totally corrupted by original sin, and that in its present state, such as we see it, You could never have created it, for it was unworthy of You, Holy Church laid hold of these accursed doctrines, in their passage, and condemned them. It is not true that the Creation in which I find myself has become wholly bad. It is broken down. A wounded man is not a dead man.

Since this creation is Your work, I can discover in it the marks of Your fingers; since it comes from You it returns to You, and the aroma of Your eternity is wafted over all these transient things. I wish to pray this evening with all Your creatures. Why have we not as yet got the Feast of Creation in our Christian calendar? I know indeed that this idea has been defiled, and that unbelievers have attempted to substitute the Author of the Universe for the Divine Father who is in heaven, that they wished to put nature in the place of Your grace. But is not that all the more reason why we should restore to Your work the honour that belongs to it, just as we organize magnificent ceremonies of expiation, and as we pray solemnly in our Churches when some public act of impiety has for a time profaned them?

I hear around me the protracted lamentations of all those people who are, they say, disabused; they find that everything is wearisome, and they can discover no good reason for living. They have never learnt to look, in quietness and in truth on the beautiful side of simple things; they do not know in what divine splendours their lives are incessantly bathed and they will die without having opened their eyes.

No, Your work is not faded. The phrase which You uttered when creating all things, that phrase which the Universe sends back to us in echo, is so beautiful that we almost fear to cling too much to it and take it for Your whole discourse. When we consent to allow ourselves to be delighted by the works of Your hands, life becomes a perpetual wonder, and without even penetrating into the world of souls, in the realm of nature alone we find reason for unceasing adoration. Tell me, O my God, were they quite mistaken, those far-off ancestors of ours, who prostrated themselves before century-old trees and threw their offerings to the waterfalls? Yes, they were mistaken, of course, to confound the work and the Workman; they were mistaken in adoring the effect, without, as they say in books, rising up to the Cause; but between the work and the workman there is not, after all, an absolute separation, the effect only subsists through all that it has received from the cause. My ancestors were mistaken, not because their movement went in a wrong direction, but because they stopped short too soon, like the Crusaders who set out all right for the Holy Land, but loitered at the first port and never saw Jerusalem.

I have not enough respect for things. I do as those Roman soldiers did in the sack of Corinth, playing at dice on the priceless pictures of the old Greek masters. I do not hear the modest voices of those million messengers, who from the wind-flowers to the shooting-stars speak to me of You and invite me to love You, because I am still coarse and brutal, and my selfish dream of happiness haunts and degrades me. When some great personage preaches on simplicity or on confidence and when he cleverly knits his serried arguments, I listen, and I admire and I feel more or less convinced. But is it really necessary to disturb great personages to teach me or to re-teach me these ancient truths? Did You not Yourself recommend us in the Gospels to consider the flowers of the field and to put ourselves to school with the homely sparrow? Are not the scorpions, the serpents, the eggs and the hens, the ox and the ass, the well and the lamp, the bread and the oven, the lake, the net, the tempest, the reaping hook and the harvest, are not all these simple things from the crowing of the cock to the glow of the setting sun, enriched with lessons for us through You, and full of memories? When the cocks crow, should not I, a Christian instead of thinking of them as humble fowl of the poultry-yard, recall the palace of the High Priest and the triple denial? Should I not, in presence of the glowing embers of a wood fire, think of the soldiers of the cohort and hear from afar the voice of the servant maid? Should not the silent night be filled for me with the low grave tones in which, in those far-off days, You made known to Nicodemus the necessity of being born again in order to escape from death—*Nasci denuo?*

You are everywhere and to whatever side I turn, it is Your Truth and Your love that I meet. Creator, Redeemer, You are the Word by whom all things were made; it was then suitable, as theology inrorms us, that the One who made the World should come to repair it. It was best that the Workman should not entrust to any other the care of setting His own masterpiece to rights again. And thus it is The Word who became Incarnate. In the Universe I find then no trace of a double plan, no lines of a two-fold design as in our feeble architecture, in which successors come and complete, according to their own ideas, that which the original builders, carried off by death, had no time to finish. All has been made by You, and all has been remade by You. Your hands, those which upheld Peter on the waters, and which the soldiers fastened to the blood-stained wood, are the hands of Him who created the world and who alone can save me at the last day.

> *Tuae sanctae manus istae*
> *Me defendant, Jesu Christe,*
> *Ultimis in periculis.*

> (*Hymn—Salve, salve Jesu bone.*)

Grant that I may adore these divine hands everywhere throughout Your work; grant that admiration may purify me and never allow that from my lips or from my heart words of contempt should fall for this marvellous Universe in which You have found a place for me, for me whom, along with all the rest, You pronounced to be very good at the moment You created me.

XCII

YOU have forbidden us to put out our own light. You have not even wished that we should be voluntarily dwarfed. You have prohibited the suppression of that which shines. I admire Your command, but I fear that I may not understand it, and may make use of it in order to canonize the most wretched ambitions and to stimulate the most conceited pretensions. To shine is to appear. All upstarts will make use of Your precept, Lord, and the discontented will talk of the bushel as soon as authority, or tradition imposes salutary restraints on them. Chatterers will no longer consent to keep silence. They are always persuaded that their discourses are rivers of enlightenment. Beginners will each claim their own candlestick—*supra candelabrum*—and all modesty, all effacement, all reserve will become ridiculous and evil things. . . . It is so easy when we are smoky and flickering to lay the blame of our weakness on one or another importunate bushel; it is so easy, in order to excuse our cowardice, to incriminate circumstances and to compare ourselves with what we might have been, if we had but found the "candlestick." It is not the humble who glorify You, and did You not Yourself recommend those who were invited to a feast to place themselves of their own accord at the lower end of the table?

The bushel with which we have no right to muffle up our virtue or our talents is not that of modesty or reserve. These are always necessary. The bushels forbidden to us to use are pusillanimity, distrust, cunning lies and cowardice. It is the bushel with which the avaricious flame covers itself, not in order to be protected from the draught, or to give itself time to increase, but in order to withdraw itself from others and to keep its light to itself. Selfishness is the summing-up of all our powers of extinction, and many have gone through life most uselessly, who with a little self-sacrifice could have enlightened a world. The bushel is a life of comfort and slackened effort; it is the little handscreen which we use to limit our horizon artificially; the refusal to illuminate the whole house and to work to the utmost of our powers. The flame hidden under the bushel, the talent wrapped up in the napkin, the buried treasure, all teach the same terrible lesson; we shall be forced to render an account of the good we have omitted to do, and of the good which our cowardice made us incapable of accomplishing.

A holy spirit of adventure is at the bottom of the Christian temperament. Why should we fear the light? Why preach slackened virtue? Why should we only occupy ourselves in sheltering, in a poor way, those who believe, while neglecting the immense multitudes who are waiting in the darkness? My God I cannot bear that the world should be thus divided; that they should make compartments in the one home and say: Here is for us, there for our adversaries; here for the believers, there for the unbelievers; here for our friends, there for the sons of the devil. . . . These cruel frontiers were not sanctioned by You, when You said that we owed our light to all eyes, and that our love should extend itself as far as the penetrating action of Your Grace. Our adversaries of to-day! You perhaps, are preparing them in secret, as You prepared Saul, the persecutor, to carry Your name throughout the world, and our believers have no reason to give themselves airs of importance, they have to work out their own salvation, taking care lest they fall—*qui stat videat ne cadat.* (1 *Cor.* x. 12.) To have faith in the Truth is to bring it fearlessly face to face with lies and errors: darkness is incapable of killing a flame. To have faith in Grace is fearlessly to ask heroic virtue from men, it is to measure their obligations, not by their own powers, nor their duties by their resources; but to bring into our calculations the inexhaustible reserves of divine power, and to call upon Christians to be worthy of Christ—*ut ambuletis digne Deo.* (*Col.* i. 10.)

Pagan fears put the finishing touch to our corruption. We are all encumbered by people who refuse, as they say, to compromise themselves and who only rally to the combatants after the victory. One would say that everything that belittles is welcome to them. They have never been willing nobly to run the risk of the magnificent adventure of universal charity. They have never consented to burn unreservedly for the good of all. Their virtues are narrow and distrustful, and their first care, like that of mediocre soldiers, is to find themselves a good shelter, before they set out to do anything.

Ut luceat omnibus.—I belong to all, I have no right to use my mind as if it was of no concern to anyone but myself. Dilettantism is always very culpable. My physical vigour, my moral health, and everything for which others might envy me, is part of the "lamp" and should shine *in domo.* Mediocre ways are always full of fascination for our laziness, and when a duty is irksome to us, we immediately conclude it is not meant for us.

Lord, I know, perhaps, something of the men of my day. You caused me to be born among them, I assure You they are not so bad as some pretend, nor even so perverse as they themselves say. There is in them, as there was in their ancestors, an immense capacity for self-sacrifice, a real desire not to live an aimless life. They wish for a job, a hard one if needful, but one which is worth the trouble they would take to do it well. They do not refuse to work, they accept even to die, so long as the work is not useless and their death has some meaning. That which is lacking to them is not Your Grace. They need, as the attacking units in an army, an objective and a field of action, rising ground on which they can open out freely, giving full play to all their energies. Those who will speak to men in the language which Your Grace whispers to them, those who will enlighten the work that lies before us by a ray of that light which You cause to burn in the depths of all minds, those who will have faith in Truth which delivers, in Justice which saves, in Christ who forgives, those who will say all that should be said, and do all that should be done will shine as stars *in perpetuas aeternitates*.

A bimatu et infra
Of two years old and under
(*Matt. ii.* 16.)

IN order to make quite sure of getting rid of You, they massacred all around who might be like You, and Bethlehem heard the cry of mothers weeping. The tactics of Your enemies have in no ways changed. Their methods have made no progress, and it is by laying waste their own countries that they endeavour to free themselves from You.

Before You had spoken they tried to destroy You. Brutally, cruelly, they wished to strike the new-born Christ, so much did they fear to be disturbed later on by the true King of the one Israel.

My God, I know these ridiculous and destructive tyrants; I know where they are, those who crush, in their country the country of their own souls, the yet tender shoots of Your inspirations and who wish to close Your mouth before You have said a single word. We are so jealous of our independence and, not daring always to withstand You, when You thunder from the heights of Sinai, we take cowardly revenge on Your humble advents, and we overthrow the beginnings of Your work in us.

You are born within our will each time that a good impulse, coming from Your Grace, makes us better. And we fear to be better, because we have no love for austere perfection. We are afraid lest, having become stronger within us by reason of our earlier concessions, You may raise Your voice; we fear to find a Master in You, and to be ousted from the royal palaces which our selfishness has usurped, and in which we have established our lives most comfortably. Your inspirations are so frail! Those good desires which flash across our minds can be so easily suppressed! No one will know anything of it, and none will even hear in Rama, the lamentations of Rachel. When a generous thought is born within us, we have but to make a little sign and it will cease to be. My God, I begin to think that the worst disloyalties are brought about through the injury done to these little things. I ask myself whether it is not to this fundamental ruthlessness of souls, exteriorly very correct, that we must look, in order to explain the secret of their little worth. What should we not gain if we allowed Christ to speak and to grow within us, if we respected the first, still timid invitations of His Grace! In the things of life it is always the most feeble element that is the most effective. Plants shoot up through the tiny extremities of their buds, and it is by means of the fragile point of the combatants of the first line, that an army with all its immense resources in the rear, goes onward to its victory. When a needle has been broken, it is but an invisible fragment that has been shattered, but the needle is no longer of any use, for it is by its point that it pierces through the stuff and nothing can replace this point. Your initial graces are almost imperceptible, but they are decisive. The whole of a life can be changed under their modest impulse.

But we cut them down mercilessly. We are always on our guard against You, and our fidelity is very deceitful. We do not like a God who inconveniences us, we do not tolerate a God who dethrones us. Grant that I may welcome Your birth within my soul and all that silent, tender meekness by which You bend my ridiculous obstinacy towards good.

For if I do not allow You to become my Master, I shall be obliged to injure myself very much, and through fear of You I shall kill within me all promise of the future and all flowers of innocence. The massacre of the Innocents is a sinister story and a terrible symbol. To cut down within myself all that seems like Your inspiration, all the companions of the Christ of Bethlehem, is a cruel butchery. When we wish to protect ourselves from Your pretensions, we must turn whole regions of our souls into desert places. All generosity must be looked on with suspicion by him who fears to see You coming under the disguise of some inspiration to charity; all noble love is disquieting to him who does not wish to be disturbed in his repose, and who wishes to continue his ridiculous dreams in peace. I know in truth that should I wish to cut You out of my life, I should have to abolish, to kill, everything that reconciles me to my duties and enables me to be not altogether vile. I know that I should have to sacrifice much innocence to be delivered from You and that I cannot drive You out unless I massacre *en bloc* my good desires.

And I also know that these infamous manœuvres could never crush You, but would make me gravely guilty. You never cease to be the true King of souls, even of those who persecute You, deny You and drive You away. Our clever strategies are but the play of naughty children, and when we refuse to let You speak we deprive ourselves of eternal life. This terrible truth fills me with consolation. If You are always the King of souls, it is because they are always made for You, and that in this life Your Grace never abandons them. When they are guilty it is not because Christ, their Saviour was massacred before He had been able to redeem them it is because they do not accept the salvation which is always offered, and they treat their God as an intruder. We have not, here below, the power of destroying You; You are at times driven from souls be grievous sin, but from the other side of the frontier, in Egypt,

u*

You watch for the moment when the tyrants will be dead—*defunct sunt enim qui quaerebant animam purei*—and as soon as the land is freed You return to Your country. In spite of my infidelities, which have lasted long perhaps, come back to me, O Lord! The tyrants are dead or dying. I have had enough of laboriously trying to establish my own system of home politics; I can make nothing of all these combinations, and I have a horror of my meanness. I no longer wish to kill my good desires or to suppress so many dawning graces. Come back to me and reign within me, and do with me what You will according to the measure of Your infinite mercy.

XCIV

De laqueo venantium
From the snare of the hunters
(*Psalm xc. 3*.)

YOU have been very hard, O Lord, towards all those who place their hopes in riches. In spite of the care that we have taken to soften down Your words they still wound us, when we re-read the Gospels. All our exegesis has been powerless to blunt their sharp edges. They remain, as on the first day You uttered them, piercing after the manner of a sharpened sword-blade—*penetrabilior omni gladio* (*Heb.* iv. 12). I can easily imagine that if I refuse to understand them, my life will be stamped with a great falsehood. I can perceive indeed that between your disciples and pagans there ought to be an absolute difference in their manner of considering wealth. It is not possible that we and they should view in the same light, and weigh in the same balance, that which You have called by a word that cannot be translated, the "mammon of iniquity," that strange thing which is Your rival and which we cannot serve without ceasing to belong to God.

So I come back to that eternal lesson of poverty, like fireflies which hover round the lamps at night. It is fascinating and consequently dangerous. I know that there have been extravagant views with regard to wealth which were heretical, and I fear equally the solutions which are too simple and dispense us from thought, and those which are too clever and allow us to keep everything. There is such a thing as religious poverty, but this poverty cannot be totally confined to the cloister any more than obedience or chastity or the apostolate. Its spirit can be no man's monopoly, since all virtues should exist in some form in the faithful, and all spiritual goods are shared in Your Church.

Lord, there are people who have this word poverty for ever on their lips, but the thing of which they speak, and which they recommend to us, is not poverty at all, but stinginess. They say that we are always mistaken in spending much, and I do not find that there is anything very supernatural in that opinion. Doubtless we should not spend much on our own selfishness, and our own sensual gratifications; even nothing at all should be spent on the support of these old enemies. But when I am enjoined to respect money, and to gaze with awe upon the signs of wealth as on a thing that is almost sacred, I allow myself to believe that Your blessed words have been perverted, and that we are being induced to adore images. There are two ways of showing that we hold very much to money; the first is to accumulate it to such an extent that we seem to think we can never have enough; the second is to spend so little that we seem to imagine we are always spending too much. To acquire greedily or to keep jealously are both forms of vile cupidity, they are genuflections before hollow idols; they show the soul made captive to a god of metal. Poverty is royally magnificent. It is founded on an immense liberty, and acknowledges no other value in wealth but that of being used. When poverty, so wide, so great in itself, is narrowed to the spare proportions of petty middle-class economies; when we count out every farthing parsimoniously, and part with them with difficulty as if they were beloved children, precious Benjamins; when we speak of a poverty which is crabbed, and anxious and calculating, we travesty the noble reality, and we blaspheme the Beatitudes. Nothing should cling to our souls, nothing should adhere to our hands. Parsimony has no sense unless it is practised in view of ultimate alms-giving. The truly poor spits in the face of idols, as did the martyrs of olden days. This action is not perhaps in very good taste, but it is sincere and pleases God and contains some useful lessons. There are many among us who would consent, indeed, to spit upon an idol made of wood, or a fetish of cloth and feathers, but who would no longer exhibit this supreme contempt were the Baals well gilded or the false gods of solid silver.

De laqueo venantium. We fall back so easily into the snares of the old tempter. We hold to wealth. We prefer opulence with slavery to the hard, poor, frugal liberty of the prophets in the desert. We are penetrated and contaminated by the ideas of slaves. We do not like to empty our two hands, without even taking the inventory of what we abandon on the high-road. Everything, even our merits and our rewards, has become for us a matter of reckoning and of valuation.

What wretchedness! My God, I aspire to the divine liberty of the poor. Whether they are in religion or in the world, Your faithful followers should look on money as nothing more than a means to which we do not attach ourselves, and the foolish joy of great profits should be unknown to us. Grant that my wealth may consist in possessing You and do not suffer that the goods of the earth should accumulate themselves around me. All great things that have been accomplished here below owe their realization to the poor. The spiritual treasures of humanity are not kept in safes, but in souls empty of all attachment and filled only with the joy of heaven. I have neither gold nor silver, but what I have, I give to thee, arise and walk! Thus did Your Apostle Peter speak; thus do the priests speak who absolve in Your name and who give heaven to sinners for nothing. It is always for nothing that we give and receive the only things which are worth being prized. I received grace for nothing; the very word says this, grace is gratuitous, and Your Church condemned the Pelagians who denied it. I receive also for nothing, my pardons and Your lights and also those beneficial ideas which have restored health to my weakened will. It is for nothing too that I shall receive my Paradise, and it was for nothing that so many kind friends, so much good example, wise love and prudent advice came to meet me on my road, like the brethren from Rome going out to meet Paul of the old Appian way.

Dives sum satis.—My riches are overflowing. To whom shall I give in my turn? To men now on earth and to the dead. To those who are to come and to those who now surround me, to all; to God Himself even, my praise and my thanks and the treasures of my two hands, now quite empty. We can only clasp empty hands. It is just that which makes their value. May mine be only filled with You.

XCV

YOU have never loved that which agitates us. Feverish activities are not to Your taste. As soon as You enter a house You seek to establish peace in it. All Your movements tend towards calm.

And I! I struggle unceasingly in the midst of all my fevers. Good desires themselves in my soul are full of frenzy. I strike out to right and left, just as sick people do in delirium, and when all is quiet I say that everything is wearisome. Can my fever be ever really cured?

See, O Lord, how in the hearts of Your disciples, faith is often in such confused alarm. One would be tempted to tell them to occupy themselves less with it, so wrongly are they pre-occupied about it. They mingle scruples or terrors with it; they want to criticize everything without respect, or to accept everything without reflection; they do not know as yet, how eyes are opened gently to the light, nor by what supernatural harmony, good will and right thinking can mutually rest upon each other. They fear reason as an enemy, and science as an intruder: their soul's diet is like that of the fever-stricken, who change the choicest food into poison and are obliged to submit to all sorts of curtailments in their nourishment. The good health of a strong and tranquil faith has been lost in their paroxysms, and it is by fits and starts and by crises that it acts or wakes up within them. These are the tumultuous of heart, and there are many among Your followers.

Their apostolate knows nothing of moderation. When this word is uttered in their presence they become indignant, and are unwilling to see anything in it but cowardly concessions or sceptical sloth. Ah! if You had let them have their way they would long since have torn up all the roots of cockle from Your furrows, but they would at the same time have exterminated the good seed. These restless and vehement people have done much harm to Your work. They have no skill in handling the finer things of the soul; they refuse to watch patiently for the moments of Your Providence, and when You have neither condemned nor forbidden, by precaution as they say, they forestall You, and pour themselves out in violently preventive measures.

My God, these fevers kill me. Could You not restore me to health? When my ears are buzzing I hear Your voice so badly, and when nightmares of delirium trouble my sight how shall I be able to discern Your presence and to recognize Your messengers? My life thus passes in panting activities, which leave no clear remembrances. There are many sudden starts with little progress, and jerks which dislocate me without managing to make my any more supple. Everything, down even to my repentance is feverish. I hasten to put order in my innermost soul, but without giving myself the time to do it thoroughly, a little like those writers who weary of the pell-mell and disorder of their bureau, open wide every drawer, pitch in all their papers, and then seated in front of their tables now swept clear, imagine that their affairs are quite in order.

It is not easy to accept the long delays that are necessitated by every work of true education. To change an idea, a minute is some-times enough, but to organize our convictions and to establish a coherent system in the centre of our lives, persevering, quiet labour is indispensable. I have a horror of everything which does not follow the law of my imperious caprices, and I stamp impatiently when things go slowly, and when Your Will beats the rhythm of events to a measure other than that which I desired.

Cure me of my fevers! They have so often hindered my prayer. They have prematurely exhausted my reserves of generosity. After taking the most marvellous resolutions, instead of setting off quietly, I have run like a fool, I have reeled at the first shock and collapsed in the ditches, a pitiable, ridiculous, incorrigible and incapable object.

Take me by the hand—*apprehensa manu ejus*. It was thus that, in olden days, You cured the fever-stricken. At this contract with Your pacifying virtue, the trouble within them disappeared. You have not ceased to be the physician, the sole physician, and Your hand in mine, or better still, my hand in Yours, we could still accomplish something for Your glory. It seems to me that if my eyes could once again become clear, without terror, without hatred, without agita-tion, I should never again cease to see You. Exorcize my phantoms and abolish my nightmares!

When I shall see things in their true bearings shall I not again give to You, quite tranquilly, the one place which is Your own. There must be somewhere in my soul, as in the vaults of those old castles in the stories, a treasure of generosity and self-sacrifice that no one has as yet discovered. My true resources, all the beauty which I could develop by Your Grace; all *that* is ignored through the delirium of my fevers, and I shall never get hold of this treasure with my poor half-conscious efforts. Lead me, and when I shall have ceased to shiver, to tremble and to see nothing, show me what You have deposited within my life, and the divine work which, in spite of my age and my miseries, remains still to-day, by Your will, the reason of my existence.

Imperavit febri.—I am not alone and I hear around me other fever-stricken patients whose teeth chatter, who shiver with cold, who cannot stand erect, whose sight fails, and on whose foreheads the beads of perspiration form. For all of these, O my God, be the physician. For the scrupulous, whom our unkind mockery ridicules so cruelly, and who suffer so much, because they cannot live in peace; for the discouraged who torture themselves at the remembrance of what they have neglected to do; for those fiery people who have never tasted the beatitude of calm horizons and the serene joys of silent nights. Ah! if only You would do away with all our fevers, and if only our perpetual health of body and of soul could at last glorify You in Your Church! If we would look at our own faults calmly in order to destroy them, and at those of others in order to support them! If we had no more bitterness in our memories, no more venom in our ambitions and no more harmful fire in our delights, Your Redemption would fulfil itself in us and we should become like Your desire.

Psalmi graduales
What is sung on the steps

EACH of our actions is a symbol. You speak to us in the language of things and Your lessons come to us continuously, hidden beneath the most humble appearances. I have so often gone upstairs during my life. How is it I have not noticed that this simple action is a whole gospel, and that I need only understand it aright to become heir of the wisdom of olden days and to be illumined with purifying light? After all I have nothing else to do here below than to mount up above! The Ascension was the final mystery of Your visible existence, and in spite of my native heaviness, I must accomplish this miracle, of raising myself up to You *in excelsis*.

I have despised these humble lessons. A staircase seems to me a prosaic thing. Saint Alexis had to hide himself under one in order that I might consent to think about it. And yet it is grave and gentle as an old teacher; it is religious and solemn as a priest; those stairs before which we stop short when beginning Mass, those stairs at the foot of which we say the Confiteor and on which we may only take our place in prayer . . . *ut ad sancta sanctorum puris mereamur mentibus introire*. Was it not towards the steps of the Temple that Your disciples were hastening at the night hour, when You allowed Peter to cure the paralytic? Do not those very steps recall the feast of the Presentation to us, and was it not by steps that You went slowly up to meet Pilate "in the place called Lithostrotos." It was a staircase also up which Eliseus, the prophet, went, when he entered the house of the Sunamitess, to restore the little child to life, who was lying on his bed upstairs, . . . and it was down a flight of stairs that Saint Paul went in haste when he perceived that the young man sitting on the window sill, while he was long in preaching, had fallen—*somno ductus*—oppressed with deep sleep, on the hard ground outside. And Your martyrs have known what it was to mount the steps of the scaffold, and the chosen people sang psalms on the steps, as we still say the gradual, after the epistle. All has been made holy by Your presence in the midst of us; and just as we celebrate the Last Supper in memory of You, so too could we, without saying a word, go up our flights of stairs with devotion. . . . For this action transports us, slowly, just as we are, full of desires and of heaviness, and only able to raise ourselves with difficulty. We are the *aggravati*, the heavily burdened, and our knees tremble and bend, and our hearts beat in our breasts, when, in

addition to our burdens we have also to carry ourselves and to
establish ourselves on some plane above us. And we do it! By steps
we have succeeded in scaling the dizzy heights of towers; by making
holes in the snow, by cutting footholds in the rocks, slowly, we the
ants, have attained to the summits of mountains. Shall it be said, O
Lord, that in order to go up to You we have not this same courage,
and that, timorously, we never dare scale Your Sinai to speak to
You and see You face to face? When I think of the immensity of the
effort, I feel crushed. What shall I do to attain to the inaccessible?
But that which we cannot do by one single act, we shall manage to
accomplish by dividing the burden, and faithful to my duty, I need
but mount the steps of my days, keeping my face turned towards
You. Since You descended into our humanity, a road has been
opened by which to reach You.

> *Haec est scala qua descendit*
> *Calceata deitas.*

You shod Yourself in our heavy traveller's shoes. You knew well,
when You made Yourself man, that the business was a rough one,
that it would necessitate going up and going down, and toiling
under the weight of weariness. It is with You that I wish to reascend,
and it is towards You that I cry *de profundis*, from the depths of my
weakness. At each step I shall be nearer to You. Do we not say that
virtue has its *degrees* and prayer too, like the heirarchy of the Church
and the nine choirs of the Holy Angels?

A flight of steps is a teacher of patience and of energy. If we do
not go up to the top, it was useless to have begun the ascent. To
stop short half way is to nullify all previous effort. It is possible on a
road to go no further. We can take a walk, that is all, and having
given a glance at the landscape we can turn back and go home. We
are not ridiculous for so doing. But who is the fool who takes walks
on the stairs and who turns back before he has reached the landing,
the storey, or the door or the terrace, which alone gives a meaning
to his whole expedition? Each step involves the one that is to follow
it a little more imperiously, and we are the more ridiculous the
later we give up the project.

I look behind me. The number of my days already traversed has
caused my life to ascend towards its term, and the years of my childhood are lost there below in the haze, all diminished like the valleys
on which we look down from the heights. I am no longer on a level
with that former life. I can stop short and bemoan myself, but I can
no more go back, My whole future is above me.

My God, I ask but one thing of You this evening. Grant that death
may not surprise me half way on my ascent towards You, but rather,

that like the patriarchs of old, the number of my days may be complete when You come to demand my great reckoning from me. The number of my days complete, that is to say every step taken, all the ascensions ended, all the duties accomplished and my life culminating at the height which Your Providence had eternally foreseen for me in the plan of the Redemption. I do not want my soul to stop short half way; I do not wish, above all, that with age, and almost without adverting to it, I should begin to descend.

And when I go up our humble stairways, ten, twenty times a day, I shall try to sum up my whole life in this action; I shall put into it the fullness of its meaning and I shall give glory to You because, notwithstanding my native heaviness and the weight of my weakness, in spite of it all, in order to render service or to please You, I struggle up by steps towards heaven.

XCVII

Unigenitus . . . primogenitus
The only begotten Son . . . the First-born
(*John i.* 18. *Col. i.* 15.)

THE apprenticeship of wisdom is long and adventuresome. It is only after having wasted many hopes, after having sown disappointments like acorns on the roads of our life that at last we resign ourselves to hoard all our treasure of desires in God alone. We have not yet, perhaps, understood that the only Begotten Son is also the First-born of all creation, and we do not even know the reason of our existence.

My God, very opposite preachers have attempted to make me understand that, with all Christians, I belong to Jesus Christ, and they have added that Christ being my Master by right of inheritance, by right of election, and by right of conquest, His possession of me was unassailable, and that all resistance on my part was a rebellion and an injustice. This sermon is undoubtedly to be held in reverence, because of the truth which it contains and because of the remote times to which it takes us back. It is quite certain that we are the heritage, the conquest and the people of Christ. But why does my devotion find itself ill at ease in these juridical theories, like a traveller who is shod with only a single shoe, no matter how excellent a one? It seems to me that "natures" come before "rights," and I cannot believe that it is by some sort of "deed of conveyance" that I began one day to belong to You. Heritage, election, conquest, these are titles which allow us to enter a claim to a thing which we have not ourselves made, and which does not belong to us from its first beginnings. You are the only Begotten Son, but You are also the *Primogenitus*, and it is for You that all has been created. As the Word made Flesh, You have been from all eternity the object of the complacency of the Father, and Your Incarnation cannot be only a chance accident in the order of events as willed by God. It is this Incarnation which gives their meaning to all things, just as it is the end which gives worth to all the means.

I am for You; if You had not existed I should never have received my being, the stars would never have shone in the firmament, the light would never have been divided from the darkness, and chaos itself would never have lain dormant, as a child, under the tutelage of Your Spirit, in the first days of the world. You are the reason o the existence of all creatures—*propter quem . . . omnia.* (*Heb.* ii. 10).

I have no need of title-deeds and archives, it is my being that I owe to You; and I shall not keep repeating, as those stubborn

Christians of whom Saint Ignatius of Antioch speaks: *Nisi in archivis reperero non credam:* let the papers be shown to me, else I refuse to believe. If You were not the very reason of my life; if from the mere fact that they are men, all my brethren were not traced back to You alone as to their necessary end; if the insects, the birds, the plants, the storms had not in You their explanation and their meaning, You Would be to me and to the world, a stranger of distinction, a personality of noble descent, and we should receive You with courtesy, perhaps with cordiality, but never with that utter transport of a being which finds itself again in its goal, and which comes to rest in the ultimate. That which is final must also be first. I can only stop short at my fulfilment, and fulfilment is the realization of the first idea which gave me my being. The end, the goal is at all the beginnings, invisible but active. All things prepare Your way, because all things awaited You. I do not wish to belong to You by title deeds, or by links and bonds of law, and by adventitious obligations. I know well that my being has but one supreme law: to belong to You as deeply, as utterly as possible, and only to become myself through You. Words too receive their meaning from the very phrase for which they exist, and stones are cut for the building in which they must take their places. You did not arrive after the event, as a mere corrective of the initial work, but all was ordained in view of You in the first Divine plan, and in every order it is You who hold the precedence. I shall leave to theologians the praiseworthy task of showing that these truths take nothing from Your unique and necessary role of Redeemer, and I shall repeat with the contemplatives of olden times in our monasteries:

> *O Sanctorum Sancte mirabilis,*
> *Toti mundo de iderabilis,*
> *Homo potens et Deus humilis,*
> *Non est tibi nec erit similis*
> > *Deus meus.*
> > > (*Medieval Hymn.*)

O Thou who art holy, admirable among all holy ones, Thou whom the whole universe pursues with one sole desire, Thou in whom was brought to being this miracle, of all-power in a Man and humility in a God, there is not, and there never will be one like to Thee, O God, who art my own.

I shall go towards You as towards my state of rest and my eternal life. In Your two hands You hold my being and You are my reward, because the perfection of my being lies in You. Between us two there is not only a legal link and an obligation defined by lawyers, there is the absolute exigence of my life, which is incapable of sustaining or understanding itself unless it flows into Your immensity.

For long ages now have I sought You with eyes bandaged by my capricious follies; laying hold to right and left on my passage of all that my groping hands could reach. I have done great damage in the course of my mortal days. In my blind wanderings I have often overstepped the lines drawn by men in chalk upon the ground and which they call their rights and privileges; I have oftentimes offended these men, my fellow-men; I have entered into their domains, and transgressed their rules; I have broken down the enclosures behind which they were sheltering themselves, and they have made me pay dear for my follies. If I had devoted all this energy which I have poured out in roaming among other men, to bringing myself nearer to You, if I had understood more clearly that apart from You I had no value and that I existed for You, as the soldier does for victory, I should be less of a slave to my mediocrities and less unworthy to call myself Your witness—*Eritis mihi testes*. (*Acts* i. 8.)

Qui diligunt adventum ejus

Those who delight to see Him coming

(2 *Tim. iv.* 8.)

I CALL You my God. This possessive seems strangely ambitious, but when I reflect upon it, the perspective changes. It is no longer the ambition of man which stands out before me, but the condescension of God. By showing me the heights to which I may pretend, this possessive makes me see from whence You have come towards me. There are then, leading from me towards You roads of light; there are paths of peace which convey my prayer to God, more surely than the postal service carries things sent by the roads of earth. Communication between my Redeemer and the one whom He has ransomed is never interrupted. He has come, He will return.

Where are those who love this mysterious Advent? Christ enters into our life like the ploughshare of the plough, and the glebe of our desires is impenetrable, and the clods resist. We do not accept to be broken and reduced to dust by Providence, it is quite enough for a thing to be painful, for us to refuse to recognize the divine action in it. And yet the Heavenly Father is a husbandman, He has said so, *agricola est.* (*John* xv.1.) For long the sight of widely broken-open furrows has delighted us. Why do we become on a sudden, so mistrustful, when it is we ourselves who serve as furrows for the great work of the Eternal? Why these revolts, when He turns us over at His pleasure, when His will searches deeply into us, and investigates us, and with one stroke reveals our miserable desires to the light of day.

Love His mysterious advent? To do so needs at times heroic courage. The injured tooth that see the pliers of the surgeon drawing near! The giants of the forest that behold the woodmen coming! The walnuts in September that see the gang of farm labourers armed with long poles approaching! All those who are about to be shaken, stripped, cut down, lopped, torn up perhaps from their natural surroundings, beaten by trials that they may give all their fruit, all these need a cloudless faith in their souls, an unfaltering fidelity, when Christ, exacting, unexpected, strong, shall come towards them as a thief. I am willing to give things of my own accord, but I do not like others to take from me without consulting me, and yet this is what God does every day. I perceive that He despoils me unknown to myself, and forces me to ratify these divine depredations when the thing has been done. My plans which had been so carefully laid, and which have collapsed so pitiably, by reason of one little unforeseen detail; my enterprises, so perfectly enshrined in the frame of my desires, like teeth in their sockets in the jaw and which He has come roughly to lay bare and to break to pieces . . . and all those things to which I cling, and on which I dread to see Him fix His gaze; all my little, humble joys, and my peaceful diversions! Ah! when He came, He carried them away, all to the very last and I had not even time to stammer my objections. He came, and at once I understood: There is no help for it, Lord! I must give that with all the rest. My evenings to works of charity, my days to labour, my free time to the poor, my nights to prayer, my holidays to self-sacrifice! Take all!

Qui diligunt adventum ejus. Where are those who rejoice when He comes into their lives; where above all, are those who rejoice to bring nearer the hour of His coming into souls who do not know Him, and who wish to prepare His way before Him, in the continents which are still without the Faith. The Propagation of the Faith should be our perpetual solicitude, the chief of our desires and the cause of our joy. How many are there among us whom this anxiety, at times, prevents from sleeping? When we are expecting news, when we watch for the arrival of a friend, we do not sleep. Evening comes down, night falls, but at the window-sill the watcher listens, facing the stars. Are there many among us, who thus in the silence, lie in wait for the stealthy steps of the Redeemer, as He descends by our terrestial roads towards the sheep of His fold?

We have installed ourselves in a very fairly comfortable life and the delays of the Second Coming can be prolonged without causing us inconvenience. This "Valley of Tears!" we have worked to make it as smiling a valley as possible, and it is in spite of us that suffering still lingers there. If we were told that in place of that heaven which is to come we were to be allowed to remain for ever on earth, and that we had permission to make ourselves a nest here, I imagine that many among us would joyfully take part in that adventure, regretting only that they could not, in addition, bring down heaven itself here below. The arrival of Christ is joyful tidings only to the pure of heart. But the further my life advances the more I see that it is covered with spots and, as it were, striped with faults; this ordinary life of a weak and indolent man, without much consistency, more rich in floating illusions than in solid worth, quick to assume that his desires are his actions, and his self-esteem his real value. It is all this falsehood that keep us far from Christ, that prevents us from longing ardently for His arrival, and from exulting when we are assured that at no distant date we shall meet Him. *Laetus judicem sustinet.* (*St. Gregory the Great in Rom. Brev.*)

Our first fathers in the faith, O Lord, watched for You as for the dawn. You will come at the end of time, in Your own hour, when You choose and when all is ready for the last judgment. What have You still to put into my hands and in what will my eternal lot consist. You must grant me my pardon . . . this pardon given by You! I shall remain upon my knees in the invisible sanctuary, until I have obtained this pardon, just as those to be ordained are commanded not to leave the Church, where they are being consecrated, until the Mass is finished and they have received the blessing of the bishop—*nisi Missa finita et benedictione Pontificis accepta.* You will grant me my forgiveness and also my perseverance, that supreme gift, which You hide as a pearl beneath the bitterness of death, the liberating seal of Your predestined ones. I await it, I must prepare myself more fully for it and live in this blessed expectation—*corde suspenso*—. My God, in view of Your final coming cut down in me all that hinders Your work, break all that serves as a screen, and triumph over all that checks You. Come in Your hour, as a Master long desired.

XCIX

THIS is the crowning desire, the last word sent forth by the Church
to entreat Your mercy, in favour of the dead; and as one day all the
living will become the dead, it is to this goal that our life should
attain, if we are called to final happiness. . . . In meditating on it I
do not go astray . . . I survey this Requiem, as the pilot surveys
the narrow opening between the two ends of the break-waters, at
the mouth of the harbour. . . . It is through this Requiem that all
must enter into Paradise, and I look to see if I am able to pass
through, if my superfluous desires do not bulge out on every side,
and if the divine austerity of this word of blessing can accommodate
itself to all my fantastic luxury and to all my selfish bawbles.

Requiem aeternam . . . final rest! Your holy Church, notwithstanding all conjectures of theorists, had already described Purga-
tory in terms of repose; in the Canon of the Mass she called it "rest in
Christ,"—*in Christo quiescentibus*—"the sleep of peace"—*in somno
pacis*. Does not the very word cemetery itself signify that our dead
are asleep? And when the universal Church spoke in Greek, no one
could have understood it otherwise. Yes, Your elect, in proportion
as they make their way towards You, progress in peace; and the
repose of the militant souls who trust, who abandon and resign
themselves, is a beginning of Paradise. The repose of the suffering
souls is deeper still. They are no longer agitated or disquieted, they
have no movements of revolt, no desires contrary to Yours, no
guilty resistance. Their entire will is conformed to Your law. These
souls know that peace which surpasses all feeling, and they give
themselves into Your purifying hands as we yield to love and
surrender ourselves to truth. . . . A mysterious suffering, at the
same time most keen and most gentle, which can cause neither shock
nor start, neither dread nor shrinking, a suffering of waiting rather
than of change, and one in which the repose of the soul is not
disturbed.

Heaven will be a still more complete and still more absolute
repose—*Requiem aeternam*. My God, can my perfection be to work
no more? Is the term of my existence inaction? How could idleness
satisfy me? And shall I be happy having nothing more to do? I am
afraid I do not understand the full meaning of this ancient Requiem,
and I dread lest my want of comprehension may make me disdain
Your gift.

For though it is doubtless true that work exhausts us, yet You know well that we are trained through it alone, and we have sunk down towards deceptive baseness, each time that we have slackened in this healthful effort, which holds us in and supports us, just as the unseen string tightens up the stalks of a bouquet, which opens out so widely. It is true that, at times, our shoulders have been flayed by this daily labour, and that we have drawn weary weights, like the barge-men on the towing-path, who with the breast-collar over their chests, drag the heavy boats along. But if I had not been obliged to work hard I should have become most abject. It is not in Capua that we should seek for warriors. Could rest, without work, ever be completely satisfying? I am indebted for so many benefits to this austere toil. To cut out of my life the hours which were laborious ones for me, would be to sweep away nearly all my merits, and certainly to efface my most precious memories.

And yet, to possess is better than to desire; to be one with You is better than to be tending towards You; to know You is better than to conjecture You, and that is doubtless what You wished to say when You inspired Your Church with these soothing words, sung to so sad a tune. *Requiem aeternam.*

Rest in You is not like our precarious halting places. Our rest down here below is always full of corruption, of defilement and of death; it is a rest brought about by cessation and scarcely ever a repose through plenitude. A full glass and an empty glass are two forms of completion, they are two terms, and it is always towards the second form that I descend. My rest is not that of the full tide but that of the ebb, and it is by arresting effort and by diminishing results that I endeavour to refresh myself.

Your rest is a fulfilment. Your creative rest, that of the sabbath without evening which still endures and will endure eternally—*requievit die septimo*—who could dare to speak of it as of a kind of idleness? Who would presume to blaspheme this divine activity which gives us our being. The creation in which I find myself is the work of Your repose; and my eternity will be the work of Your rest, when I shall belong so completely to You that nothing in me will be void of You, and in union with You I shall love all Your work and its uncreated Cause, One in Three Persons.

Your rest is a harmony; my earthly rest is always reached by suppression; I attain to unity by putting aside that which I cannot bring into line, but You know how the most discordant things can yet agree, and You need destroy nothing in order to establish eternal order. *Nihil eorum odisti quae fecisti.* (*Wisdom* xi. 25.)

All that is final reminds us of You. Grant me to find my end in You for ever. I never asked You that I might exist; my nothingness

did not protest when You gave me being. It was not I who asked
for Baptism. When my mind awoke, I found that You had already
taken possession of my life and that I was sealed with Your seal. I am
nothing except through You, and my sole worth lies in this, that I
can attain to You, and that since my beginnings You have drawn
me towards Your self-existent love. Complete Your work and slay
all my resistance. When the new-born babe, Moses, was floating on
the Nile, shut up in his little wicker skiff, You alone knew that this
child would one day lead Your people, would come to speak to
You upon the mountain and would die in Your embrace—*in osculo
Domini*. In spite of my misery You have obliged me to believe that
a divine mission has been entrusted to me. You do not wish that I
should keep mean thoughts upon my ledgers; and in my act of hope
I repeat each day that I await, from Your mercy, the vision of
Paradise. I am less even than a child in a wicker basket, I have none
of its freshness, and long since my life has fled into the past. Lord,
my days fall one after one like the fruits of autumn on the stormy
evenings in the devastated orchards. Lead me by Your paths to
Your own rest. Give me the repose of detached and trustful souls;
if You deem well, make me pass, as it will please You, through the
purifying rest of souls who after death prepare themselves to possess
You for ever; and finally—You will do it as You have done all the
rest, through Your measureless mercy—finally grant on my behalf
the immense desire of Holy Church, my mother, that of all my
Christian ancestors, and of Your Spirit the Comforter; yes, to me
and to all Yours grant this great *Requiem aeternam*, with the *Lux
perpetua* which You Yourself will be, and the *in pace*, which I beg of
You upon my knees.

END OF THE THIRD AND LAST SERIES